Marginalisation and Events

This book is the first to take an in-depth examination of marginalisation and events. Marginalisation has been the subject of academic research for some time now. For example, marginalisation and exclusion have been identified as problematic in fields as diverse as geography, public health, education and media studies. However, little research has been carried out within the field of event studies.

Using a range of different theoretical and methodological approaches from a variety of disciplines, the volume applies a critical approach to events as they relate to marginalisation that seeks to address the 'how' and 'why', and to provide a holistic picture of their place and influence in the lives of marginalised individuals and communities.

International through authorship and examples, it encompasses case studies from around the world, including South Africa, the United Kingdom, Italy, Afghanistan, the United States, Brazil, Portugal, Australia and New Zealand. This is essential reading for students and researchers in the fields of critical event studies, anthropology, cultural studies, tourism, sociology and management.

Trudie Walters, PhD, is a Lecturer in the Department of Tourism at the University of Otago, Dunedin, New Zealand. Her research interests include media representations and individuals' experiences of leisure phenomena, with a particular focus on events and second homes. She serves on the World Leisure Organisation Board of Directors and is the Member Engagement Officer on the Board of the Australia and New Zealand Association for Leisure Studies. She is also Associate Editor and Reviews Editor of the journal *Annals of Leisure Research*.

Allan Stewart Jepson, PhD, has contributed widely to event studies literature within the realm of community festivals and events. His seminal work investigated power; hegemony; and the construction, representation and consumption of culture(s) at a community festival, and was the first to reveal marginalised local communities trapped and under-represented in a community cultural festival. Allan has three key texts in event studies (*Exploring Community Festivals and Events*; *Managing and Developing Communities, Festivals and Events*; and *Power, Construction and Meaning in Festivals*), all edited with Alan Clarke, University of Pannonia, Hungary.

Routledge Advances in Event Research Series

Edited by Warwick Frost and Jennifer Laing
Department of Marketing, Tourism and Hospitality, La Trobe University,
Australia

For more information about this series, please visit: www.routledge.com/
Routledge-Advances-in-Event-Research-Series/book-series/RAERS

Marginalisation and Events

**Edited by
Trudie Walters and
Allan Stewart Jepson**

Routledge
Taylor & Francis Group

LONDON AND NEW YORK

First published 2019 by Routledge

2 Park Square, Milton Park, Abingdon, Oxon OX14 4RN
605 Third Avenue, New York, NY 10017

Routledge is an imprint of the Taylor & Francis Group, an informa business

First issued in paperback 2022

British Library Cataloguing-in-Publication Data
A catalogue record for this book is available from the British Library

Library of Congress Cataloging-in-Publication Data
A catalog record has been requested for this book

ISBN: 978-1-138-58356-6 (hbk)
ISBN: 978-1-03-233863-7 (pbk)
DOI: 10.4324/9780429506697

Typeset in Times New Roman
by codeMantra

Trudie:

This book is dedicated to my husband, Richard – thank you for your love and support over the last 25 years, and for encouraging me into academia.

I would also like to thank Allan Jepson, first for saying yes, and then for being a wonderfully easy person to work with to bring this project to fruition.

Lastly, special thanks must go to the contributing authors and the marginalised communities whose voices they represent through their research. It has been a joy to work with you all.

Allan:

I dedicate this book to my wonderful wife, Joanna – whose love and support is never-ending – and to the three amazing little people in my life (Henry, Freddie and Ellie), who fill my days with happiness, love and laughter.

Thank you to Trudie; it was an easy project to say yes to, but your determination and organisation have made it possible, and together we have produced a very important addition to the *Routledge Advances in Event Research* series.

Thank you to all of our contributing authors for coming on this journey with us and for presenting your research to the highest standard, and to those who have contributed anonymously to this book in order for your voices to be heard.

Event Studies and Critical Event Studies are coming of age and beginning to tackle issues of marginalised communities, and give a voice to those who may be seen but not heard; as researchers this is our duty in our constant quest to make contributions to knowledge.

Contents

Figures

Tables

Contributors

Anna Baeth is a PhD student in Kinesiology, studying Sport Sociology, at the University of Minnesota. Her focus is on gender and coaching, resiliency in the coaching profession, coach development, masculinity in sport and socially responsible sport practices. She earned her MS from Smith College in Exercise and Sport Studies, with a focus on collegiate coaching, and her BA from Swarthmore College in Sociology, Education, and Peace Studies.

Christina Ballico is a researcher at the Queensland Conservatorium Research Centre, Griffith University (Australia). She is presently a Research Fellow on the Australian Research Council Linkage Project *Making music work: Sustainable portfolio careers for Australian musicians.* Her research broadly examines the relationship between music and place, including aspects such as creative and cultural capital, business and career development, popular music culture and policy, and creative and cultural clusters. She has spent time engaged with community radio and not-for-profit print media while also undertaking policy research for not-for-profit music advocacy organisations and has assisted on funding reviews for state and federal government.

Willem JL Coetzee is a Senior Lecturer in the Department of Tourism at the University of Otago, New Zealand. His research theme is within the nexus of tourism, with a focus on (i) protected areas, sustainability, small-town tourism and World heritage sites; (ii) mega and hallmark events; and (iii) small-scale sporting and food events. In this context, he has explored specific issues among attendee experiences in New Zealand as well as stakeholder engagement in and around protected areas in Southern Africa, and the impacts of nature-based tourism on surrounding communities. His recent publications evolve around the perceptions and consumer behaviours of attendees at sporting events (ranging from the 2010 FIFA World Cup in South Africa to the Masters Games in New Zealand) as well as food and music events, such as the Cape Town & Johannesburg Jazz Festivals and the Dunedin Craft Beer Festival. He has been involved in a range of tourism supply-and-demand projects in small towns and the formulation of tourism master plans for many of these communities.

Katie Deverell is a Visiting Lecturer on the MA Event Design and Management programme at the University of Westminster, London. With a background in research and social science she has a long-standing theoretical interest in liminality and margins. In 2001, Routledge published her PhD research investigating issues of professionalism, identity and boundaries as 'Sex, Work and Professionalism: Working in HIV/AIDS'. With a career spanning academia and public and private organisations, since 2010 she has worked as a ceremony designer and celebrant, helping to create and deliver many funerals.

Sudiipta Shamalii Dowsett is an anthropologist, mother and part-time emcee. She completed her PhD in 2017 at the National Institute for Experimental Arts (UNSW Art & Design). Her PhD thesis is a phenomenological ethnography of hip-hop in Khayelitsha, Cape Town, South Africa, and explores collectivity, embodiment, language, locality, traditional poetry (imbongi), identity and politics. Her research interests include decolonial research methods; phenomenology; social justice; folklore, storytelling and narrative; experimentation with tradition; music therapy; identity, space, and place; and social justice.

Amanda Elliott is an Events Management BA (Hons) graduate from Queen Margaret University, plus-size style blogger and fat studies writer. Born in Kansas City, Missouri, and matured in Edinburgh, Scotland, she is a comic book nerd, lipstick hoarder and mac and cheese enthusiast. She is passionate about social justice, body liberation and intersectional feminism. In her spare time, she enjoys local coffee shops, posting selfies on Instagram and smashing the patriarchy.

Rebecca Finkel is an urban cultural geographer and Reader of Events Management in the School of Arts, Social Sciences and Management at Queen Margaret University, Edinburgh. The main focus of her research frames critical events studies within conceptualisations of social change. Her main research interests centre on equality and diversity, social justice and cultural identity as it relates to urban festivals and major events. Her new research investigates post-humanism in events, tourism and leisure contexts.

Erin Flores is an undergraduate research assistant at the University of Montana Research and Training Centre on Disability in Rural Communities. She graduated in 2018 with a Bachelor of Arts degree in sociology, with a concentration in inequality and social justice, from the University of Montana and plans to pursue a career in social justice and human rights.

Amanda Ford is a doctoral researcher in the Department of Management, Sport and Tourism at La Trobe University, Melbourne, Australia. Her research interests include event strategies for city development; the connections between events and liveability; and events as instruments of social change. She is also interested in craft beer and its implications for tourism, hospitality and events industries and research.

Warwick Frost is an Associate Professor in the Department of Management, Sport and Tourism at La Trobe University, Melbourne, Australia. His research interests include heritage; events; nature-based attractions; and the interaction between media, popular culture and tourism. He is a co-editor of the *Routledge Advances in Events Research* series and has co-edited five books and co-authored five research books.

Allan Stewart Jepson, PhD, has contributed widely to event studies literature within the realm of community festivals and events. His seminal work investigated power; hegemony; and the construction, representation and consumption of culture(s) at a community festival, and was the first to reveal marginalised local communities trapped and underrepresented in a community cultural festival. He has three key texts in event studies (*Exploring Community Festivals and Events*; *Managing and Developing Communities, Festivals and Events*; and *Power, Construction and Meaning in Festivals*), all edited with Alan Clarke, University of Pannonia, Hungary. He, along with colleagues, is currently pursuing a research agenda investigating the well-being impacts of local community festivals and events, which has centred on families and Quality of Life, and more recently has begun to investigate arts participation events and collective memory creation amongst the over 70s and how these events can reduce the common psychosocial impacts associated with older age.

Jennifer Laing is an Associate Professor in the Department of Management, Sport and Tourism at La Trobe University, Melbourne, Australia. Her research interests include travel narratives, the role of events in society, rural and regional regeneration through tourism and events, and health and wellness tourism. She is a co-editor of the *Routledge Advances in Events Research* series and was recognised in 2017 as an Emerging Scholar of Distinction by the International Academy for the Study of Tourism.

Chantal Laws is a Senior Lecturer in Events and Course Leader for the MA Event Design and Management within the College of Design, Creative and Digital Industries at the University of Westminster, London. Her research interests centre on consumer culture and experience design, with a particular interest in fringe eventscapes, dark experiences and symbolic interactionism. Alongside her academic work, she helps to organise an annual fringe festival and has a background in heritage and arts management.

Xiang Liu is a Masters of Tourism alumni of the University of Otago. His research interest focusses on LGBTQ tourism, specifically the impacts of gay events at international tourist destinations on participants' behaviour and perceptions. His recent research analysed the motivation and perception of Asian gay participants in Gay Ski Week at Queenstown, New Zealand. He is interested in the development of gay events, including their effects on the change of LGBTQ culture, participants' behaviour and the development of LGBTQ community. He has researched the difference in the Asian gay community and the changing perspectives in the past and the present.

Jared Mackley-Crump is a Lecturer in event studies in the School of Hospitality and Tourism at Auckland University of Technology. His areas of research and teaching include contemporary issues in event management, Pacific festivals, popular music festivals, queer events, gender and sexuality, diaspora and culture.

Paulo Cezar Nunes Jr is a Lecturer in Humanities at Federal University of Itajubá, Brazil, and PhD candidate in Sociology, Cities and Urban Cultures at University of Coimbra, Portugal. He has acted as a Visiting Fellow at Amsterdam School for Cultural Analysis, University of Amsterdam (The Netherlands, 2018); at Humanities Institute, University College of Dublin [Ireland, 2017]; and in the Department of Social Psychology, Universitat de Barcelona [Spain, 2008]. He develops investigations and community projects linked to culture, festivals, city and urban planning. He is a member of the European Sociological Association.

Madeleine Orr is a PhD student in Kinesiology (emphasis in sport management) at the University of Minnesota. Her research focusses on sport event impact and legacy, and the relationships between sport and its geographic, economic and social environments. She earned an MS in International Events Management from the University of Brighton, an MS in Natural Resource Science and Management from the University of Minnesota and a BSocSc from the University of Ottawa.

Ana Paula Cunha Pereira is currently lecturing in History of Education at Centro Universitário de Volta Redonda (UniFOA), Rio de Janeiro, Brazil, where she is also associated with the Master Professional in Health and Environmental Sciences. Her research interests include the phenomenon of second homes upon leisure lifestyles, leisure and the concept of social capital, and symbolic violence. In 2011 she was a visiting researcher at Leeds Metropolitan (now Beckett) University, UK (under the supervision of Professor Jonathan Long), with the funding of Brazilian Federal Agency for Support and Evaluation of Graduate Education (CAPES). She is a member of the Leisure Studies Association.

Rayna Sage is a rural sociologist at University of Montana (UM) Research and Training Centre on Disability in Rural Communities. Utilising primarily qualitative methods, she studies gender and economic inequality, and the vitality of rural labour markets and community support systems for marginalised and oppressed people. She completed her PhD at Washington State University in Sociology in 2012, focussing on rural direct care workers in an increasingly feminised rural labour market. Prior to joining the UM faculty in 2016, she was faculty in the Department of Human Development at Washington State University, where she conducted community-based participatory research to study rural food insecurity, youth programming and college-based experiential learning.

Trudie Walters is a Lecturer in the Department of Tourism at the University of Otago, Dunedin, New Zealand. Her research interests include media representations and individuals' experiences of leisure phenomena, with a particular focus on events and second homes. She serves on the World Leisure Organisation Board of Directors as the Member Engagement Officer on the Board of the Australia and New Zealand Association for Leisure Studies, and is Associate Editor and Reviews Editor of the journal *Annals of Leisure Research*. She is also a Trustee of the Vogel Street Party Charitable Trust in Dunedin.

Nicholas Wise is a Senior Lecturer in the Faculty of Education, Health and Community at Liverpool John Moores University, UK. His research focusses on social regeneration, community and place image/competitiveness. His current research focusses on social regeneration linked to community change and local impacts in Southern and Eastern Europe.

Kirsten Zemke is a Senior Lecturer in ethnomusicology in the Department of Anthropology at the University of Auckland. Her areas of research and teaching include hip-hop, New Zealand hip-hop, gender and popular music, rock history and Pacific popular music.

1 Understanding the nexus of marginalisation and events

Trudie Walters and Allan Stewart Jepson

Introduction

In developing this book, our aim was to bring together a collection of work that drew from many disciplines and applied a critical approach to events as they relate to marginalisation, that delved deeper and sought to address the 'how' and 'why' rather than the 'what', and that made use of a range of different theoretical and methodological approaches. The authors who have contributed chapters have engaged with these themes enthusiastically and critically, and this book will appeal to both emerging and established scholars working in a range of discipline areas – from fat studies to event studies to geography and anthropology.

This first chapter seeks to help the reader understand the nexus of marginalisation and events. It begins with a discussion of some of the myriad ways in which groups and/or communities may be marginalised, along with some of the consequences of marginalisation. This provides the necessary context for an examination of events and the ways in which they may engage with the margins and the marginalised, drawing out the contributions of subsequent chapters.

The margins

The expression of power commonly determines who lies 'at the margins' (Smith & Pitts, 2007), and by definition those 'at the margins' are not 'in the centre', which is where the seat of power is located (Kwong, 2011). Here, we borrow the eloquent words of Deenabandhu Manchala (2017: p. 202), who states that the term 'margins'

> belongs to the language of the centre. It seems to hold the marginalised people as objects, as a category, often referring to them as 'the poor.' But their faces and names are many – discriminated, despised, exploited, and kept disempowered so that the centres of power and privilege remain intact in the hands of a few. Secondly, this categorisation hides the many causes of their marginalisation. Thirdly 'margins' is

a fluid concept. Some experiences of marginalisation are not the same as those who experience multiple or intense forms of marginalisation.

Groups and/or communities may experience marginalisation for a number of reasons and in a number of ways. Manchala's words highlight the inter-sectional nature of marginalisation – often more than one factor is involved, which compounds the intensity of being marginalised (Smith & Pitts, 2007; Kwong, 2011; Manchala, 2017). At the same time, it is very uneven: those marginalised in one place or time may not experience the same marginalisation in another. Let us now turn to the literature dealing with the marginalised to understand who they are and how they experience marginalisation.

The marginalised

Marginalised groups and communities are commonly subject to derision, threats, exploitation and explicit and implicit discrimination, and/or are treated as objects rather than people (Smith & Pitts, 2007; Kauff, Wölfer & Hewstone, 2017; Manchala, 2017). This results in a sense of powerlessness and has significant impacts on all areas of the lives of the marginalised – social, economic, health and well-being (both physical and mental) and cultural. In order to contextualise the research presented in this volume, here we discuss the lived experiences of a selection of groups and communities marginalised for reasons of age, religious beliefs, sexuality, race/ethnicity, socio-economic status, disability, refugee/migrant status and geographic location. It must be noted that for each of these there is a wide body of literature, and it is impossible to cover it in any real depth while working within the word limits of a book chapter (or indeed a book). Rather, we treat this chapter as a mere starting point; we bring a very small selection of the available research and encourage interested readers to use the studies cited here as a springboard from which to dive into the pool of knowledge.

Age

Young and old alike may be unheard and rendered powerless, and both groups are marginalised as being dependent and unproductive (Angus & Reeve, 2006; Smith & Pitts, 2007). Arguably, the latter group has received more attention in the academic literature in light of increased life expectancies and an ageing population in most countries (Gratton & Scott, 2016). In reality, older people can be mentally and physically fit, healthy, active and contributing members of society. However, negative stereotypes of people over the age of 50 persist – they are often described as 'over the hill', frail and incapable of living independent lives in their own homes (Angus & Reeve, 2006; Roscigno et al., 2007; Altmann, 2015). Indeed, Angus and Reeve (2006: p. 138) state that, 'discrimination against individuals based on their age – is widespread, generally accepted, and largely ignored'. Studies have found age discrimination in the workplace (Roscigno et al., 2007; Lahey, 2008) and in medicine (North & Fiske, 2012). When age does intersect with other factors, such as ill health, reduced mobility, reduced social networks (through death of friends or partners, or the need to relocate to be closer to services) and economic independence, the level of marginalisation intensifies (Angus & Reeve, 2006). For example, elder abuse is reported within families and nursing homes, and loneliness and social isolation are commonplace (North & Fiske, 2012).

The intersectionality of age and gender in the marginalisation of older people is apparent, with women reporting more ageist discrimination in the workplace based on their appearance and/or sexuality (Clarke & Griffin, 2008). While limited research focusses specifically on 'invisible woman' syndrome (where women report feeling invisible from their late 40s on), many participants in Clarke and Griffin's (2008) study did note that 'you don't exist' in the eyes of society as you gain the physical markers of age, such as grey hair, wrinkles and sagging skin (p. 661). Certainly, the phenomenon has gained attention in the popular media in recent years (see, for example, Holmgren, 2014; Tufvesson, 2016; Jones, 2017). This gendered age-based marginalisation is very real and takes a variety of forms: as Tufvesson (2016) notes, 'Women may be passed over for service in a department store, overlooked for a spare seat on the train or passed over for a promotion in the office'.

Religious beliefs

Marginalisation based on religious belief remains a significant issue for many faith communities. A comprehensive study on religious discrimination conducted in England and Wales in 2001 found evidence of unfair treatment and overt hostility for believers of all religious faiths (Weller, Feldman & Purdam, 2001). However, the experience of marginalisation was not consistent across religions – some (Christians, Buddhists, Jews) face ignorance, while others (Sikhs, Hindus, Muslims) suffer verbal and physical abuse, damage to property and hostility (Weller, Feldman & Purdam, 2001).

Muslims in particular have been the target of discrimination since the Al Qaeda attacks in Washington and New York in 2001, Madrid in 2004 and London in 2005 (Brüß, 2008). Yet Islamic migrants have been marginalised in many European countries since the 1950s through their exclusion from mainstream society (Brüß, 2008; Karlsen & Nazroo, 2013; Pauly, 2013). They have been relegated to the periphery of cities and towns, their mosques are frequently situated in squalid locations, they are often working in unskilled labour and have low incomes, and unemployment rates amongst Muslims are at least twice the national average (Brüß, 2008; Pauly, 2013). Despite governmental attempts at integration, the Islamic community remains the subject of misrepresentation in the media in many places

(Karlsen & Nazroo, 2013). Furthermore, there is little understanding of ethnic diversity in the Muslim faith, and people often associate all Muslims with Islamic fundamentalism and terror attacks (Brüß, 2008; Pauly, 2013). Similarly, and despite its foundational ideal of freedom of religion, the United States exhibits strong anti-Muslim sentiment (Council on American-Islamic Relations, 2018). Under the Trump regime, in 2017, changes were made to the federal government visa waiver programme to discriminate against those from Muslim countries, while hate crimes against the Islamic community reportedly rose 15 percent in 2017 (American Civil Liberties Union, 2018; Council on American-Islamic Relations, 2018).

Sexuality

Homosexuality has a long and complex history; it has existed across time, societies and cultures, and in some times and places, it has been accepted, while in other times and places, it has not (Valentine, 1993; D'Emilio & Freedman, 1997). It remains tightly bound with power relations, notions of gender identity and the social construction of sexual norms. For decades being gay was illegal in many countries, while heterosexuality was institutionalised in life (weddings, television, suburban family living) and in legislation (marriage, tax laws, welfare systems) (Valentine, 1993). This heteronormativity has resulted in stigmatisation and negative attitudes (including verbal and physical abuse) towards the LGBTQ (lesbian, gay, bisexual, transgender and queer) community (Lyons et al., 2015). Decisions that may be straightforward for heterosexual singles, couples and families, such as where to rent or buy a home, are more difficult for others due to the heteronormativity of place and a perception of intolerance (Valentine, 1993).

Like other communities discussed here, the consequences of marginalisation are far-reaching – including higher rates of depression and anxiety – and are exacerbated by age. Research with older gay men has found a sense of invisibility and being devalued (akin to that of older straight women, discussed earlier) due to the youth-oriented culture of the gay community and report new forms of institutional discrimination as they find themselves needing aged-care and/or hospital services (Lyons, Pitts & Grierson, 2013). Indeed, an ex-manager of a residential aged-care facility notes from experience that 'the rainbow [LGBTQ] community in Australia was, as it aged, subjected to a huge amount of discrimination … Many people found that to get access to aged-care services, they felt they had to go back into the closet' (Harford, 2018: p. 30).

Gay rights around marriage and parenthood have been brought to the public's attention by the media in many places, especially in the last decade. Some countries, such as Northern Ireland have introduced marriage-like frameworks (civil partnership legislation), although these offer fewer economic and legal benefits (Jowett & Peel, 2010). The Netherlands was the first country to legislate same-sex marriage in 2001, and in recent years gay marriage has been legalised in a number of other countries, including New

Zealand (2013), the United Kingdom (2014), the United States (2015) and Australia (2017). There has also been an increasing visibility of gay lives in the media and popular television programmes, such as *Modern Family* (United States), *Coronation Street* (United Kingdom) and *Neighbours* (Australia) (Jowett & Peel, 2010; Goldberg, 2012). These changes indicate a widespread change in attitude since the 1970s (Lyons et al., 2015). One survey found that the percentage of Americans who believed gay relations were morally acceptable had risen from 40 percent in 2001 to 52 percent in 2010 – although this does not extend to their acceptance of same-sex couples adopting children (Goldberg, 2012), and marginalisation thus remains. Participants in Lyons et al.'s (2015: p. 2237) Australian study report that while society has become more 'accepting' of gay relationships, there is 'still a lot to change', and the level of acceptance is context specific – some industries and social situations are easier to be 'out' in than others.

Race/ethnicity

The issue of racial and ethnic marginalisation unfortunately needs no introduction. In many countries, indigenous and non-white people have been, and continue to be, marginalised in a number of ways. Racial inequality and exclusion persist, such that in the United States in 2014 African Americans were twice as likely to be unemployed as white Americans, more than twice as likely to be living in poverty (28 percent compared to 11 percent) and less likely to be university graduates (21 percent compared to 35 percent), and they faced a narrowed choice of housing areas due to unwelcoming (white) neighbourhoods (Mele & Adelman, 2015). Discrimination is also evident in the US criminal justice system, where African Americans and Native Americans are over-represented in criminal activity and experience the highest rates of victimisation (Walker, Spohn & Delone, 2012). Following atrocious treatment during the colonisation of Australia and pervasive ongoing racism (indigenous Australians were only granted citizenship in 1967), it is perhaps not surprising that health outcomes and life expectancies for indigenous Australians are poor, and unemployment rates are high (Brennan, 2011; Waterworth et al., 2015). Research from New Zealand shows media representations of indigenous and non-white people to often be narrowly stereotyped and negative, illustrating the power of the press to reinforce the marginalisation and exclusion of certain groups and communities from mainstream society (Allen & Bruce, 2017).

Marginalisation based on race and ethnicity is also evident in the education system, in both structural inequality and racial discrimination. In South Africa, despite the overturning of apartheid in the 1990s, structural inequality in the education system continues to discriminate against black youth, and the 52 percent dropout rate helps to perpetuate disadvantage (Chetty, 2014). The underachievement of black children from poor areas in South Africa is significant. A 2004 government report found that while 80 percent of children in former white schools were reading at the appropriate level for their age, just 4 percent of children in black schools achieved the same level of literacy (WCED, 2004). Furthermore, Chetty (2014: p. 99) reports that 'black youth are being asked to learn in contexts of humiliation, betrayal, hunger and disrespect'. Research in the United States and Australia has found that children and adolescents from indigenous and ethnic minority (non-English) backgrounds report higher rates of racial discrimination than those from white majority backgrounds; consequences of this include poorer mental health; loneliness; low self-esteem; lower academic achievement; and more behavioural problems, such as aggression and substance abuse (Priest et al., 2014; Umaña-Taylor, 2016). Given the importance of childhood and adolescence for predicting future mental health outcomes over the life course, and the importance of educational achievement to overcoming inequality, these findings are deeply concerning (Chetty, 2014; Priest et al., 2014) and illustrate the serious long-term ramifications of marginalisation.

Racial marginalisation is also experienced in everyday situations, including access to simple leisure activities that many people take for granted. An article in *The Guardian* tells the stories of three African American hikers and the fears and stereotypes they have had to overcome in order to participate in this popular pastime (Pires, 2018). The first, a male in his 30s, discussed the abundance of representations of white, athletic, attractive people in outdoor recreation advertising and magazines, and how that led him to feel excluded. The second, an older woman, had fear instilled in her as a child that if she went into the woods by herself (as a black person) she might not come back – this fear remains with her today, and she feels that white people on the hiking trails look at her as if she should not be there. As a result, she is unable to hike alone and only goes with people she knows. The third person, a younger black woman, reports feeling more uncomfortable since Trump's election as racism has become more overt. She and her white boyfriend went hiking together in a conservative area, and she was unable to hold his hand because of the stares of white hikers (Pires, 2018). The mental and physical health benefits of contact with nature through hiking are therefore being denied to marginalised groups.

Socio-economic status

The poor have been marginalised throughout history, but poverty is often associated with other factors, such as age, gender, race and ethnicity, and geographic location. For example, McCurn's (2018) research investigated how young African American women negotiate and manage the emotional impacts of the stigma of being poor. For the individuals in her study, personal appearance was key to disrupting prevailing notions of what 'poor' should look like – being neat, tidy and stylish was very important. Expensive clothing and accessories were obtained from informal (possibly illegal) sources and were a vital part of the women resisting their 'impoverished class status' (McCurn, 2018: p. 2).

Socio-economic marginalisation may also intersect with other factors and have broader consequences for the marginalised. Low-educated workers often face higher rates of unemployment, and even when they are employed they are often in low-skilled jobs that are correspondingly low paid and insecure (Gesthuizen, Solga & Künster, 2011). For all people but especially for indigenous groups, studies have shown that socio-economic marginalisation increases physical and mental health risks (see, for example, Subramanian, Smith & Subramanyam, 2006; de Jong & Schout, 2013; Eliassen et al., 2013).

Disability

The United Nations Convention on the Rights of Persons with Disabilities was adopted in 2006, and 161 countries have since become signatories (UN Department of Economic and Social Affairs, 2018). Its purpose is to 'promote, protect and ensure the full and equal enjoyment of all human rights and fundamental freedoms by all persons with disabilities, and to promote respect for their inherent dignity' (United Nations, 2006: p. 4). Despite this, people with physical, intellectual, mental or sensory impairments still form a marginalised group within society. This is especially true for children with disabilities, whose voices are still largely unheard in policy and planning issues that affect them (Conder, Schmidt & Mirfin-Veitch, 2016).

People with disabilities are marginalised at school, at work and at play as a result of exclusionary practices and attitudes – whether deliberate or unconscious. One study found that just 48 percent of people with disabilities are employed, compared with 81 percent of people without disabilities, while another found that over twice as many people with disabilities worked part-time as those without (Shakespeare, 2014). Those with disabilities also face multiple barriers to achieving full participation in everyday life experiences, such as leisure, tourism and events. For example, venues are not always accessible, information is not always presented in an accessible manner (such as screen readers), dietary requirements are not always catered for, or assistance animals are not always permitted on flights. The everyday life experience has not always been designed for independent wayfinding and staff have not always been adequately trained (Darcy, 2012a, 2012b). Even where places are physically accessible, they may not be socially accessible – nightclubs cater to the young and beautiful, while care facilities may not take into account the need for intimacy with a partner (Shakespeare, 2014). For a person with disability, these (and more) factors highlight inequitable practices, impinge on their dignity and may result in increased levels of anxiety and humiliation (Darcy, 2012a).

Refugee/migrant status

Many countries around the world offer asylum to refugees and migrants fleeing war, famine and political instability in their home country. However, even in countries with official government policies that welcome them, their citizenship status means that refugees and migrants from ethnic minorities frequently face discrimination by members of their new communities (Kwong, 2011; Paxton et al., 2011; Goodman et al., 2017; Kauff, Wölfer & Hewstone, 2017; DeMarco, 2018). In China, there is also internal migration from countryside areas to major cities, but government policies have, until recently, been far less welcoming and excluded migrant children from the public-school system (Kwong, 2011). Migrants' citizenship status often combines with low socio-economic status and/or rural origins to intensify and reinforce their marginalisation (Kwong, 2011; Paxton et al., 2011; Goodman et al., 2017). Media commentary about refugees and migrants (especially ethnic minority migrants) is often negative (Paxton et al., 2011; Olvera, 2016; Triandafyllidou, 2018). These groups are disproportionately represented in low-wage employment, even when they hold educational qualifications, which marginalises them further and has longer-term consequences for them and their families (Olvera, 2016; Goodman et al., 2017).

The intersectional nature of marginalisation is also evident here as age and gender both influence how marginalisation is experienced for these diaspora communities. For example, school has an important role to play in identity formation for children. Kwong (2011) found that when school-aged migrants are socially excluded (even if they were born in their new country or city), it shapes their sense of identity – they identify with the home place but wish to live in the new place. Their marginalisation means they belong to neither and instead inhabit an in-between place. Adolescent ethnic minority diaspora groups who experience discrimination are more prone to depression and low self-esteem, which, in turn, can lead to poor academic outcomes, dropping out of school and increased unemployment (Kauff, Wölfer & Hewstone, 2017). A study of older refugees in Sydney, Australia, found different concerns related to marginalisation. The most significant was that the needs of ageing refugees were not addressed: changing family dynamics as a result of having to move to a new country, coupled with no longer having their 'ordinary' community available to them for support, meant that many felt they were ageing in 'the wrong' place (Hugman, Bartolomei & Pittaway, 2004: p. 148–149).

Refugees are more likely to be female, and as a result more research has been carried out on their experiences (Papadopoulos & Gionakis, 2018). One study identified a number of stressors faced by refugee women, including economic and employment stressors, where they faced discrimination from social services employees and potential employers (Goodman et al., 2017). Refugee men, on the other hand, and particularly fathers, have been largely overlooked by professional services and academic literature alike (Papadopoulos & Gionakis, 2018). Whereas mothers may be able to adapt more easily to their new daily domestic routines as a result of caring for children (taking them to school, medical appointments), refugee and migrant fathers tend to stay at home and thus are very vulnerable. Their experience of resettlement commonly includes loss of employment, financial independence and social status; loss of authority within the family; and loss of identity as father and family leader/protector (Papadopoulos & Gionakis, 2018).

Geographic location

Geographic marginalisation is often perceived to be related to remoteness and is generally associated with peripheral rural areas, a reliance on agriculture or other primary industry, poor infrastructure, an ageing population, outmigration of young/educated/skilled workers, rising unemployment and a lack of 'connectivity' (Bock, 2016). In the rural US region of Appalachia, outmigration of the able and capable (in terms of work skills, academic ability and entrepreneurial drive) led to declining populations, which, in turn, resulted in business closures, institutional/public-sector decline, infrastructure decline and an erosion of social networks (Adelman, 2015).

The rapid pace of technological change in recent years, particularly with regards to information and communications technology, has exacerbated the nature of geographic marginalisation. For example, the uneven nature of access to broadband has been shown to be problematic for communities living in isolated areas. Such access is an increasingly important determinant in the location decisions of entrepreneurs looking to start new companies. However, if broadband access is found in combination with higher levels of education amongst the population, even in a remote rural location, new businesses are more likely to be formed (McCoy et al., 2018).

It is also possible to be geographically marginalised in an urban area – particularly where it intersects with other factors, such as race and poverty. For example, spatial exclusion can occur along racial lines, as was the case with segregation policies in the United States and South Africa, forcing black people to live in specific places and excluding them from others. In US cities, residential segregation has resulted in ghettoes that isolate poor Latinos and African Americans (Adelman, 2015).

Events and marginalisation

The preceding discussion has highlighted the ways in which groups and communities may be marginalised and the deleterious consequences of this. It has identified vulnerability to increased health problems and unemployment, decreased incomes and mobility, and generally a reduction in their overall quality of life as a result of their marginalisation. So, turning to the central question of this book, how do events intersect with marginalisation? The research presented in this book highlights the ways in which this may occur: events may help cause marginalisation, they may help perpetuate it, they may help resist it or they may help overcome it. These outcomes are an outward manifestation of power relationships and whether event managers choose to adopt inclusionary or exclusionary approaches to event organisation (Clarke & Jepson, 2011). The chapters in this volume speak to each of these outcomes, and we have divided them into three broad themes that deal with: (1) identity, cohesion, well-being and quality of life; (2) empowerment, resistance and transformation; and (3) managing events at the margins of life, death and the universe.

Identity, cohesion, well-being and quality of life

Events can assist people in overcoming (at least to some degree) their experience of being marginalised by helping them maintain a sense of identity, create a more cohesive community and improve their sense of well-being and quality of life. The chapters in this first section highlight these benefits of events for a variety of marginalised groups and communities. While all quite different in their demographic characteristics and in the types of events held or attended, these groups each gained positive social and well-being benefits from participation. These chapters show the value of events held in, by and for marginalised communities, which extend far beyond the economic. In Chapter 2, Nunes and Pereira highlight the complex and often contradictory relationship between gentrification and marginalisation, using events in São Paulo, Brazil, and Lisbon, Portugal, as case studies. An examination of festival programmes reveals the social control of marginalised groups while at the same time offering opportunities for inclusion and improved well-being.

For a low socio-economic suburb in Dunedin, New Zealand (Walters, Chapter 3), the annual street festival was perceived by attendees and organisers alike to be good for the community – it provided a focus; showcased the leisure and support services available to them; put community groups in touch with each other; and promoted a sense of place identity, pride and belonging. Importantly, it did so in such a way that the community could celebrate its uniqueness without drawing attention to its marginalised status.

Rural events are important tools in creating and maintaining social networks, connectivity, community identity and self-development, and therefore need to be inclusive and accessible for people with disabilities. Sage and Flores examined this in western Montana, United States (Chapter 4), and found that people with disabilities want to participate in the events held in their rural community but that it requires extra effort on their part to attend.

Participatory arts events in the United Kingdom are the focus of Jepson's work (Chapter 5). He argues that, for the over 70s living in sheltered housing or attending community centres in rural areas, such events can help overcome a sense of social isolation and loneliness that is a consequence of marginalisation through poor mobility and a loss of independence. Attending participatory arts events helps reduce the negative impacts of marginalisation on the health and well-being of the over 70s, and improves their quality of life.

Empowerment, resistance and transformation

De-marginalisation is also the focus of Mackley-Crump and Zemke's work (Chapter 6), although they approach this through the lens of peripheralisation. They examine the experiences of FAFSWAG, an Auckland, New Zealand-based collective centred around their uniquely fluid, Pacific gendered identities. Mackley-Crump and Zemke argue that the FAFSWAG events' celebration of the margins is emancipatory; the events create highly public statements and assertions about belonging and authenticity, recentring their stories and thus disrupting and subverting marginalisation.

Similarly, transformative effects are identified in Dowsett's work on hip-hop events held in a marginalised township on the outskirts of Cape Town, South Africa (Chapter 7). Hip-hop events are enabling the youth of Khayelitsha to connect with the global experience of historically oppressed Black people and marginalised youth living in ghettoes. Live performance events take place in public places and spaces within the community, and this embeddedness helps transform the experience of the township by remaking space and countering negative stereotypes.

In Chapter 8, Wise argues that the empowering and transformative effects of events such as the European Capital of Culture (ECoC) are not being harnessed effectively for one marginalised group: refugees. Using Matera, Italy (host of the ECoC in 2019), as a case study, Wise puts forward a compelling case for the potential of the event to integrate refugees rather than serve to further marginalise and position them as 'outsiders', and uses the literature to identify a variety of ways in which this could happen.

Events may serve to exacerbate marginalisation, and this is particularly the case for homeless people. Ford, Laing and Frost (Chapter 9) discuss this with regards to Melbourne, Australia. This is a city that has adopted an event-led destination development strategy but where the central city area's 'cleansing' of homeless people prior to two major events in 2017 drew high levels of media attention. Organisers of the White Night event subsequently chose homelessness as a theme, but Ford, Laing and Frost argue that if major events wish to increase the visibility of social issues then marginalised communities must be involved in the messaging.

Managing events at the margins of life, death and the universe

The chapters in this section offer useful insights for event managers to consider based on rigorous, critical research with marginalised communities and peripheral locations. Queenstown, New Zealand, has cleverly positioned itself as a gay-friendly tourist destination through the creation of a popular winter event – Gay Ski Week. Coetzee and Liu (Chapter 10) investigate the experiences of gay Asian men who attended the event. Key learnings for event managers include recognising that participants are seeking more than just 'bright lights and mirror balls'.

Working at the intersection of event accessibility research, fat studies and fashion event literature, Elliott and Finkel (Chapter 11) critique fashion events and their marginalisation of plus-size women. Their research found that constraints to attendance are both physical (such as the accessibility of seating and toilets) and psychological (a lack of representation of the diversity of plus-size women's bodies). These barriers serve to marginalise plus-size women further, and Elliott and Finkel conclude by suggesting that fashion event managers and organisers should address these constraints in order for their events to be inclusive.

An event that has successfully negotiated constraints to participation for a marginalised group (women) in a marginal location (Bamyan) is the Marathon of Afghanistan. In Chapter 12, Orr and Baeth use safe space theory to frame their investigation of this event. They found that the building of relationships was fundamental to all five dimensions (political, sociocultural, physical, psychological and experimental) of safe space, and this was intentional on the part of the event organisers.

Ballico (Chapter 13) focusses on music festivals in Western Australia, examining the challenges associated with staging these events in peripheral and geographically isolated locations. Hosting music festivals 'out west' incurs a high financial investment, and changes in the nature of music events coupled with increasing competition have led to some festivals' becoming unviable. Ballico concludes that these factors may be limiting the ways in which the geographical isolation can be overcome.

In the last chapter of this section, Laws and Deverell (Chapter 14) appropriately shine the spotlight on our final event: the funeral. End of life events are becoming increasingly personalised experiences imbued with meaning, and celebrants need to respond to these changing expectations and demand for their services. A vignette highlights the key themes; illustrates contemporary practice in the death care industry; and provides celebrants with ideas about how to enhance funerals through layout, staging and flow.

Our book ends with our conclusions on marginalisation and events (Chapter 15), drawing together the contributions to knowledge with respect to the three themes: identity, cohesion, well-being and quality of life; empowerment, resistance and transformation; and managing events at the margins of life, death and the universe.

References

Adelman, R. M. (2015) Social inequality and spatial exclusion. In: Adelman, R.≈M. & Mele, C. (eds.) *Race, space and exclusion: segregation and beyond in metropolitan America*. New York and London, Routledge, pp. 166–172.

Allen, J. M. & Bruce, T. (2017) Constructing the other: news media representations of a predominantly 'brown' community in New Zealand. *Pacific Journalism Review*. 23 (1), 225–244.

Altmann, R. (2015) Who are you calling old? Let's ditch ageist stereotypes. *The Guardian*, 4 February. Available from: www.theguardian.com/society/2015/feb/04/old-ditch-ageist-stereotypes [Accessed 6th July 2018].

American Civil Liberties Union. (2018) Anti-Muslim discrimination. Available from: www.aclu.org/issues/national-security/discriminatory-profiling/anti-muslim-discrimination [Accessed 12th July 2018].

Angus, J. & Reeve, P. (2006) Ageism: a threat to 'aging well' in the 21st century. *Journal of Applied Gerontology*. 25 (2), 137–152.

Bock, B. (2016) Rural marginalisation and the role of social innovation; a turn towards nexogenous development and rural reconnection. *Sociologia Ruralis*. 56 (4), 552–573.

Brennan, E. (2011) On this day: indigenous people get citizenship. *Australian Geographic*, 27 May. Available from: www.australiangeographic.com.au/blogs/on-this-day/2011/05/on-this-day-indigenous-people-get-citizenship [Accessed 15th July 2018].

Brüß, J. (2008) Experiences of discrimination reported by Turkish, Moroccan and Bangladeshi Muslims in three European cities. *Journal of Ethnic and Migration Studies*. 34 (6), 875–894.

Chetty, R. (2014) Class dismissed? Youth resistance and the politics of race and class in South African education. *South-North Cultural and Media Studies*. 28 (1), 88–102.

Clarke, L. H. & Griffin, M. (2008) Visible and invisible ageing: beauty work a response to ageism. *Ageing and Society*. 28 (5), 653–674.

Clarke, A. & Jepson, A. (2011) Power and hegemony within a community festival. *International Journal of Event and Festival Management*. 2 (1), 7–19.

Conder, J., Schmidt, L. & Mirfin-Veitch, B. (2016) *Listening to the voices of children with disabilities in New Zealand*. Available from: www.donaldbeasley.org.nz/assets/Voices-of-Children.DBI-Report.pdf [Accessed 16th July 2018].

Council on American-Islamic Relations. (2018) *Targeted: 2018 Civil Rights report*. Washington, DC, Council on American-Islamic Relations.

Darcy, S. (2012a) (Dis)embodied air travel experiences: disability, discrimination and the affect of a discontinuous air travel chain. *Journal of Hospitality and Tourism Management*. 19 (1), 91–101.

Darcy, S. (2012b) Disability, access and inclusion in the event industry: a call for inclusive event research. *Event Management*. 16, 259–265.

de Jong, G. & Schout, G. (2013) Breaking through marginalisation in public mental health care with family group conferencing: shame as risk and protective factor. *British Journal of Social Work*. 43 (7), 1439–1454.

DeMarco, N. (2018) Government plan promotes refugee integration in Italy. *Borgen Magazine*, 2 April. Available from: www.borgenmagazine.com/refugee-integration-in-italy/ [Accessed 5th July 2018].

D'Emilio, J. & Freedman, E. (1997) *Intimate matters: a history of sexuality in America* (2nd ed.). Chicago and London, Chicago University Press.

Eliassen, B-M., Melhus, M., Hansen, K. L. & Broderstad, A. R. (2013) Marginalisation and cardiovascular disease among rural Sami in Northern Norway: a population-based cross-sectional study. *BMC Public Health*. 13, 522–532.

Gesthuizen, M., Solga, H. & Künster, R. (2011) Context matters: economic marginalisation of low-educated workers in cross-national perspective. *European Sociological Review*. 27 (2), 264–280.

Goldberg, A. E. (2012) *Gay dads: transitions to adoptive fatherhood*. New York and London, New York University Press.

Goodman, R. D., Vesely, C. K., Letiecq, B. & Cleaveland, C. L. (2017) Trauma and resilience among refugee and undocumented immigrant women. *Journal of Counseling and Development*. 95, 309–321.

Gratton, L. and Scott, A. (2016) *The 100 year life*. London and New York, Bloomsbury.

Harford, J. (2018) Ageing rainbow community focus. *The Star*, 12 July. Available from: www.thestar.co.nz/digital-edition/?edition=STR_2018_07_12 [Accessed 13th July 2018].

Holmgren, K. (2014) 5 reasons to enjoy being an older 'invisible' woman. *Huffington Post*, 11 November. Available from: www.huffingtonpost.com/2014/11/11/older-women-feeling-invisible_n_6140494.html [Accessed 6th July 2018].

Hugman, R., Bartolomei, L. & Pittaway, E. (2004) It is part of your life until you die: older refugees in Australia. *Australasian Journal on Ageing*. 23 (3), 147–149.

Jones, L. (2017) Now we know the real cost of being an invisible woman… *Daily Mail*, 11 June. Available from: www.dailymail.co.uk/femail/article-4592444/Now-know-real-cost-invisible-woman.html [Accessed 6th July 2018].

Jowett, A. & Peel, E. (2010) 'Seismic cultural change?': British media representations of same-sex 'marriage'. *Women's Studies International Forum*. 33 (3), 206–214.

Karlsen, S. & Nazroo, J. Y. (2013) Influences on forms of national identity and feeling 'at home' among Muslim groups in Britain, Germany and Spain. *Ethnicities*. 13 (6), 689–708.

Kauff, M., Wölfer, R. & Hewstone, M. (2017) Impact of discrimination on health among adolescent immigrant minorities in Europe: the role of perceived discrimination by police and security personnel. *Journal of Social Issues*. 37 (4), 831–851.

Kwong, J. (2011) Education and identity: the marginalisation of migrant youths in Beijing, *Journal of Youth Studies*. 14 (8), 871–883.

Lahey, J. N. (2008) Age, women and hiring. *Journal of Human Resources*. 43 (1), 30–56.

Lyons, A., Pitts, M. & Grierson, J. (2013) Factors related to positive mental health in a stigmatised minority: an investigation of older gay men. *Journal of Ageing and Health*. 25 (7), 1159–1181.

Lyons, A., Croy, S., Barrett, C. & Whyte, C. (2015) Growing old as a gay man: how life has changed for the gay liberation generation. *Ageing and Society*. 35, 2229–2250.

Manchala, D. (2017) Moving in the Spirit: called to transforming discipleship. Reflections from the vantage points of the marginalised people. *International Review of Mission*. 106 (2), 201–215.

McCoy, D., Lyons, S., Morgenroth, E., Palcic, D. & Allen, L. (2018) The impact of broadband and other infrastructure on the location of new business establishments. *Journal of Regional Science*. 58, 509–534.

McCurn, A. S. (2018) 'Keeping it fresh': how young Black women negotiate self-representation and controlling images in urban space. *City and Community*. doi: 10.1111/cico.12274.

Mele, C. & Adelman, R. M. (2015) Racial exclusion and spatial inequality in metropolitan America. In: Adelman, R. M & Mele, C. (eds.) *Race, space and exclusion: segregation and beyond in metropolitan America*. New York and London, Routledge, pp. 1–17.

North, M. S. & Fiske, S. T. (2012) An inconvenienced youth? Ageism and its potential intergenerational roots. *Psychological Bulletin.* 138 (5), 982–997.

Olvera, J. (2016) The state, unauthorised Mexican migration, and vulnerability in the workplace. *Sociology Compass.* 10 (2), 132–142.

Papadopoulos, R. K. & Gionakis, N. (2018) The neglected complexities of refugee fathers. *Psychotherapy and Politics International.* 16. doi: 10.1002/ppi1438.

Pauly, R. J. (2013) *Islam in Europe: integration or marginalisation?* Abingdon, Ashgate.

Paxton, G., Smith, N., Win, A. K., Mulholland, N., & Hood, S. (2011). *Refugee status report: a report on how refugee children and young people in Victoria are faring.* Melbourne, Victorian Department of Education and Early Childhood Development.

Pires, C. (2018) 'Bad things happen in the woods': the anxiety of hiking while black. *The Guardian*, 13 July. Available from: www.theguardian.com/environment/2018/jul/13/hiking-african-american-racism-nature [Accessed 17th July 2018].

Priest, N., Perry, R., Ferdinand A., Paradies, Y. & Kelaher, M. (2014) Experiences of racism, racial/ethnic attitudes, motivated fairness and mental health outcomes among primary and secondary school students. *Journal of Youth and Adolescence.* 14, 1672–1687.

Roscigno, V. J., Mong, S., Byron, R. & Tester, G. (2007) Age discrimination, social closure and employment. *Social Forces.* 86 (1), 313–334.

Shakespeare, T. (2014) *Disability rights and wrongs revisited* (2nd ed.). London and New York, Routledge.

Smith, A. & Pitts, M. (2007) Researching the margins: an introduction. In: Pitts, M. & Smith, A. (eds.) *Researching the margins: strategies for ethical and rigorous research with marginalised communities.* Basingstoke, Palgrave Macmillan, pp. 3–41.

Subramanian, S. V., Smith, G. D. & Subramanyam, M. (2006) Indigenous health and socioeconomic status in India. *PLOS Medicine.* 3 (10), 1794–1804.

Triandafyllidou, A. (2018) A 'refugee crisis' unfolding: 'real' events and their interpretation in media and political debates. *Journal of Immigrant & Refugee Studies.* 16 (1/2), 198–216.

Tufvesson, A. (2016) Invisible woman syndrome: do you have it? *The New Daily*, 30 July. Available from: https://thenewdaily.com.au/life/relationships/2016/07/30/invisible-woman-syndrome/ [Accessed 6th July 2018].

Umaña-Taylor, A. J. (2016) A post-racial society in which ethnic-racial discrimination still exists and has significant consequences for youths' adjustment. *Current Directions in Psychological Science.* 25 (2), 111–118.

United Nations. (2006) Convention on the rights of persons with disabilities and optional protocol. Available from: www.un.org/disabilities/documents/convention/convoptprot-e.pdf [Accessed 16th July 2018].

UN Department of Economic and Social Affairs. (2018) Convention on the rights of persons with disabilities (CRPD). Available from: www.un.org/development/desa/disabilities/convention-on-the-rights-of-persons-with-disabilities.html [Accessed 16th July 2018].

Valentine, G. (1993) (Hetero)sexing space: lesbian perceptions and experiences of everyday spaces. *Environment and Planning D: Society and Space.* 11, 395–413.

Walker, S., Spohn, C. & Delone, M. (2012) *The colour of justice: race, ethnicity and crime in America* (5th ed.). Wadsworth, Cengage Learning.

Waterworth, P., Pescud, M., Braham, R., Dimmock, J. & Rosenberg. M. (2015) Factors influencing the health behaviour of indigenous Australians: perspectives from support people. *PLoS One.* 10 (11). doi: 10.1371/journal.pone.0142323.

Weller, P., Feldman, A. & Purdam, K. (2001) *Religious discrimination in England and Wales.* Home Office Research Study 220. London, Home Office Research, Development and Statistics Directorate.

Western Cape Education Department (WCED). (2004) *Grade six learner assessment study 2003: final report.* Cape Town, Western Cape Provincial Government Printers.

Part I

Identity, cohesion, well-being and quality of life

2 Marginalised groups and urban festivals in São Paulo and Lisbon

Between social control, urban renewal and gentrification processes

*Paulo Cezar Nunes Jr and
Ana Paula Cunha Pereira*

Introduction and background

Lisbon, 25th November 2016. The eighth edition of Mexefest, one of the city's most emblematic music festivals, begins with the reopening of a classical entertainment complex, the Cine-Teatro Capitólio. The first concert, in which the Cape Verdean musician Mayra Andrade collaborated with the Portuguese rapper Valas, signalled the festival's objective: to discover the city through new music.

São Paulo, 18th May 2014. The ninth incarnation of Virada Cultural, the city's main cultural festival, begins with a hip-hop and street art event at the Municipal Theatre, surprising the audience. Groups from different peripheral areas enthusiastically greet performances by artists such as Thaide, DJ Hum, Code 13, MC Jack and The Creed, who acted at this central venue for the first time.

What do these two episodes have in common? Through unusual music concerts, both associate emblematic urban cultural spaces with marginalised publics. This basic act of bringing together particular places with particular publics raises questions explored throughout this chapter: how are marginal groups present in urban festivals? How are they socially repositioned through these events, and what are the implications of these processes for the development of contemporary cities?

Seeking to understand how cultural events intervene in contemporary social dynamics, we focus on the marginalisation processes at work in urban festivals, through dialogues between the Mexefest (Lisbon) and the Virada Cultural (São Paulo). To establish the main theoretical background to this chapter, we will now discuss processes of gentrification, renewal projects and the way in which cultural festivals have been used as a tool for social control.

Gentrification and renewal process

Recent critical writing has approached festival events as potentially having social agency, through which they shape, define or interrupt urban topographies (Sassatelli & Delanty, 2011). Accordingly, much of scholarly debate about festivals focusses on the intrinsic connections among festival events, social structures and spatial arrangement. The social dynamics and spatial organisation of many cultural events can be read in terms of the governmental policies under which festivals take place. As such, cultural events can be grasped as dynamic modulators in contemporary cities (Deleuze, 2000): points of intersection that mediate and shape social issues (Miles, 2007); urban planning and cultural practice (Zukin, 1995); governmental strategies aimed at marginalised groups (Líndon & Hiernaux, 2012). Mindful of the multiple socio-spatial dynamics at work in urban festivals, contemporary critical scholarship attends to the disputes that arise in festival contexts. Urban renewal projects are often particularly at stake in these discussions.

Rena, Berquó and Chagas (2014) argue that this subject is directly linked with cultural processes of social segregation, particularly in urban areas. Consider how governing classes often develop deteriorated spaces into creative circuits, irrespective of the interests of unprivileged groups. Facilities such as museums, libraries, galleries and theatres installed in urban centres like São Paulo and Lisbon, for instance, send a signal about how space is to be used and who it is constructed for, as part of a classist urban planning.

As Kara (2007) and Fix (2000) have shown, since the 1990s, Brazil has enacted a policy programme named the public-private partnership. Implemented in urban contexts, this strategy has become the 'magic potion' of governmental policy in São Paulo. It has been applied to a variety of emblematic cultural sites in the city: the Bairro da Luz, for example, and the historical centre, where Virada Cultural takes place. The urban renewal of São Paulo's historical centre began in 2005, helping to construct a new cultural image for the city. It has moved from a stigmatised neighbourhood (modest, insecure, marginal) to a creative site, meeting governing expectations (fancy, safe and alive areas).

In line with urban tourism over the last decades, Lisbon has developed an increasing number of festivals and cultural events. Following the Expo 98 World Fair, central and north-eastern areas of the city were reoriented or redeveloped (Ferreira, 2010). As an indirect consequence of this, Mexefest festival today functions as a kind of public celebration that aims to reinforce the image of a cosmopolitan and tolerant city, which the Portuguese government first promoted in the 1990s to both internal and international publics. During the third weekend in November each year, the Liberdade Avenue neighbourhood is strategically transformed into a unique site for the Mexefest. This has a dramatic effect on how the area is imagined, especially because the development has concentrated tourists in the heart of Lisbon, following the idea that 'the Mexefest fits like a glove', widespread among its stakeholders. While transforming the Liberdade Avenue into one of the city's gentrified tourist districts (which also include Chiado and Príncipe), Mexefest seeks to mitigate cultural differences between tourists and immigrant neighbourhoods around the festival area (especially the Intendente and Martim Moniz).

In connection with the theme of immigration and urban space, Líndon and Hiernaux (2012) describe how suburbs were historically constructed on the grounds of moralising discourses that saw ghettos and outskirts as poor and brutish areas in need of transformation. In addition, they argue that all state projects function in terms of these axes of value, transforming deteriorated neighbourhoods on the urban peripheries through gentrification. Metaphorically, it works as a form of enchantment or fetishism, 'allowing new urban policies and attracting new marketing trends to urban centres but also implementing international tourism' (Líndon & Hiernaux, 2012: p. 97). In line with this, Miles (2007) notes how the image of creative neighbourhoods is a strategy meant to attract celebrities, investment and tourism, and inflate property values.

This discussion prompts us to consider how urban development materialises in festivals and cultural events. How do these events function not just to bring marginalised groups into urban centres but also as masks through which the centre maintains its distance from – and power over – the margins? This paradoxical question suggests that contemporary governmental force operates through a logic of stabilising conflict, of controlling outsiders through cultural mediation. In this situation, festivals act as an inverted diaspora, encouraging marginalised groups to occupy central areas and established venues. At the same time, the institutionalisation of marginality in events programming allows such groups to be recognised, generating a sense of belonging and mitigating possible social conflicts that may emerge from urban renewal.

To illustrate this argument, over the last ten years in São Paulo, for instance, a variety of cultural events have proliferated in the historical centre, such as the case of Festival Baixo Centro and SP na Rua. In the same period, equivalent festivals in Portugal such as Festival Todos and Lisboa Mistura sought to bring marginalised groups closer to upper class neighbourhoods. Black people, immigrants, gypsies, refugees, street dancers, rappers, hip-hop artists and other members of the lower classes and minorities are being attracted to urban centres through offers of specific cultural actions. This has been achieved through careful cultural programming, public transportation facilities, raffle tickets for events and targeted marketing campaigns. The goal is to ensure that different marginalised groups are guaranteed access to culture, as well as building a good social image of the city through the event. Over this process, urban festivals have combined with public-private partnerships to socially reposition different marginal groups through cultural practice.

This mechanism can act in many ways. As part of government programmes of urban renewal, festivals play a prominent role in practices of social control, particularly in the 'least developing countries' (LDCs). The acceptance of graffiti, the promotion of marginal poetry slams and rap battles at official cultural events, also offers programming for specific ethnicities. These and other strategies strive to include marginal cultures in institutional documents in both of the cities addressed in this chapter, as in the case of the 'Programme Vai – Valorisation of Cultural Initiatives in São Paulo' and the 'Strategies Program for the Culture in the city of Lisbon' (Costa, 2017). Attending to the practice of public festival events allows us to analyse how urban renewal programmes have sought to shape patterns of sociability, conviviality and city planning strategies (Ferreira, 2010).

Having laid out the theoretical context in which our discussion is situated, we now mean to examine a range of mechanisms that serve to create spaces of inclusion for marginalised groups in cultural events, redefining urban centres and margins. As explained earlier, there are in these mechanisms contradictory processes of cultural production, gentrification, urban renewal and social integration. Marginal groups appear at the same time as agents of urban revitalisation and as objects of governance to be controlled through cultural policy.

Night and security

The intersection between cultural festivals and the night is especially interesting, because most festival conflicts take place at night, when their participants experience liminal atmospheres. At Virada Cultural in São Paulo, for instance, police interventions, disputes between groups, physical violence and even deaths are common. Theft and alcohol and drug abuse are also frequent, especially at dawn. To mitigate the risk of nocturnal violence, festival programmers have avoided scheduling marginal cultural activities at night.

This example indicates how security discourses impinge on cultural events in Brazil. This is the point broached by Matarasso when he asks (2009: p. 20), 'If security is part of popular engagement and the key element of citizen participation, why are the festivals events still reproducing rhetoric about isolation?' This question resonates with a prominent concern affecting LDCs where security represents a central governmental goal. However, new forms of occupying urban space are directly associated with the sense of security and the presence of marginalised groups on the street. Nightlife has value as a site of political dispute and is thus an important aspect of the Virada Cultural festival circuit.

In light of the increasing commodification of nocturnal cultural practices, and the intensity of their regulation, it is possible to envisage the development of urban lifestyles based on acts of 'being out' (Liempt, Aalst & Schwanen, 2015: p. 412). In a majority of cases, people imagine street space as far removed from the experience of being safe, as unable to provide friendly encounters. 'People see the street as a frightening space, a space for disputes. An important sign of this is that people feel safer when there are less people on the street' (Dimenstein, 2014: p. 132). We believe that there is a very close relationship between the street, safety and cultural practices that needs to be understood if inclusion policies aimed at marginal groups are to succeed. Holding events indoors and institutionalising marginal practices can be important steps in building new networks and social places for these groups. However, we believe that it is the activities carried out on the street that work best in building more democratic sociabilities among different actors in the city.

The question about how to integrate marginalised groups has a bearing on cultural events, festivals and other celebrations, which act as an important bridge in bringing people onto the streets and thereby facilitating cultural encounters in a secure shared ambiance. On this point, Hughes (1999) explains how the interest in festivals that arose among cultural practitioners and policymakers in the 1990s amounted to governmental strategies aimed at dealing with urban alienation and the sense of insecurity shared by citizens in public spaces. Over different stages of urban development, festivals provide a mechanism for including different discourses, facilitating interactions among different groups and affirmed different cultural identities. These strategies evoke a sense of community, by which we mean 'people bound by a particular identity defined by ethnicity or race, religion, sexuality or profession' (Mulligan et al., 2006: p. 18).

Social control and ethnicity marketing

Actions related to the inclusion and integration of peoples and representativeness of different social groups became important in the curation of cultural events, especially since the 1990s, when debates about inclusivity, ethnicity and social minorities intensified (Costa, 2011). Since then, Lisbon has been embedded in cosmopolitan cultural rhetoric, and today represents an important example of a city that has been renewed and reoriented by discourses of multiculturalism.

Based upon data from Borders and Foreigner Services (SEF, 2010), 2 percent of foreign residents in Portugal are concentrated in cosmopolitan areas. The results gathered by the survey reveal that the largest immigrant population is Brazilian (unsurprising given the history of Portuguese colonisation), Angolan, Cabo Verdean and Mozambican. In response to this multicultural population, the government adopted strategies of 'ethnicity marketing' (Costa, 2011), which we believe are directly linked to the reorganisation of marginality in this city. Accordingly, groups of African and Asian immigrants now have specific events in the local city hall's annual calendar, such as the Lisboa Mistura and Festival Todos. In São Paulo, the programme of multi-ethnic events held all year-round across city districts includes Brazilian north-eastern culture fairs, rapper battles and hip-hop gatherings. What emerges from this scenario is how governmental policy makes use of cultural practice to establish urban security strategies. Through convivial rhetoric, inviting marginalised groups to participate in a common and (supposedly) democratic programme, festival events enrol aesthetic difference and multi-ethnic participants in the programme of urban governance.

Beyond the context of Lisbon and São Paulo, the 70th year of the well-known International Festival of Avignon in southern France illustrates this curatorial discourse by emphasising the African feminine style. In drawing on marginal cultural traditions and practices, these festivals both enact and are determined by at last three factors: (1) cosmopolitan cultural and governmental discourses; (2) tensions between socio-spatial margins, borders or peripheries and centres of urban power; (3) the popular, intercultural appeal of artistic practices.

Moving forward, this chapter examines how festivals can function as strategic tools in redefining marginalised groups in contemporary cities. We critically explore how festivals control cultural production and marginalised groups. These events, we argue, function as a device of social control in contemporary cities, while also 'serving the public good, [...] providing space for the benefit or well-being of the public' (Deleuze, 2000: p. 20; Glover, 2015: p. 97). In so doing, we will emphasise themes of security; gentrification; strategies of urban renewal; conflicts within urban space; cultural cosmopolitanism; and the marketing of ethnicity as a form of social control as they play out in two different contemporary festivals: the Virada Cultural, which takes place in São Paulo, Brazil, and the Vodafone Mexefest, which takes place in Lisbon, Portugal. Both festivals exploit and attempt to manage existing social disputes.

The Virada Cultural and Mexefest

The Virada Cultural has been described popularly as the 'big party of the city', which brings an average of four million people to participate in 100 cultural practices over two days (data gathered from São Paulo Council in 2018). All these activities are financed by São Paulo Council and the programme is designed to be unique. Since 2005 the festival has included 36 stages sited in São Paulo's historical centre and after 2013 it went through a process of decentralisation, expanding to include 37 venues in other, less central urban neighbourhoods (Spot 1 to Spot 37, First List – Figure 2.1). Into these areas, the programme brought a wide variety of music: popular cultural bands, chorus, forró bands, rock bands, samba, rap, popular Brazilian music, children's programmes, international music and orchestras. Besides this, the festival also featured forms of circus, dance and theatre. Virada Cultural is today one of the main cultural assets of the country, which is why it was replicated in at least 26 other Brazilian cities.

Virada Cultural de SP

Veja o mapa dos lugares onde serão realizadas as atividades culturais

1. **Sambódromo do Anhembi** - Shows
2. **Autódromo de Interlagos** - Shows, circo e oficinas
3. **Chácara do Jockey** - Shows
4. **Parque do Carmo** - Oficinas de arte
5. **Praça do Campo Limpo** - Shows e oficinas
6. **Largo do Rosário** - Shows
7. **CEU. Paz** - Shows
8. **Ceu Butantã**
9. **CEU Parque Veredas**
10. **CEU Heliópolis**
11. **CEU Azul da Cor do Mar**
12. **CEU CEI Navegantes**
13. **CEU AT COM JAMBEIRO - JOSE GUILHERME GIANETTI**
14. **CEU VILA DO SOL**
15. **Céu São Mateus**
16. **CEU QUINTA DO SOL**
17. **CEU EMEF PERA MARMELO**
18. **CEU Jaçanã**
19. **CEU Alvarenga**
20. **Centro Cultural Palhaço Carequinha** - Shows
21. **Centro Cultural da Juventude** - Shows
22. **Centro Cultural Tiradentes** - Shows
23. **Centro Cultural da Penha** - Shows
24. **Centro Cultural Jabaquara** - Shows
25. **Centro Cultural Tendal da Lapa** - Shows
26. **Centro Cultural Santo Amaro** - Shows
27. **Centro Cultural São Paulo** - Shows
28. **Casa de Cultura do Butantã** - Shows
29. **Casa de Cultura da Brasilândia** - Shows
30. **Casa de Cultura Freguesia do Ó** - Shows
31. **Casa de Cultura do Ipiranga** - Shows
32. **Casa de Cultura M'Boi Mirim** - Shows
33. **Casa de Cultura Vila Guilherme** - Shows
34. **Casa de Cultura de Guaianases** - Shows
35. **Casa de Cultura Campo Limpo** - Shows
36. **Casa de cultura Itaim Paulista** - Shows
37. **Casa de Cultura Raul Seixas** - Shows

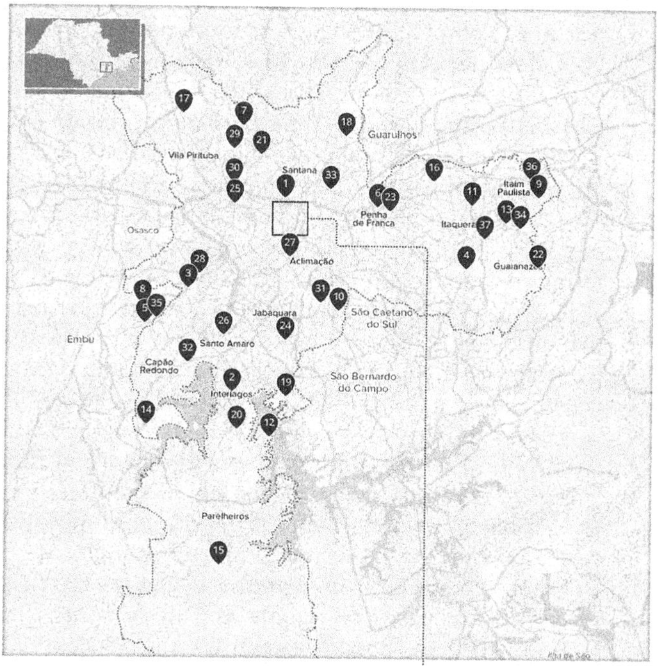

Virada no Centro

Shows, leitura e arte vão agitar a região central na Virada Cultural

1. **Vale do Anhangabau** - Musicais
2. **Copan** - Cabaré Queer
3. **Edifício Itália** - Cabaré República
4. **Boulevard São João** - Tributos
5. **Ipiranga com São João** - Samba
6. **Praça do Patriarca** - Forró
7. **Praça Roosevelt**
8. **Largo do Paissandú** - Lona e Circo
9. **Largo São Bento** - Hip Hop
10. **Rua 24 de Maio** - Hip Hop
11. **Rua do Tesouro** - Refugiados e Imigrantes
12. **Largo São Francisco** - Iberoamericano
13. **Praça Dom José Gaspar** - Piano
14. **Xavier de Toledo x 7 de Abril** - Cultura Popular
15. **Rua José Bonifácio** - Risadaria
16. **Viaduto do Chá** - Batalhas de improviso
17. **República x Pedro Américo** - Kombódromo
18. **Rua Aurora x São João** - Virada
19. **Álvares Penteado x São Bento** - Latino Americano
20. **Deck São Bento** - Brasil 360
21. **Avenida São Luís** - Big Bands
22. **R. dos Gusmões** - Teatro de Container
23. **Dr. Falcão Filho** - Tablado Test
24. **Praça Pedro Lessa** - Virada Oriental
25. **Rua do Tesouro** - Mágicos
26. **Praça Padre Manuel da Nóbrega** - Dança
27. **Galeria Olido** - Palhaçaria
28. **Conselheiro Crispiniano** - Shakespeare
29. **Theatro Municipal** - Shows, coral e balé
30. **Praça das Artes** - Variados
31. **Biblioteca Mário de Andrade** - Música e leitura
32. **Praça da República** - Soul Funk
33. **Largo do Arouche** - Jazz
34. **Barão de Itapetininga x República** - Virou Mix
35. **Três de Dezembro** - Pregão
36. **Biblioteca Monteiro Lobato** - Viradinha

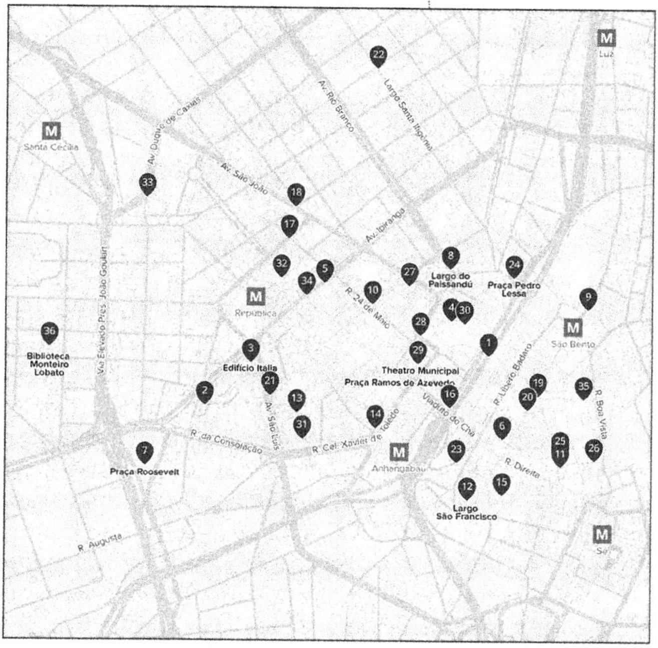

Figure 2.1 Virada Cultural 2017 venue map.
Source: G1 News Portal.

Although the programming of Virada Cultural is multifaceted, it is important to emphasise that in its more peripheral venues, such as the Parque do Carmo (Spot 4 of First List – Figure 2.1) and Praça do Campo Limpo (5 of First List – Figure 2.1), which are about 30 km from the city centre of São Paulo, the cultural activities are geared for specific publics. Rap and hip-hop concerts closely match local audience profiles. Most are young men aged between 15 and 25 years of age. Some of them do not have a family life, and are descendants of migrants from other parts of the country. Street dancing and skateboarding provide the sense of cohesion that is not easily found in these group's other spaces of everyday sociability.

Having premiered in 2008, the Mexefest is one of the most important urban festivals in the Europe in terms of musical variety. On average, its programme includes 50 concert performances, and these make use of 25 eclectic spaces around Lisbon's historical centre. The guiding idea behind this event is to provide a cultural circuit through which the public can move from one place to another within the heart of the Portuguese capital. In this way, the festival organisers aim to facilitate the exercise of participant choice based on an eclectic programme of simultaneous activities, juxtaposed on Liberdade Avenue (Figure 2.2).

When we mention marginalised groups participating in Mexefest, we refer in most cases to female and male youths living in peripheral districts of Lisbon, aged between 20 and 35 years. They are, in large proportion, Latin American and African immigrants, which helps explain the considerable number of African and Brazilian artists in the festival's programming.

Overall, both Virada Cultural and Mexefest enrol cultural discourses promoting diversity, multiculturalism and aesthetic syncretism in order to work with different marginalised groups. Both festivals promote events aimed at so-called marginal cultures (the Voices of Writing Project in Mexefest and the Rap Stage on Rua 24 de Maio over the Virada Cultural). It is because of their explicit focus on urban marginality that these festivals have been chosen as the subject of this chapter. These festivals celebrate hybrid and heterogeneous cultural forms, and this explains the range of concerts and artistic styles offered in their programmes. Therefore, the festivals reflect cultural strategies aimed at constructing social cohesion, displaying the well-being of marginalised groups and (at least symbolically) reconciling social conflicts. Simultaneously, however, they reveal strategies of social control and appeasement, since they institutionalise marginal cultures through policies of financing; fresh thematic foci; the creation of professional networks in and among periphery groups; immigrant activism and representations of minorities more generally. From this perspective, both of the festivals that we are discussing in this chapter can function as devices of social control while also maintaining a multicultural discursive image in which different nationalities and groups can be together.

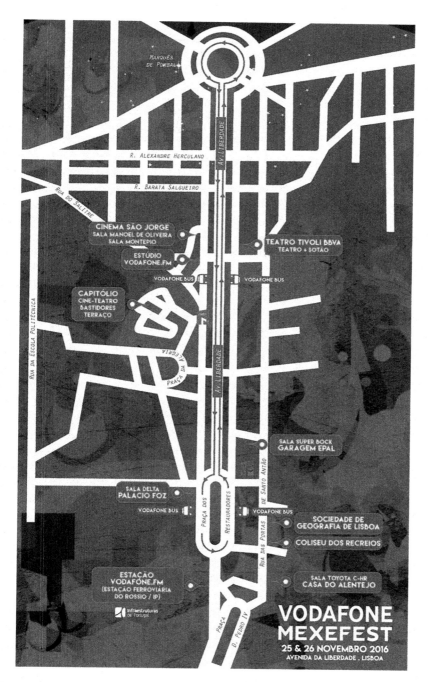

Figure 2.2 Vodafone Mexefest 2016 venue map.
Source: Mexefest Festival Official Website.

Methodology

This research takes a qualitative approach based on Actor-Network Theory (Latour, 2005), using data gathered at both festivals (Mexefest in Lisbon, held on 25th and 26th November 2016 and Virada Cultural in São Paulo, held on 20th and 21st May 2017). We draw on Latourian theory because it represents the views of research subjects in as rich and multivocal a way as possible. This line of thought suggests that researchers must be rigorous in recording the views of research subjects, sharing findings with them and claiming no authorial privilege in writing up the research (Greener, 2011), which thus becomes a collaborative process. It attempts to capture the complexity of the research site through strategies such as multivocal writing and the use of images and primary resources. Thus, we have carried out documentary analysis, interviews and direct observation, focussing on (1) formal events of the programme announced in both festivals and (2) pre-production meetings (media conferences, brand marketing campaigns and related forms of promotion).

We began our immersion in the research field of the festivals by contacting their planning representatives, requesting rights to collect data in the three months running up to each event. Discussion of the results with participants will be conducted through six interviews with festival organisers, curators and journalists, each of whom are associated with a specific aspect of the festivals. In addition to these events professionals, to address issues of cultural actions and urban marginality, an urban activist was consulted during the data collection phase, and later interviewed. Each interview had an average duration of 50 minutes. In keeping with ethical standards of interview investigations, all were recorded, transcribed verbatim and manually coded. In the following discussion of the transcripts, the interviewee identified (1) by reference to the city in which he or she was involved during the research; (2) the sequence of interviews; and (3) their occupation. 'L1- Musical Production', for example, refers to an interviewee who relates to the case study of Mexefest in Lisbon, was our first interview and makes music. S2 signals a participant related to another case study, São Paulo's Virada Cultural, and was our second interviewee.

During our field research into both case studies, an on-site investigation was carried out over a period of six months (three months for each study case), during which we followed key actors and scenarios (Latour, 2005) and observed relations among the festivals, marginalised groups and the city. Three categories of analysis were created, seeking to discuss associations between renewal issues, gentrification process and social control by urban festivals.

Findings and discussion

Gentrification processes

This research considers the relationship between festivals and gentrification processes in both cases, Mexefest and Virada Cultural. If these festival's programmes allow the movement of the marginal groups to urban centres, we also noticed precisely the opposite movement, especially in the case of São Paulo. This is shown by the decentralisation of venues in Cultural Virada, visible in Figure 2.1 (Spot 1 to Spot 37, First List – Figure 2.1). The removal of several venues from the city centre was justified through arguments about improved public control and that it would democratise access to cultural activities in different parts of the city. This aligns with our discussion of social control and urban gentrification (Miles, 2007; Líndon & Hiernaux, 2012), in that thematic venues were linked to marginal cultures in peripheral areas of the city, with the effect that marginal groups stay in those locations.

A distinct form of gentrification took place during the 13th Virada Cultural. Although this is a striking instance of exclusion, it can be seen as an isolated case. Groups of homeless addicts were removed in Cracolândia and surrounding areas over the festival weekend, in an operation that amounts (in our view) to urban cleansing. It occurred between Palcos da Praça da República and Rua dos Gusmões e Largo do Arouche (see the triangular area designed by Spots 22, 32 and 33 in the Virada Cultural map at the centre of São Paulo – Figure 2.1). This operation was directed by the Military Police and displays similarities with actions of urban renewal discussed by Kara (2000) and Fix (2000), reflecting how festival spaces are embedded of social conflicts.

In Lisbon, evidences of gentrification appeared in different ways. Compared to the first incarnation of the Mexefest ten years ago, many spaces were no longer available to participants because they were transformed into hotels. Accordingly, the range of festival performances declined. The reason was to maintain a quiet atmosphere in a tourist area, Liberdade Avenue and surrounding areas, as this interviewee pointed out:

> There is one important thing that has been affecting our work in terms of the production of the Mexefest. I'm talking about the huge concentration of hotels located in Liberdade's Avenue because we have to be friendly with our neighbour, I mean the hotel business is important for us.
>
> (L1 – Musical Production)

Another interviewee expands on this consideration:

> Every year we miss strategic spaces on the map for the concert performance [...] So, every year these spaces are replaced by new ones.
>
> (L2 – Musical Production)

The interviewees' statements demonstrate that gentrification processes in Lisbon impact the spaces available for recent festivals. One prominent example is the Cabaré Maxime, a bar located in the hub of Liberdade

Avenue, which has been incorporated of an important hotel network well known as 'Read'. Another interviewee noted the gentrification of culturally significant spaces:

> The gentrification process persecutes all spaces which became attractive for people.
>
> (L3 – Urban Activist)

Through direct observations (made by day in the two weeks preceding the festival and by day and night during the festival) around Liberdade Avenue, we noted an intense movement of tourists, but a decreased movement of commuting office workers. In the point of view of one interviewee:

> Nobody wants to get in conflict with the hotels. That is a sort of noble Avenue and the main concentration of people is clearly tourists, isn't it? This famous Avenue belongs to the tourists.
>
> (L1 – Musical Production)

The appearance of hotels and other innumerable services of lodging in most central areas of Lisbon is related to the displacement of local residents, producing higher rents. In addition to the rent market regulations and housing policies, gentrification processes stemming from the eight years of Mexefest and other cultural initiatives in Lisbon also manifest themselves in smaller and more everyday issues, such as commercial services and urban mobility management during the events. Here, numerous practical examples have appeared both in Portugal and in Brazil as well: car and pedestrian routes adapt to the festival; restaurant and bar menus are redesigned; and temporary street fairs and services appears for the festival public.

Security and outdoor nightlife

Festival organisers put on concerts aimed at more marginal groups during the afternoon, thus avoiding nocturnal schedules and minimising the risk of fights and excess alcohol consumption. Two other interviewees expressed their feeling of freedom and security they had during the event:

> I think that the Virada Cultural is a sort of key, but nobody recognises that because until this existence of this event we never experienced the possibility of being on the street [...] before of the Virada Cultural we felt secure in parks and some events that were always held in closed spaces.
>
> (S2 – Musical Production)

> I notice that Virada Cultural is a support to get in touch with the city, because we do not panic anymore, now that we started a relationship

with the city. We had misunderstood our city, I mean, if in the past we were frightened by our city now we are thinking different.

(S3 – Journalist)

The sense of security described by our interviewees suggests how the Virada Cultural (and consequently general cultural events) can produce a security perception of being in the street. From them, São Paulo city centre is more secure during the festival because there is a constant presence of people outdoor. The security provided by cultural events like festivals re-establishes nightlife and makes marginalised groups more visible. The issue of integration, therefore, intersects with cultural events, festivals and other celebrations bridge social divides, allowing for the resumption of street culture and the meeting of different groups in a secure atmosphere.

The reclamation of the night in São Paulo's historical centre serves to position Virada Cultural and urban festivals more broadly as key agents in a rhetoric of street security (Dimenstein, 2014; Liempt, Aalst & Schwanen, 2015). Activities that attract groups of people, and facilitate their mobility, ensure the vitality of the centre.

Social control by festival programme

In the field, we observed that these festivals, by connecting different cultural styles, aesthetic senses and artistic practices, act as spaces of visibility for different groups. For example, hip-hop, rap, breakdance and the marginal groups with which they are associated have been well represented at the Virada Cultural in several recent years. The same is evident in the case of musical groups of African origin at Mexefest. This occasions reflection on how festivals channel aesthetic-political resistance and provide subtle forms of social control (Miles, 2007) by means of its programme design.

Social control is evident in how festivals institutionalise marginal cultures. We observed this process in the inclusion of different aesthetics in the festivals' programmes: the marginal poetry of the Vozes da Escrita project at the Coliseu dos Recreios in Lisbon; the hip-hop performances at the Venue Rua 24 de Maio Stage in São Paulo; the Brazilian singer Elza Soares; and the American MC Talib Kweli in Lisbon (both Soares and Kweli are representatives of the black music linked to immigrant groups in Portugal).

Alongside these situations, which, together, characterise a multiculturalist discourse, a key question arises: is the Mexefest programme available to marginalised groups? If, on the one hand, the organisers curate a multi-ethnic performance context, which includes the well-known rapper Portuguese called Vala and the Cabo Verdean singer called Mayra Andrade, on the other hand we can identify how spaces are restricted by high ticket prices.

In São Paulo, great emphasis was placed on setting up the extensive programme of activities at the Chácara do Jockey (Spot 3, First List, Figure 2.1) during the 2016 Virada Cultural, which was centred around issues of gender, negritude and marginal culture, such as the concerts of the group Liniker e os Caramelows and the Orquestra Brasileira de Música Jamaicana. In the Parque do Carmo (Spot 4, First List, Figure 2.1) the performances of the Acadêmicos do Tatuapé group, the singer Alcione and the duo Wilson das Neves and Germano Mathias foregrounded the samba and other popular Brazilian performance genres. In Praça do Campo Limpo (Spot 5, First List, Figure 2.1), the Sarau Marginal do Binho, the Bonnie & Clyde Rappers battle and the MV Bill performance combined to consecrate marginal culture as a key part of the official festival programme, emphasising the character of local communities (Mulligan et al., 2006; Matarasso, 2009) of these activities.

In addition to programming activities, the link between the festival and marginal groups appeared indirectly in the discourse of cultural intermediaries in Lisbon. 'This festival is made up of many worlds', said a member of the Mexefest programming team at a press conference on 2nd November 2016, referring to the fact that the festival includes very different styles such as hip-hop, fado (Portuguese traditional music), spoken word or indie music.

Together, the strategies carried out by the organising team of Virada Cultural recognised marginal artistic expressions, but restricted them to specific groups and spaces. When they are incorporated into a big event like the Virada Cultural, Brazilian north-eastern culture, breakdance, punk and hip-hop begin to acquire new significance and bolster new discourses among the public while building and strengthening the identity of various marginal groups. Over the years, some of these strategies, which first seemed spontaneous, have recurred, not only in São Paulo's centre but also in the battles of rap and marginal poetry slams in the city's peripheries. Certainly, the creation of opportunities through festivals could facilitate social cohesion by including marginal groups. However, if the festival allows inclusivity and cultural conviviality, it also generates conflicts in public space.

Final remarks

This chapter has explored the different social roles that our selected festivals play with marginalised populations in both countries. Cultural events are often planned to further urban renewal policies, particularly the symbolic redesign of historical urban centres and creation of social labels. This may explain why governments emphasise discourses aimed at approaching and including marginal cultures, rediscovering an unusually insecure city. These aims justify the transformations of the Cine Teatro Capitólio and the Teatro Municipal we mentioned in opening this chapter into stages for the expression of marginal culture in Lisbon and São Paulo.

The connection between urban festivals and gentrification processes can be seen in two significant examples in our field research. In the Mexefest, the accessibility of festival events to marginal groups was controlled through the concentration of activity in a single central site, with expensive ticketing policies. Although the Virada Cultural programme, by contrast, is entirely free of charge to the public, other forms of controlling marginality occur, such as the setting up of specific venues in peripheral neighbourhoods of the city to control the audience movement. Therefore, gentrification and control of marginal groups are facilitated through the decentralisation of events in the Virada Cultural, and the restrictive prices make it, for many, difficult to access Mexefest venues.

How do discourses of inclusivity and marginality play out in urban festivals? The festivals we have studied both promote cosmopolitanism and their cities' unique identity. In São Paulo, festivals highlight cultural hybridity, drawing on Brazil's many regions and cultural traditions in performances and other thematic events in the Virada Cultural. In addition, night and the street appear as important liminal space-time, in which marginal groups socialise, as our observations and interviews made clear.

As our interviews revealed, cultural workers involved in the festival in São Paulo emphasise the positive role of the festivals as mediators of urban conflicts, facilitating new sociabilities and ideas. Thus, Virada Cultural contextualises itself as a valuable space of difference and inclusivity, suggesting different ways of doing things in the city and new ways of existing and resisting, subtly increasing social tolerance, security and well-being for different urban actors.

In Lisbon, we observed an important nuance: the election of artists so as to musically represent immigrants and alternative music scenes. Lisbon's association with multiple marginal identities and migrants (SEF, 2010) is reflected both in its regular festival programme. In addition to Mexefest case, it is possible to redeem here two other important events about this aspect: the Festival Todos and Lisboa Mistura.

The approximation between city and marginal communities can occur with the intention to generate positive results according to the creation of a friendly, diverse and hospitable atmosphere (Matarasso, 2009). Providing the city with a cosmopolitan sensibility is often a key factor in ensuring the well-being and inclusion of marginal groups, attracting new people and, therefore, new businesses to service them.

If, some decades ago, the concept of marginalisation was associated with specific antagonisms, such as centre-periphery, rich-poor or black-white, today we might say that marginalisation is bound up with new immigration dynamics, refugees, cultural policies and digital technologies. The design of a festival programme offers important hints about the kinds, and spatial distribution, of contemporary social marginality in the city. Such reflections can relocate the marginalised groups while presenting the first risks of the re-signification of their culture through the proliferation of creative circuits (Miles, 2007).

As an important device of social control in their respective cities, both festivals represent more than a site of cultural experience. They are a product of broad cultural policies that aim to brand and establish the value of urban centres though their controlled occupation by marginalised social groups. These festivals, overall, have the potential to generate new urban topographies (Sassatelli & Delanty, 2011), activate new social dynamics and recalibrate boundaries and margins in the city.

References

Costa, F. L. (2011) Globalização, diversidade e 'novas' classes criativas em Lisboa. Economia etnocultural e a emergência de um sistema de produção etnocultural. *Sociologia, problemas e práticas.* 67, 85–106.

Costa, P. (2017) *Estratégias para a cultura da cidade de Lisboa 2017.* Lisboa, Câmara Municipal de Lisboa.

Deleuze, G. (2000) *Post-scriptum sobre as sociedades de controle: conversações.* Rio de Janeiro, Editora 34.

Dimenstein, G. (2014) Entrevista. In: Colaboratória, Grupo Interdisciplinar (2014). *Manifesto da noite.* São Paulo, Invisíveis Produções.

Ferreira, C. (2010) Cultura e regeneração urbana: novas velhas agendas da política cultural para as cidades. *Revista Tomo.* 16, 29–56.

Fix, M. (2000) A 'fórmula mágica' da parceria público-privada: operações urbanas em São Paulo. *Cadernos de Urbanismo.* 3, Rio de Janeiro, Prefeitura Municipal do Rio de Janeiro.

Glover, T. D. (2015) Animating public space. In: Gammon, S. & Elkington, S. (eds.) *Landscapes of leisure: space, places and identities.* London, Palgrave Macmillan, pp. 96–109.

Greener, I. (2011) *Designing social research: a guide for the bewildered.* London, Sage.

Hughes, G. (1999) Urban revitalisation: the use of festival time strategies. *Leisure Studies.* 18 (2), 119–135.

Kara José, B. (2007) *Políticas culturais e negócios urbanos. A instrumentalização da cultura na revitalização do centro de São Paulo 1975–2000.* São Paulo, Annablume, FAPESP.

Latour, B. (2005) *Reassembling the social.* Oxford, Oxford University Press.

Liempt, I., Aalst, I. & Schwanen, T. (2015) Geographies of the urban night. *Urban Studies.* 52 (3), 407–421.

Líndon, A. & Hiernaux, D. (2012) *Geografías de lo Imaginario.* Barcelona, Anthropos Editorial.

Matarasso, F. (2009) A place in the city recognising creative inclusion. *Creative Communities Conference.* Surfers Paradise, Australia, 16 April.

Miles, M. (2007) *Cities and cultures.* London and New York, Routledge.

Mulligan, M., Humphery, K., James, P., Scanlon, C., Smith, P. & Welch, N. (2006) *Creating community: celebrations, arts and wellbeing within and across local communities.* Melbourne, The Globalism Institute, RMIT University.

Rena, N., Berquó, P. & Chagas, F. (2014) Biopolíticas Espaciais gentrificadoras e as resistências estéticas biopotentes. *Lugar Comum.* 41, 71–88.

Sassatelli, M. & Delanty, G. (2011) *Festivals in cities, cities in festivals.* In: Giorgi, L., Segal, J., Delanty, G., Sassatelli, M., Santoro, M., Solaroli, M., Magaudda, P. & Chalcraft, J. (eds.) *European Commission, European Arts Festivals: Strengthening cultural diversity.* Luxembourg, Publications Office of the European Union, pp. 47–55.

SEF. (2010) *Relatório de Imigração, Fronteiras e Asilo, 2009.* Oeiras, Serviço de Estrangeiros e Fronteiras Portugal.

Zukin, S. (1995) *The cultures of cities.* Cambridge, MA, Blackwell Publishing.

3 'Proud to be South D'

Perceptions of a street festival in a marginalised community in New Zealand

Trudie Walters

Introduction

Individuals and communities may be/feel marginalised in a variety of ways and for a number of reasons, including socio-economic status, ethnicity, race, gender, sexuality, family status, religion and/or age (Smith & Pitts, 2007). These are not discrete categories however, and the intersectionality of factors is acknowledged; individuals have multiple identities which may compound issues of marginalisation (Smith & Pitts, 2007). Planned events at all scales (from mega-events such as the Olympic Games to small community events) may purportedly seek to include those at the margins, with varying degrees of success or inadvertently work to further marginalise individuals and/or communities.

This chapter presents the findings of a research project focussed on an event in a marginalised suburb of Dunedin, a city in the South Island of New Zealand. The aim of this research is to understand how an event in a marginalised community could contribute to community celebration, pride, cohesiveness and well-being for its residents. It uses a case study approach and focusses on the South Dunedin Street Festival, held annually since 2011. South Dunedin is a low socio-economic suburb with high rates of unemployment, disability, drug use, sole parents and elderly residents, coupled with low levels of educational achievement and home ownership. Local government is perceived to have neglected the infrastructure needs of this community over the years, and a significant flood in the area in 2015 exacerbated the sense of neglect. In order to achieve the research aim, three members of the South Dunedin Street Festival organising committee were interviewed, and 'in the moment' conversations were had with 12 people attending the 2017 event.

Community events and the marginalised

Jepson and Clarke (2013: p. 7) define community events as:

> [A] themed and inclusive community event or series of events which have been created as the result of an inclusive community planning process

to celebrate the particular way of life of people and groups in the local community with emphasis on particular space and time.

This definition is broad enough to capture those community events that target an external audience, and indeed much previous research on community festivals and events has focussed on their role in driving tourism and regional development across urban, regional and rural contexts (see, for example, Derrett, 2003; Rusher, 2003; Quinn, 2005; Barrie, 2008; Kalkstein-Silkes, Cai & Lehto, 2008; Clark & Misener, 2015; Luonila & Johansson, 2015). This focus on tourism and regional development has resulted in a number of studies on economic impacts, motivations for attendance, participant profiles and levels of satisfaction (see, for example, Çela, Knowles-Lankford & Lankford, 2007; Axelsen & Swan, 2010; Getz & Robinson, 2014). Other studies have found that community events frequently make a significant contribution to destination image, and in so doing may generate a sense of pride amongst the local community (Quinn, 2005; Lee & Arcodia, 2011; Laing & Frost, 2014; Getz & Page, 2016).

Less studied are community events that are aimed at residents rather than tourists (in other words, those that are inwardly focussed). Such events are often developed by local government, not-for-profit organisations or community groups and are strongly associated with local identity, values and traditions, and thus are said to be representative of place and culture (Gibson, 2010; Jepson & Clarke, 2013; Cleave, 2016). However, a number of researchers have recently begun to critically examine the role that power plays in the organisation and evolution of community events, resulting in questions about 'who' events are held for – even where they are inwardly focussed (for example Clarke & Jepson, 2011; George, Roberts & Pacella, 2015; Batty, 2016). A new book edited by Jepson and Clarke (2018) has drawn together a broad range of research centred on the topic, with many studies identifying exclusionary rather than inclusive practices. The expression of power also dictates *who* is considered marginalised (Smith & Pitts, 2007), which may manifest itself in the stigmatisation of various sectors of the community and, in turn, a lack of events held in, by and for those communities.

In addition to representing and affirming local identity and values, community events may also be created to achieve a range of other social outcomes. These may include building a sense of community, improving civic engagement, enhancing social cohesion and boosting resilience – and as such they are recognised as contributing to residents' quality of life (Derrett, 2009; Jepson & Clarke, 2013; de Brito & Richards, 2017; Jepson & Stadler, 2017; Duffy & Mair, 2018). For example, in their investigation in drought-affected rural communities in Australia, Gibson and Connell (2015) identified the important emotional role that events played in lifting the spirits of the local population at a time of crisis. In a similar vein, Derrett (2003) argued that communities recognise the value of creating events that foster residents' feelings of ownership and belonging.

These more socially driven event aims and objectives, along with issues of power, may be of particular importance to marginalised individuals and those living in marginalised communities. Events held in, by and for marginalised communities could provide a platform for such communities to redress imbalances of power (and associated stigmatising) through the celebration of their way of life (Clarke & Jepson, 2011; Jepson & Clarke, 2013). These aspects of events have been largely overlooked by critical event studies researchers to date, and this chapter aims to address this lack by furthering our understanding of the social role and value of community events in marginalised communities.

Contextualising the research setting

Before continuing with the analysis, it is important to provide the context of the research by situating myself within it and introducing the city, the suburb and the event. Previous to entering academia, I worked in a bank in the marginalised community of South Dunedin, a suburb of Dunedin City in the South Island of New Zealand. I worked there full-time for 1.5 years, and then part-time for a further 3.5 years while studying at university. I observed and was immersed in both the lives of my customers and the wider South Dunedin community (on reflection, this period of my life constituted something of an ethnographic study). As a result, I developed a strong affection for many of the former and a protective attitude towards the latter. I therefore cannot help but carry these emic perspectives and experiences into this research; they have been instrumental in the conceptualisation of this project; have shaped how I think about marginalised communities; and have (I believe) helped me to be a more empathetic, compassionate researcher. At the same time, I remain an outsider through my privilege as an educated, home-owning, white, middle-class woman with a stable income.

The population of South Dunedin is just under 2,500, with a more culturally diverse population and a higher proportion of older residents than the overall Dunedin population, lower levels of income and education qualification, higher unemployment, twice the number of single-parent families and lower levels of home ownership (Table 3.1) (Statistics New Zealand, 2013). Access to communication technologies (the internet and mobile phones) is also lower than for Dunedin City residents as a whole, and their physical mobility is more limited due to lower rates of car ownership (Table 3.1). These statistics provide a picture of the intersectional nature of this marginalised community, and while powerful, the numbers only tell part of the story.

Local residents are reported in the media to feel 'uncared for' by local government, particularly after a significant flooding event in the area in 2015 in which many residents were adversely affected and perceived the response from local government to be insufficient and unnecessarily drawn out (Morris, 2009; Price, 2012; George, 2015). Until approximately 2011 the

Table 3.1 Census data (2013) comparing South Dunedin and Dunedin City as a whole across a range of demographic measures (Statistics NZ, 2013)

Demographic statistic	South Dunedin	Dunedin City
Median age	48.8 years	36.7 years
Over 65 years old	28.4%	14.9%
European ethnicity	82.5%	88.3%
Maori ethnicity	12.8%	7.7%
Pacific ethnicity	3.7%	2.5%
Asian ethnicity	6.1%	6.2%
Most common language spoken after English	te reo Maori (4.4%)	French (1.8%)
Married	23.5%	41.0%
Separated, divorced, widowed	35.0%	16.1%
Formal education qualification	60.5%	81.9%
Hold Bachelor's degree or higher	10.9%	22.7%
Unemployment rate	11.3%	7.5%
Most common occupational group	Labourers	Professional
Median income	$20,100	$23,300
Earning over $50,000	7.6%	22.0%
One parent with children families	34.9%	16.0%
One-family households	36.9%	62.5%
Single-person households	56.3%	27.9%
Access to internet	48.3%	77.8%
Access to mobile phone	66.8%	83.4%
Access to three or more vehicles	3.2%	14.1%
Home ownership	39.4%	67.9%

local retail precinct and infrastructure had received little funding and was looking rundown with a number of empty shops and a lack of public facilities (Morris, 2009; Loughrey, 2011; Price, 2012).

Against this backdrop, the South Dunedin Street Festival was first held in 2011 and has become an annual event (with the exception of 2016 when it was cancelled due to the unforeseen personal circumstances of one of the organising committee members). The promotional poster for the 2017 event (held on 4 November, and the focus of this research) states that the Festival is 'a celebration of all things South Dunedin; all the fantastic variety and diversity of cultures, community groups, families and striking individuals that make up this special part of town. The Festival aims to both build a stronger sense of community, and to showcase the amazing resilience that's already here, at times almost hidden...' The Festival is supported (both in-kind and some financial) by the South Dunedin Business Association and has received some funding from the Dunedin City Council and the Otago Community Trust.

Methods, limitations and challenges

Given the research aim and the visual nature of events, a multi-methods approach was adopted (Pauwels, 2013; Zuev, 2016). It was important to understand the perceptions of both the organisers of the South Dunedin Street

Festival and those who attended, and to capture the material culture of the event. In early October 2017, emails were sent to the members of the organising committee explaining the purpose of the project and requesting an interview – three out of six responded. The interviews were semi-structured (which allowed flexibility for deeper questioning and to explore related topics; see McGehee, 2012) and took place after the event in late November and early December 2017. They ranged from 27 to 40 minutes in duration and were digitally recorded and later transcribed by the researcher. To supplement the information gained through interviews and give a richer and more holistic understanding of the South Dunedin Street Festival, including its material culture, participant observation and photographs were used during the event (Zuev, 2016). This captured the event and the attendees 'as they were' and allowed the nuances of social interactions and the event experience to be recorded through detailed field notes.

The collection of event attendee perspectives was more problematic, however. Perhaps because of my supposed familiarity with the community through working at the bank, and my familiarity with conducting research interviews (including some with members of this community), I did not fully comprehend the challenges I would face. Initially I intended to approach attendees during the event on 4 November 2017, ask them to read and sign the project consent form and then verbally survey them using a list of Likert-scale questions followed by open-ended questions. I envisaged these conversations being 10–15 minutes long and being able to digitally record them. Three obstacles presented themselves almost immediately.

First, the power inherent in my new academic role presented a barrier to people's willingness to participate (Smith & Pitts, 2007). As the Street Festival began, I approached a woman walking past. She glanced at me (and my official-looking clipboard and name badge) and declined to engage in conversation, saying 'I don't want to talk to a university person' and walking quickly away. Second, it became evident that not all event attendees were able to read the consent form, and third, those with children were not willing or able to spend time talking to me. My preconceived notions of my familiarity with the community were clearly flawed and a new approach was needed: event attendees were approached (without the clipboard), given a brief verbal overview of the project and asked whether they would be interested in a quick chat about the Street Festival. If so, I verbally conveyed the contents of the consent form and asked them to sign it, and the 'in-the-moment' conversation (Quinn & Wilks, 2013: p. 20) ensued. These conversations were semi-structured and lasted 3–8 minutes. Immediately after the conversation, I quickly took detailed field notes about the thoughts and experiences that they shared with me, and included as many quotes as I could capture. In this way, the perspectives of 12 attendees at the 2017 event were gained (Table 3.2) – not as many as hoped for, and perhaps not in as much detail as initially envisaged, but arguably adequate in terms of data saturation (Guest, Bunce & Johnson, 2006).

Table 3.2 Demographic information of event attendees who participated in the study

Pseudonym	Gender	Age bracket	Place of residence
Laurel	F	40s	South Dunedin
Colette	F	70s	Musselburgh (neighbouring suburb)
Ailsa	F	70s	South Dunedin
Yvette	F	60s	Visiting family, from a different city
Philip	M	30s	Caversham (neighbouring suburb)
Aaron	M	30s	Caversham (neighbouring suburb)
Adrienne	F	80s	South Dunedin
Peter	M	40s	South Dunedin
Nerolie	F	40s	Broad Bay (further away suburb)
Clarissa	F	30s	Sawyers Bay (further away suburb)
Robert	M	40s	Visiting family, from a different city
Martin	M	70s	South Dunedin

The interview transcripts and notes from the 'in-the-moment' conversations were examined using inductive thematic analysis, which is a qualitative method that allows the researcher to generate meaning from the material itself rather than preconceived ideas (Braun & Clarke, 2006). It is also a flexible tool that can be applied to visual material; therefore the analysis of the photographs was undertaken using the same method (Walters, 2016).

Findings

Four significant themes were identified from the analysis of field notes and interviews with organisers and attendees at the 2017 South Dunedin Street Festival: (1) good for the community; (2) it gets people out; (3) the stigma of South Dunedin; and (4) a diverse community. Each will be unpacked and critically examined, in turn.

Good for the community

The South Dunedin Street Festival was perceived both by organisers and attendees alike to be good for the community, and the analysis identified three main reasons for this. The first was through showcasing local community groups, activities and service organisations – indeed, this was one of the goals of the organising committee:

> We tried to keep stalls and that from round the local area so that we were showing off locals that availability of things and what we do out here and what people do.
>
> (Organiser 1)

Likewise, the benefits of the Festival for local retailers were recognised by event attendees:

> It's great for South D, great to have a focus, get the community together, helps keep the shops on this strip going.
>
> (Nerolie, event attendee)

> It's right *in* the community, amongst the shops so it has positive benefits for them too, rather than being in a carpark isolated somewhere. I have been into quite a few of the shops and the owners are happy to be having a busy morning, it's not just the stall holders outside [who are benefitting].
>
> (Robert, event attendee)

This focus on the 'local' provided event attendees with an understanding of the diversity of activities and services in the area that were available to them for leisure and support:

> It gave the community a little bit more understanding of what is going on around the place, and what is available, and where it's available.
>
> (Organiser 1)

Indeed, some of the most popular stalls were the local Member of Parliament, Blind Foundation, Dunedin City Council (who provide a range of support services), Social Services (a social services and counselling agency run by the Catholic Diocese of Dunedin) and the open day held by the community dance group. People were observed queuing to ask questions of the organisations and taking information brochures about services available to them. The guide dog at the Blind Foundation stall drew a great deal of attention, and he and his owner were clearly known to many of the event attendees.

The Street Festival also facilitated networking opportunities between smaller activity and support groups that wouldn't ordinarily occur due to a shortage of time and resources:

> Um, one of the ideas of the festival was to try and bring together some of those groups to…see what each other were doing, um, to share a bit, and one of the things we always tried to have as part of the festival was a strong community group presence. Um, so…for that reason alone, yes I think it's really good to get those people seeing each other, knowing about each other, um ah in a practical way rather than just reading a list.
>
> (Organiser 3)

Along one side of the street the tents had been joined together to form a single strip of shelter with a line of trestle tables set up for each community group (Figure 3.1). This layout facilitated conversations between groups,

Figure 3.1 A line of community stalls.

and I observed a sense of camaraderie and genuine interest between them –
even though many had clearly not met before. Stallholders were seen swap-
ping stories, introducing each other to event attendees, pointing attendees
in the direction of other stalls whose services they may be interested in and
looking after each other's stalls during short absences.

The South Dunedin Street Festival sought to showcase its unique qualities to a largely internal audience – those living in the suburb or with connections to it. It aimed to foster a sense of community and pride, through
highlighting what there was on offer in terms of businesses, support services
and creative talent. While some of the marketing may have resulted in people from neighbouring suburbs attending the festival, this was not the main
focus. As one organiser pointed out,

> we're faced with this sort of dilemma, if we, people have made the com-
> ment that there's no stalls that sell posh stuff, so nobody wanting posh
> stuff comes - well this is not our neighbourhood, posh isn't us! Um...
> and I think if you do that the local community won't turn up, or their
> poverty will be reinforced.
>
> (Organiser 2)

In this way, a community event in a marginalised community may stand in
contrast to other forms of event – many festivals focus on showcasing their
unique qualities to external audiences and aim to attract visitors from out

of the area while still fostering a sense of community (Derrett, 2003). As an event held in, by and for the local (marginalised) community, the South Dunedin Street Festival provides attendees with an authentic and relatable event that meets their needs. Perhaps most importantly, it is an event that does not alienate them nor draw attention to their marginalised status by seeking to attract or cater to the 'other'.

The second way the Festival was seen as being good for the community was through celebrating South Dunedin, which, in turn, helped to generate or increase a sense of pride amongst local residents:

> I just think they feel it's their day, it's their chance to show off their area, and it's their…opportunity to participate as part of [being] a South Dunedinite.
>
> (Organiser 1)

> Celebrating South Dunedin is the basic goal of the festival. Um and if that engenders a sense of pride where there isn't one previously well that's a bonus…I know that in the past, performers on the main stage often would introduce themselves by way of their South Dunedin credentials. And they were proud to be associated with South Dunedin and contributing to the festival. Um, and… I think there is that sense that… that there is something to celebrate about that unique part of town…
>
> (Organiser 3)

> I think it's good for community pride, but that was already there but it helps with it.
>
> (Adrienne, event attendee)

In this sense, the South Dunedin Street Festival functions to reflect and influence place identity and to provide a forum for demonstrating one's attachment to place. Both Derrett (2003) and Jaeger and Mykletun (2013) identified these facets of community-based festivals and events in their studies of rural areas in Australia and Finland, respectively.

The final way in which the Street Festival was good for the community was through being an enjoyable and accessible event designed specifically for South Dunedin residents:

> I think it has value in terms of focusing the community's attention um on itself. And I don't think we get attention from anybody else, in the Street Festival, the South Dunedin community focusing on itself, and having some fun.
>
> (Organiser 2)

> I think it's really good that there is, there are events in South Dunedin which are accessible and affordable um, y'know, South Dunedin people have a low um low ownership of motor vehicles for instance,

so they rely on public transport a bit more and or mobility scooters and various other ways of getting round the place but um y'know, getting to the other end of town doesn't come easy for everybody. Yeah so things happening that are good, enjoyable, local, yeah um I think that's worth doing, that's the main reason to do it, some affordable fun.

(Organiser 3)

Here again we see evidence of the 'relatable' nature of the event, and the sentiments of the organisers presented were echoed by event attendees. While attendees did not provide specifics, some nevertheless made statements such as 'It's great for the community' (Laurel) and 'I've lived in this area all my life, this is good for the community' (Martin). Others commented that they could afford the bus fare from the neighbouring suburb to attend, whereas they wouldn't attend an event 'in town' (which would mean paying for one extra zone on the bus). When assessed holistically, the comments from both organisers and attendees that contribute to this theme suggest that the event was somehow empowering.

It gets people out

Related to the notion of affordability and accessibility is the second theme of 'getting people out'. There is little in the way of community events catering for those on low incomes or with limited mobility living in South Dunedin, and organisers noted that the Street Festival appeared to be valued for its ability to get people out and bring them together:

What I think it does with the festival, it brings a huge amount of people out in together, and sort of...it... it brings more of a community spirit I think?... A place where we can come together.

(Organiser 1)

Certainly, this theme was the strongest of those identified from the conversations with event attendees, and indeed, rich social interactions were frequently observed while at the Street Festival. Rather than attendees perusing stalls and listening to musicians in pairs or small groups with little interaction between groups (as I have observed at other events), at the South Dunedin Street Festival there was a great deal of interaction between groups which engendered a real sense of community. People were seen hugging each other, remarking how long it had been since they last saw each other, asking after friends and family and animatedly discussing their personal connections to the event (for example, their child, grandchild or great-grandchild was performing in the cultural event). It was clear that meeting one's neighbours, friends and relatives at the event was a catalyst for enjoyable, meaningful and important social engagement, a contention that was supported by many attendee comments:

> It's great because I've seen so many people I know.
>
> (Collette)

> It's important to me, it's a day out, I get to talk to people, get to know my neighbours. I see people I've known since they were children. That's really special, that's a South D thing.
>
> (Ailsa)

> Great way for people to mix and mingle. We've already met the other grandma! It's the spirit, the community spirit.
>
> (Yvette)

> It's good, gets you out of the house, I'm in a council flat, you know... You get to see lots of people you know, have a catch up.
>
> (Adrienne)

> Nice to see everyone out in the street. Opportunity to come out, mingle and talk to each other.
>
> (Peter)

Again, it is argued that a sense of empowerment is evident in the attendees' comments. They emphasise the role of the festival in creating and maintaining both a collective identity and a sense of belonging to place found in other research in marginal communities (Derrett, 2003; Jaeger & Mykletun, 2013). Similar sentiments were expressed by participants in Gibson and Connell's (2015) study of the importance of events in small drought-stricken communities in rural Australia. There, community festivals and events played a vital emotional role in assisting communities in dealing with shared struggles – getting people out and bringing them together to talk and have fun helped them overcome isolation and frustration, and provided them with an avenue to forget their problems for a few hours.

The importance of the South Dunedin Street Festival to the community was underscored by the observation that some people were waiting impatiently for the Street Festival to begin, even before the official starting time of 10am – much to the delight of the event organisers, who viewed this as a positive sign:

> that's the thing I've found out here, that um...not only, um, not only do they look forward to events and everything else, but they're happy to participate, happy to be part of it, they *want* to be part of it.
>
> (Organiser 1)

Alongside this, however, two of the organisers noted that residents' self-awareness of the marginalisation of South Dunedin resulted in the community taking nothing for granted – including the Street Festival. They felt that while the community may have been disappointed if the event was discontinued for any reason, it would not have surprised them as their expectations about any form of service provision for their community were so low. This contrasts with Gibson and Connell's (2015: p. 456) findings where communities expected that the annual events would continue to be held regardless of hardship imposed by the drought, thereby providing 'normalisation' in a difficult time. This points to the stigma associated with being part of a marginalised community, which is the third theme identified in the findings.

The stigma of South Dunedin

The suburb of South Dunedin has been marginalised for a number of years, largely due to the (perceived or real) demographic composition of its residents. This (and the associated disempowerment) is acknowledged as problematic by the South Dunedin Street Festival organisers, many of whom work in organisations that support marginalised individuals and groups:

> It's been an area that's been very badly neglected, um, over the years, it's... Because there's a lower socio-economic group out here, we don't seem to count... it was an eye-opener to me [when I first moved here], that people were so... should I say, they weren't down [despondent]... but they walked probably with their heads bent more often than they do now.
>
> (Organiser 1)

> South Dunedin does have a terrible reputation, its where the cr – my son he told me 'don't go live or work in South Dunedin, that's where the crazies live'! [laughs] so we have a reputation for being on the flat [land], which is the synonym for poor, and um badly housed, and um high disability, aged, mental health, physical disability, population. So there's that...stigma...attached to South Dunedin...I think it is a community that feels itself um...powerless. These are all the most powerless groups and they're in one place.
>
> (Organiser 2)

> South Dunedin has been characterised by various people as um, fragmented, um, fractionalised, factionalised, um...not integrated community...South Dunedin is often characterised by those not-so-positive statistics and people think 'oh gee it must be a real dump'.
>
> (Organiser 3)

The stigmatising of South Dunedin and the importance of the Street Festival in counteracting this for residents were explicitly voiced as a statement of fact by two of the event attendees:

> Good vibe, South D needs this 'cos no-one likes South D
>
> (Philip and Aaron)

Other event attendees articulated the stigma and neglect in a more subtle manner:

> It's nice to have something like this to encourage people to come to this area of town.
>
> (Robert)

> Nice to see everyone out in the street, 'cos it feels like this area is a bit neglected and run down.
>
> (Peter)

In 2011, as part of its South Dunedin retail strategy, the Dunedin City Council provided a one-off $53,000 fund for retailers and building owners to clean and paint the facades of buildings along the main street of South Dunedin (South Dunedin clean-up, 2011). However many are old and still in need of maintenance. Contributing to the feeling of decline are the number of empty shops, thrift shops and second-hand furniture dealers. One agency, offering art as therapy for people with intellectual disabilities, made contact with some of the owners of vacant buildings and obtained permission to brighten their windows with artworks by their clients. Generally, however, the vacant shop windows are dusty and soulless which does nothing to detract from the sense of dereliction.

Festivals and events may be one means of changing place image where a community is struggling with its reputation (Jaeger & Mykletun, 2013; Jepson & Clarke, 2013). While their argument is more related to external perceptions of place, there is some evidence here to suggest that internal perceptions of place may also be influenced by festivals and events. As noted earlier, one of the South Dunedin Street Festival organisers stated they had observed a positive change in the general demeanour of the community over the last 15 years. They then went on to credit the festival with playing at least some small part in that due to the positive media coverage.

A diverse community

At the same time as the demographic characteristics were a source of stigma, the diversity of the South Dunedin community's demographics was equally a point to be celebrated, and this is the final theme to be explored. The organising committee deliberately sought to make the South Dunedin Street Festival an inclusive event that represented the diversity of its residents and their interests:

> That was one of the things that I think made it more South Dunedin's festival, because there were so many schools involved, and we were really focused on that this year, y'know trying to get the different ethnic cultures and the community dancing down there like with the ceroc and the rock n roll and things like that.
>
> (Organiser 1)

[in addition to the high proportion of physically/mentally disabled and aged]...I think it's a very disparate community, and a lot of refugees too of course, um...so anything that brings them together and allows that focus, so I was in charge of the dancing, and I wanted, I wanted Chinese, I wanted Indian – I didn't get Indian but I will next time, um and Irish and y'know, I wanted a range of ethnicities and styles to be present as a representation of the community, and it was very popular.

(Organiser 2)

I think that South Dunedin's a really diverse community, and um there are a lot of, each little bit of diversity has got um...[long pause] people associating together around it.

(Organiser 3)

A number of the event attendees appreciated this diversity, with Ailsa in particular specifying some of the forms that diversity took and believing that this made South Dunedin a 'real' community:

People from all different walks of life.

(Colette)

I like to see the different groups performing.

(Adrienne)

And there's lots of elderly people live here, lots of disabled, you know, physically and intellectually...it's a real community here.

(Ailsa)

These comments demonstrate that the organisers acknowledged the importance of showcasing diversity, that they encouraged participation from a wide cross-section of the community and (perhaps most importantly) that this was valued by those attending. Participant observation revealed people from a wide array of ethnicities taking part (not only as attendees but also selling food and giving dance/cultural demonstrations) alongside groups and individuals promoting activities as diverse as religion, a not-for-profit community radio station and a cannabis museum (Figures 3.2 and 3.3). Event attendees ranged from the very young to the very old and included many with physical and intellectual disabilities (Figure 3.4).

From census data (Statistics New Zealand, 2013) and my emic understanding gained through working in South Dunedin, this seemed a fitting representation of the diversity of the community. This contrasts with the findings from Clarke and Jepson's (2011) study of the Derby Jubilee Festival in the United Kingdom, where the exercise of power by the organising committee led to an exclusive rather than inclusive event that did not reflect the diversity of the community in which it was held – despite the stated festival aims around embracing the multicultural nature of the city and celebrating its diversity.

Figure 3.2 A Christian information stall.

Figure 3.3 Whakamana Cannabis Museum information stall.

Figure 3.4 Attendees at the South Dunedin Street Festival 2017.

Conclusion

This chapter focussed on the South Dunedin Street Festival, an event in a marginalised community in New Zealand. It found that event attendees and organisers felt the event was good for the community for many reasons – it gave the community a focus; showcased the leisure and support services available to them; put groups in touch with each other; and promoted a sense of place identity, pride and belonging. Allowing South Dunedin residents to celebrate the uniqueness of the suburb and focus attention on themselves acted as an avenue to overcome the stigma of marginalisation and seemed to create a sense of pride and empowerment, even if just for one day. Having an event to look forward and a reason to leave the house was appreciated by some of the attendees, particularly the older residents spoken to, and as such the event contributed to their well-being. The event created a space and time to enjoy the company of others and the diversity of the community – both in terms of the people and the displays/activities on offer. In this way, it appears that the event met its self-reported mandate to contribute to community celebration, pride, cohesiveness and well-being.

Perhaps most significantly, this research found that if events in, by and for marginalised communities are to be successful, they must differ from other types of community events. As shown here, such events need to be inwardly focussed, authentic and relatable, and meet the needs of the community.

It is important not to alienate them nor draw attention to their marginalised status by seeking to attract or cater to the 'other' in the form of tourists or outsiders from different socio-economic groups. Through this case study, the chapter has demonstrated the value of events held in, by and for marginalised communities. However it is equally important to acknowledge that this may only occur if the event organising committee is inclusive and sensitive to the needs of local residents, and is drawn from within the community itself.

This research project has been valuable both personally and professionally; it has challenged and inspired me in equal proportions. It has provided me with a new research thread, and future work needs to expand the geographic focus to include other communities within New Zealand – and indeed, beyond. The focus will also be broadened beyond marginalised suburbs to help our understanding of other specific marginalised groups, including (but not limited to) Māori and Pacific peoples, ethnic minority migrants and refugees, rural women and older people. Each of these groups has their own issues and challenges, and particular ways in which events may contribute to, resist or overcome marginalisation. I look forward to contributing to the ongoing, necessary conversation around marginalisation and events, and welcome opportunities for collaboration.

References

Axelsen, M. & Swan, T. (2010) Designing festival experiences to influence visitor perceptions: the case of a wine and food festival. *Journal of Travel Research.* 49 (4), 436–450.

Barrie, W. (2008) Case study on the use of Scottish food events in promoting Scottish tourism and food. In: Hall, C. M. & Sharples, L. (eds.) *Food and wine festivals and events around the world: development, management and markets.* Oxford, Butterworth-Heinemann, pp. 78–84.

Batty, R. J. (2016) Understanding stakeholder status and legitimate power exertion within community sport events: a case study of the Christchurch (New Zealand) City to Surf. In: Jepson, A. & Clarke, A. (eds.) *Managing and developing communities, festivals and events.* London, Palgrave Macmillan, pp. 103–119.

Braun, V., & Clarke, V. (2006) Using thematic analysis in psychology. *Qualitative Research in Psychology.* 3 (2), 77–101.

Çela, A., Knowles-Lankford, J. & Lankford, S. (2007) Local food festivals in Northeast Iowa communities: a visitor and economic impact study. *Managing Leisure.* 12 (2/3), 171–186.

Clark, R. & Misener, L. (2015) Understanding urban development through a sport events portfolio: a case study of London, Ontario. *Journal of Sport Management.* 29, 11–26.

Clarke, A. & Jepson, A. (2011) Power and hegemony within a community festival. *International Journal of Event and Festival Management.* 2 (1), 7–19.

Cleave, P. (2016) Community festivals and events in the South West of England, UK. In: Jepson, A. & Clarke, A. (eds.) *Managing and developing communities, festivals and events.* Basingstoke, Palgrave Macmillan, pp. 179–195.

de Brito, M. & Richards, G. (2017) Events and placemaking. *International Journal of Event and Festival Management*. 8 (1), 2–7.

Derrett, R. (2003) Making sense of how festivals demonstrate a community's sense of place. *Event Management*. 8, 49–58.

Derrett, R. (2009) How festivals nurture resilience in regional communities. In: Ali-Knight, J., Robertson, M., Fyall, A. & Ladkin, A. (eds.) *International perspectives of festivals and events*. Oxford, Elsevier, pp. 107–124.

Duffy, M. & Mair, J. (2018) Engaging the senses to explore community events. *Event Management*. 22, 49–63.

George, D. (2015) Young family left homeless by flood. *Otago Daily Times*, 12 June. Available from: www.odt.co.nz/news/dunedin/young-family-left-homeless-flood [Accessed 28th March 2018].

George, J., Roberts, R. & Pacella, J. (2015) 'Whose festival?' Examining questions of participation, access and ownership in rural festivals. In: Jepson, A. & Clarke, A. (eds.) *Exploring community festivals and events*. London and New York, Routledge, pp. 79–91.

Getz, D. & Page, S. J. (2016) *Event studies: theory, research and policy for planned events* (3rd ed.). Abingdon and New York, Routledge.

Getz, D. & Robinson, R. N. S. (2014) Foodies and food events. *Scandinavian Journal of Hospitality and Tourism*. 14 (3), 315–330.

Gibson, C. (2010) Place making: mapping culture, creating places: collisions of science and art. *Local-Global: Identity, Security, Community*. 7, 66–83.

Gibson, C. & Connell, J. (2015) The role of festivals in drought-affected Australian communities. *Event Management*. 19 (4), 445–459.

Guest, G., Bunce, A. & Johnson, L. (2006) How many interviews are enough?: an experiment with data saturation and variability. *Field Methods*. 18, 59–82.

Jaeger, K. & Mykletun, R.J. (2013) Festivals, identities and belonging. *Event Management*. 17, 213–226.

Jepson, A. & Clarke, A. (2013) Events and community development. In: Finkel R., McGillivray, D., McPherson, G. & Robinson, P. (eds.) *Research themes for events*. Wallingford, CAB International, pp. 6–17.

Jepson, A. & Clarke, A. (2018) *Power, construction and meaning in festivals*. Abingdon, Routledge.

Jepson, A. & Stadler, R. (2017) Conceptualising the impact of festival and event attendance upon family quality of life (QOL). *Event Management*. 21, 47–60.

Kalkstein-Silkes, C., Cai, L. A. & Lehto, X. Y. (2008) Conceptualising festival-based culinary tourism in rural destinations. In: Hall, C. M. & Sharples, L. (eds.) *Food and wine festivals and events around the world: development, management and markets*. Oxford, Butterworth-Heinemann, pp. 65–77.

Laing, J. & Frost, W. (2014). Using fashion exhibitions to reimagine destination image. In: Williams, K. Laing, J. & Frost, W. (eds.) *Fashion, design and events*. Abindgon and New York, Routledge, pp. 148–159.

Lee, I. & Arcodia, C. (2011) The role of regional food festivals for destination branding. *International Journal of Tourism Research*. 13 (4), 355–367.

Loughrey, D. (2011) South Dunedin's makeover agreed to. *Otago Daily Times*, 1 December. Available from: www.odt.co.nz/news/dunedin/south-dunedins-makeover-agreed [Accessed 25th January 2018].

Luonila, M. & Johansson, T. (2015) The role of festivals and events in the regional development of cities: cases of two Finnish cities. *Event Management*. 19, 211–226.

McGehee, N. G. (2012) Interview techniques. In: Dwyer, L., Gill, A. & Seetaram, N. (eds.) *Handbook of research methods in tourism: quantitative and qualitative approaches.* Cheltenham, Edward Elgar Publishing, pp. 365–376.

Morris, D. (2009) South Dunedin: a tale of two cities. *Otago Daily Times*, 10 January. Available from: www.odt.co.nz/news/dunedin/south-dunedin-tale-two-cities [Accessed 30th October 2017].

Pauwels, L. (2013) Contemplating the state of visual research: an assessment of obstacles and opportunities. In: Pink, S. (ed.) *Advances in visual methodology.* London, SAGE Publications, pp. 248–264.

Price, M. (2012) South Dunedin, steaming ahead? *Otago Daily Times*, 16 January. Available from: www.odt.co.nz/lifestyle/magazine/south-dunedin-steaming-ahead [Accessed 13th April 2018].

Quinn, B. (2005) Arts festivals and the city. *Urban Studies.* 42 (5/6), 927–943.

Quinn, B. & Wilks, L. (2013) Festival connections: people, place and social capital. In: Richards, G., de Brito, M. P. & Wilks, L. (eds.) *Exploring the social impacts of events.* Abingdon, Routledge, pp. 15–30.

Rusher, K. (2003) The Bluff Oyster Festival and regional economic development: festivals as culture commodified. In: Hall, C. M., Sharples, L., Mitchell, R., Macionis, N. & Cambourne, B. (eds.) *Food tourism around the world: development, management and markets.* Oxford, Butterworth-Heinemann, pp. 192–205.

Smith, A. & Pitts, M. (2007) Researching the margins: an introduction. In: Pitts, M. & Smith, A. (eds.) *Researching the margins: strategies for ethical and rigorous research with marginalised communities.* Basingstoke, Palgrave Macmillan, pp. 3–41.

South Dunedin clean-up (2011) *Otago Daily Times*, 25 April. Available from: www.odt.co.nz/news/dunedin/south-dunedin-clean [Accessed 21st March 2018].

Statistics New Zealand (2013) 2013 Census QuickStats about a place: South Dunedin. Available from: http://archive.stats.govt.nz/Census/2013-census/profile-and-summary-reports/quickstats-about-a-place.aspx?url=/Census/2013-census/profile-and-summary-reports/quickstats-about-a-place.aspx&request_value=15068&tabname=Work [Accessed 25th May 2018].

Walters, T. (2016) Using thematic analysis in tourism research. *Tourism Analysis.* 21 (1), 107–116.

Zuev, D. (2016) Visual methods in event studies. In: Pernecky, T. (ed.) *Approaches and methods in event studies.* Abingdon and New York, Routledge, pp. 96–119.

4 Disability and rural events

The cultural reproduction of inclusion and exclusion

Rayna Sage and Erin Flores

Introduction

Since the shift from a majority rural to a majority urban population in the United States in the 1920s, there has been little investment in and preservation of rural communities in comparison to urban spaces (Lichter & Ziliak, 2017). For people with disabilities, who are more likely to live in rural places than urban ones (von Reichert, Greiman & Myers, 2014), the marginalisation of rural space means fewer resources and services. Despite the privileging of urbanisation processes that often exploit and/or exclude rural places, rural communities and their members continue to persist. It requires time, effort and a level of trust between community members to build and maintain community and one way to do this is through community events and festivals (Getz, 2010). Much of the existing literature on community events points to the development of social capital as an individual and community resource (Coleman, 1988; Putnam, 2001; Derrett, 2003; Ziakas & Costa, 2010; Quinn & Wilks, 2013).

Events such as annual festivals, rodeos and hometown celebrations develop community resources, promote social cohesion and give those involved an opportunity to collectively celebrate community together. They also contribute to and are products of the economic, social and political structures (Derrett, 2003; Arcodia & Whitford, 2006), providing a physical space for community organisations and powers to gather and interact. The planning, development and maintenance of community events create and reproduce power structures within the community that can privilege some while excluding others (Clarke & Jepson, 2011). The right to fully participate in community is one of the pillars of the Disability Rights Movement, which led to the passing of the Americans with Disabilities Act (ADA) of 1990. The ADA is designed to provide motivation and incentive for creating and modifying non-discriminating public spaces accessible to people with disabilities. This also applies to rural community events, but to date there has been very little focus on accessibility for people with disabilities and what benefits are created when participation is made possible.

Cultural reproduction

According to Bourdieu's (1993) theories on cultural production and reproduction, people with disabilities develop habitus that keep them participating in the promotion of a dominant culture that creates their oppression
(often by not participating or being exploited in their participation). The
reproduction of exclusion or exploitation of people with disabilities in
the dominant culture has taken a number of forms, including massive institutionalisation, involuntary sterilisation and the exploitation of people
with disabilities for entertainment in 'freak shows' or the circus (Chemers,
2008; Taylor, 2017). The prevalence of institutionalisation and involuntary
sterilisation dropped off sharply in the late twentieth century, following the
Olmstead Act in 1999, which ordered that people with disabilities have the
right to live, work and play in their communities, and that the government
has a responsibility to provide appropriate community-based services and
support (Olmstead v. L.C., 1999). Freak shows featuring people with disabilities were incredibly popular leading up to the Second World War, when disability became more medicalised and was seen as something to overcome or
fix (Garland Thomson, 1997; Clare, 2015, 2017). While this shift created new
human rights problems for people with disabilities, culturally Americans
viewed people with disabilities with more humanness than they had in the
past. This shift made it more difficult to justify gawking at and exploiting
people with disabilities within the freak show circuit.

Many past and present institutional facilities are located in rural places,
and freak shows and circuses often performed as road shows, travelling
through rural communities, creating rural community events where a primary focus was to objectify and 'other' people with disabilities. Thus, the
present study of rural community events and the role of people with disabilities is incredibly important in our continued effort to move towards a
more just and inclusive countryside. In the spirit of critical event studies
(Spracklen & Lamond, 2016), this project illuminates contextual factors
that contribute to the inclusion or exclusion of people with disabilities in
rural community events.

At the same time, rural community events such as annual festivals, American
Indian powwows and arts festivals provide organised spaces in what Habermas (1989) terms the 'public sphere' (p. 29) for community members to engage
in solving social problems unique to their rural place. As Sharpe (2008) states,
festivals are not just for entertainment, but to 'change things for the better'
(p. 223). This is complicated by the privileging of dominant or what Williams
(1974) calls 'high culture' that leads to behaviours and decisions that shape
what activities, events and opportunities are considered legitimate, justifying
the exclusion of certain groups and perspectives in the event planning processes (Clark & Jepson, 2011). For individuals, festivals (both the actual event
and the planning of the event) help create webs of relationships that serve as
a vehicle for acquiring resources (Coleman, 1988; Putnam, 2001) and create

opportunities for developing personal and social identities within the context of the larger culture (Jaeger & Mykletun, 2013). However, not everyone has access to this public sphere, especially those with disabilities. Festivals serve as a way to reproduce existing norms and traditions (Quinn & Wilks, 2013) and while it often seems like they take on a life of their own, it is important to remember that these events are planned, not improvised, with underlying expectations about inclusion and exclusion (Waterman, 1998).

Methods

Utilising a modified version of the methods described by Quinn and Wilks (2013), we conducted 63 'in-the-moment' interviews at six rural community festivals across the western region of the frontier state of Montana during the summer of 2017. In the United States, Montana is among the least populated and most rural states, covering 147,040 square miles with a population of about a million people (US Census Bureau, 2016). For each festival, we contacted festival organisers for permission to conduct short 'in-the-moment' interviews with their festival organisers, vendors and attendees. These interviews were conducted by both authors. At each event, we approached people with and without visible disabilities (we did not specifically target only people with visible disabilities) in a variety of physical spaces at the events and invited them to participate in a quick interview about their experiences regarding the festival followed by a request for them to read and indicate 'yes' or 'no' to a set of six dichotomous questions about impairment (see Appendix A for interview guides and disability questions). We emphasised the voluntary nature of the interview and no personally identifying information was collected. For their time, participants received a $5 gift certificate or in one case, gift coin, to a local business such as a coffee shop, near the festival. With verbal permission, the interviews, which lasted on average 8.5 minutes, were audio recorded, transcribed and coded in NVivo.

Both authors thematically coded each of the transcripts with special attention given to indicators of inclusion and social participation using attribute, provisional and values coding (Saldaña, 2013). The coded utterances tended to be clustered in participants' responses to questions about what they get out of participating in the event, what kinds of efforts they noticed being made to accommodate people with disabilities and what kinds of experiences specific people they know with disabilities would have at this event. Basic information, such as participant role, gender and disability status, was coded using attribute coding. We also used provisional coding with a 'start list' of anticipated codes such as 'seeing people' and 'getting out' related to participation and finally, we used values coding to tease out themes related to a community-based discourse around accessibility. In second cycle coding, we compared our independent coding and only included utterances in which we both coded, and we met several times to establish at least an 80 percent intercoder rate for any utterances in which we did not agree. If we could not resolve conflicted codes, we omitted them from our data. In all writing of the results, the names of the events, locations and participants have been changed to protect confidentiality.

Our events

We attended six events across western Montana representing different types of gatherings with a range of purposes to explore how discourses around disability and inclusion vary. The events, along with brief descriptions of programming and venues, are outlined in Table 4.1.

Table 4.1 Event descriptions

Event	Brief description	Venue
Arts Festival	• Two days, held over weekend • Celebrated fibre arts • Vendors sold raw and modified fibres, typically hand-spun from a variety sources • Free/low-cost classes and demonstrations	• Newer fairgrounds building. Concrete floor and no-step entry. Three rows of 10x10 spaces separated by wide aisles • **Parking:** Accessible parking nearby • **Restroom:** Meets ADA accessibility standards
Hometown Days	• Held Friday night through Saturday evening • Parade of local organisations, schools, politicians and classic cars down Main Street • Street fair with vendors, food trucks, classic cars, music, music, pie-eating contest • Street dance outside local tavern	• Outdoors along Main Street. Street and sidewalks uneven, but most intersections had curb cuts • **Parking:** No designated accessible parking • **Restroom:** Portable restrooms (one accessible unit) at end of street. Some local stores allowed the use of restrooms (not always accessible)
Powwow	• Five days • Attendees and vendors typically camp in nearby field • Events included drum performance, dance competitions, youth basketball tournaments, cooking competitions • Vendors sold jewellery, food and American Indian goods	• Historic powwow grounds. Most booths on uneven gravel and dirt. Dance area flat, no-step concrete with bleacher seating • **Parking:** Gravel or dirt, with three spaces designated 'elders' and 'handicapped' • **Restroom:** Accessible restrooms and showers near event activities, but not camping area

Event	Brief description	Venue
Ghost Town Celebration	• One day, 9am to 4pm • Hourly activities including live music, shootouts, demonstrations, exhibits and re-enactments • Local food booths and vendors	• Wild West 'ghost town' with original buildings and wooden boardwalks. Buildings with steep staircases had unmarked accessible back entrances • **Parking:** Inaccessible shuttles provided for free. Drop-off area near ghost town, but few close parking spots. Most parking over a mile away • **Restroom:** Two accessible outhouses in centre of town
Community Picnic	• One day, 9am to early evening • Parade on Main Street • Picnic at nearby local community park with BBQ competition, live big band music and vendors	• Streets and sidewalks along parade route somewhat uneven. Not every intersection included curb cuts. Picnic outside in a grassy park. All vendors located on thick grass • **Parking:** Parking was monitored and people with designated disability parking passes allowed close parking • **Restroom:** Portable restrooms, one accessible unit
Rodeo	• One day, 6pm to midnight • Rodeo held afternoon and early evening • Included men riding broncos and bulls, and children riding sheep • General concessions, a snow cone and cotton candy booth, and a beer garden • Street dance downtown (~ 1 mile from rodeo grounds) for 21+ after rodeo events	• City rodeo grounds, formerly a baseball field. No designated accessible seating area. Seating: inaccessible covered wooden stadium bleachers; wooden picnic tables behind chain-link fence in the dirt; small concrete area in walkway around the rounds. Uneven grass and pavement, with gravel and holes, throughout grounds • **Parking:** No designated accessible parking • **Restroom:** Portable restrooms, but no accessible units

Because we are interested in cultural inclusion, we do not focus on the built environment here, but Table 4.1 highlights accessibility around two of the top concerns for most people with disabilities – parking and restroom access. Our results include discussion of these two important features when they intersect with cultural discourses, but these are not the focus of our study. It is our sense that there is broad acceptance of the expectation that at a minimum, parking and restrooms should be accessible for all people (although it is certainly not always the case, especially in rural places where compliance is not asked for or enforced or buildings are deemed exempt from the ADA of 1990).

Findings

The following is a brief overview of the demographics of our participants and general views on people with disabilities, followed by three primary areas of findings. Responses to our questions from the various events are interwoven together to highlight commonalities and differences. We find there are important benefits to having access to these rural events in terms of connecting and reconnecting with family and friends, building and maintaining community, and creating alternative spaces for empowerment. We present each of these thematic areas with a consideration of cultural production and reproduction as it relates to the role of people with disabilities in these rural community settings. We find that, in line with theories of social and cultural reproduction (Bourdieu, 1993), these rural community events create spaces in which local cultural norms and expectations are maintained and reproduced. This is especially true for the events that are primarily attended by the people who live in the community (such as the Hometown Days, Community Picnic and the Rodeo). Compared to the other events that draw more regional and sometimes national attention, at these three events nearly everyone we interviewed was local. Within the frame of considering how these events create physical space where culture is reproduced, we consider accessibility for people with disabilities and what they gain from participating and the potential opportunity costs of exclusion, especially in the potential for bringing about social change (Habermas, 1989).

Participants we interviewed and how they reflect on people with disabilities

Basic demographics of who we interviewed are outlined in Table 4.2. Our intention with recruitment was to include people from a variety of backgrounds occupying different spaces at the six events. As two individuals who present as white women, we ended up with more women and completed fewer interviews at the powwow than at the other events. This was partially because the interviews we completed with the six individuals at the powwow were more extensive than the other events, but also because of an internal sense of potentially being offensive as intrusive outsiders. We acknowledge these interviews have not been drawn from a representative sample, but collectively they provide deeper insight into cultural norms and expectations around festivals and people with disabilities in rural communities.

About two-thirds of those interviewed were women and 43 percent answered 'yes' to at least one of the six dichotomous impairment questions at the end of their brief interview, with the most common disability relating to walking or climbing stairs (Table 4.2). About half of those interviewed were patronising the festival as an attendee and the remaining half were split between vendors (29 percent) and organisers or volunteers (19 percent). The average age of the respondents was just under 50 years old and those interviewed ranged from 20 to 77 years old.

Table 4.2 Demographics of those we interviewed (*n*=63)

Characteristic	n (%) or average
Primary role	
Organiser/volunteer	12 (19%)
Vendor	18 (29%)
Attendee	33 (52%)
Women	40 (63%)
Self-reported disability	27 (43%)
Average age	48.8 years
Age range	20–77 years
Event	
Arts Festival	12 (19%)
Hometown Days	12 (19%)
Powwow	6 (10%)
Ghost Town Celebration	10 (16%)
Community Picnic	12 (19%)
Rodeo	11 (17%)

When asked to think about someone they know with a disability, overall, people responded that people with disabilities are or would be accepted in the community or the event. However, it was in response to this question about a person they know with a disability that we heard a range of responses highlighting the intersection of individual and environmental characteristics and cultural beliefs about people with disabilities. In general, the most common responses included viewing people with disabilities as childlike or respondents specifically differentiating themselves from or 'othering' people with disabilities. We briefly explore these in the following.

Usually reflecting on individuals with cognitive or intellectual disabilities, some described individuals with a childish or juvenile perspective, simplifying or infantilising these individuals, pointing out how 'excited' they would be or how they would 'love it'. For example, Matthew, a 28-year-old father, noted while he watched his children play in the bouncy castle at the Hometown Days,

I have a couple of people that I know that are walking around. They got some mental, I guess, physicalities, but they seem to be having a good time. I mean, I actually I talked to both of them earlier--they were just loving it.

Dan, a 45-year-old man, who rode with the veterans group on his motorcycle in the Community Picnic parade, talked about a woman he helps out on occasion:

Yeah, I think they would really enjoy it. You have the parade, you have all the sirens, and you know this one lady that I'm helping has cerebral palsy and anything having to do with lights and sounds and stuff, it's all new to her. She just eats it up, she starts laughing. It's the sweetest thing!

Allison, a young woman in her early 20s, grappled with her own perceptions of what it means to enjoy an event when reflecting on her grandma's Alzheimer's and whether attending the rodeo could be fun, even if her grandma would not remember the experience later: 'I think that it would memorable and really exciting for them. My grandma has Alzheimer's and I think it'd just be something she would absolutely love, even with her disease, she would still remember it, hopefully'.

In other responses, there were attributes of 'othering'. Ray, an arts festival organiser and vendor in his late 50s talked about how fibre arts tend to be more accessible for people than other events because of the encouragement to touch and experience the fibres:

> I just think over the years...those are the people who really enjoy it because it is so tactile. It's not like painting fine art, or it's not an art show or something or some sort of flat art show. So, I mean, they love it.

While there is some 'othering' in Ray's choice of wording in phrases like 'those are the people...' and '...they love it...' the overall sense of the interview was inclusion. While he did not answer 'yes' to any of our impairment questions, Ray did self-identify as a 'disabled vet[eran]' during our conversation. He doesn't seem to personally identify with this group, but his dialogue demonstrates empathy and awareness of the place people with disabilities occupy within our society: 'We're at a nice public facility that already has all the accommodations that they need to get into the facility, but once they get in here, we don't look at them any differently'.

In general, events were perceived as inclusive although the frustration expressed by family members like Sandra was not uncommon, especially the way it is intertwined with tradition and attachment to place. Sandra, an outspoken 37-year-old woman we met at the street fair in her hometown, tells us, 'I was born and raised here. I don't remember not coming to this event'. She is pushing her brother in his large, tilted wheelchair through the crowd towards the vendor booths that line either side of Main Street. She described the lack of accessibility with an undertone of exclusion:

> It's, as you can see, we have all curbs. There's no ramp area except for at the end of each block and in a ramp setting we can't get him out of the van properly with the ramp that he has on his van, so it's not—it's not handicapped friendly in this town at all.

Despite beginning the conversation with indignant frustration about the lack of accessibility in her town, she concludes the interview by sharing a positive review of her community: 'There's a lot of opportunities and experiences in this town. I'm very grateful to live in this town'. This dance with a need for accessibility and attachment to home highlights a complicated relationship people from rural places have with their communities.

As we now turn to the primary themes, it is important to keep in mind how folks tended to describe people with disabilities as experiencing these events differently. Sometimes these underlying beliefs can suggest that people with disabilities might not experience the events as fully as people without disabilities and these types of beliefs can be used to justify a lack of accessibility or inclusion.

Connecting and reconnecting in physical space

By far, connecting with new people and reconnecting with people already known were the most common themes in our interviews. Regularly, as soon we asked, 'What do you get out of participating in this event?' interviewees looked up and around at the other people around and state something about people. Sometimes you could see familiarity spark on their faces or they would specifically point to people they know and proudly state, 'I know her' or, 'That's my cousin' or 'They used to live down the road from me'. For those not new to the community, community events provide a venue for them to see familiar and friendly faces, to re-energise or 'fill up their cup'. When we asked Stacey, a woman in her mid-50s with a mobility disability about who she met at the rodeo, she stated plainly with a playful smile, 'Just the whole community'. Dan, the motorcycle enthusiast, summed up his belief about why the Community Picnic is important by saying, 'The people are probably the number one thing. It's just everywhere you go, there are friendly faces. There's no strangers'. For people new to town, local gatherings provide a unique opportunity to start to integrate. Greg, an unmarried man in his mid-40s, demonstrated the importance of an event like the rodeo like this for a guy who is new to a community, 'I've been here for a month, and this is the first thing I've been to other than to go to town. Everyone's friendly and in an environment like this –', Greg then pauses and turns to a younger woman standing near us smoking a cigarette and says, 'I don't know you. Hi, my name is [Greg]'. These events provide space for people to mingle and get to know each other, putting themselves out there more publicly. There is opportunity to develop a sense of inclusion that may not be present when visiting the town grocery store or other public spaces.

Others specifically talk about these events as a venue for fostering family and family-like relationships and relational places where those lines are blurred, especially at events that are purposeful in preserving and promoting culture and community. Teresa, a vendor at the powwow in her mid-60s, shared about how her involvement and sense of community grows over time and how important it was to be seen and known.

> It's just I've been coming here for so long and so many family-friends, and the longer I come, I see people who are the same native as I am. Oh, you start talking and they become lifetime friends. I have that all weekend--people were coming up and they knew my name, they knew who I was.

Teresa's son Peter, a single man in his early 30s who made the multiple-day trip to attend this powwow for his first time, adds, 'For me, it's about family'.

Connecting and reconnecting do not necessarily mean being actively engaged in overt communication or dialogue. Sometimes attendees described just 'people watching' as how they connect. At Hometown Days, Ken, a man in his mid-60s, and Don, a man in his early 80s, both with physical disabilities that limit their ability to get around the street fair talked about '... just being with people – just watching people be happy because it is a happy occasion...' While this behaviour might be seen as less active participation, it is still important in their experiences. Similarly, Greta, a vendor in her early 60s at the regional powwow, explains, 'the fullness of my heart, seeing everybody'. For these folks, just being present in the same physical space, even without interaction, brings a sense of connectedness and fulfilment – having space to 'be seen' and 'see others' in a more communal way. Steve, a 37-year-old married father of four and an artist with a variety of learning disabilities just moving back to his hometown after being away for almost a decade, explained the importance of Hometown Days like this: 'It's nice to see a community come together and be active like this. Just chill out. It's nice. It's meaningful'. The sum of experiences – being together, active and relaxed – creates something meaningful for someone like Steve as he reconnects with his roots.

Building and maintaining community

Using these events to build and maintain community culture, practice and interactions was important to many of the participants we interviewed. This aspect was described by participants in terms of specifically investing in the reproduction of culture and maintaining practices (sometimes at the expense of making accommodations to include people with disabilities) and participating in a collective sense of communal responsibility in supporting other community members (sometimes including efforts to accommodate people with disabilities). Although the goals and activities of the different events were fairly varied, it was easy to see how culture was explicitly being preserved and promoted. Attitudes and behaviours about accessibility are interwoven into cultural beliefs within these contexts in important ways. Events and physical spaces create opportunities for both inclusion and exclusion of people with disabilities.

At the Arts Festival, participants talked about the importance of preserving an art craft (e.g. making homespun wool) and had high expectations for accommodating people with disabilities. While the festival is held in a very accessible building now, long-time organisers talked about early days of the festival where informal accommodations kept people coming and included. Linda, an event organiser in her late 40s, shared that what she gets most out of participating is, 'Really just helping the arts stay alive and being a part of that'. Ester, a 59-year-old arts festival volunteer organiser, shared similar thoughts, although she also ties accessibility and accommodations to their ability to keep the arts alive. 'What's important to me is just the satisfaction of keeping it going, keeping it alive and happening...We always need new people, fresh blood. Not just younger, it can be new old people'. The fibre arts festival was among the most attuned event to accessibility issues, perhaps because of the awareness of attracting an older demographic. Ester went on to share that from the beginning they have worked hard to both informally and formally accommodate people with disabilities.

> We've always had disabled people. Even when it was on the ranch... everybody just says, 'Oh, I'll help you with that!' I mean, you push the wheelchair out, you help them in and out of their trucks. Heaven help us! They were bringing sheep. And goats. 'You're in a walker! Okay!' Obviously at the fairgrounds here, it has improved enormously...Look at this building and look at all the sidewalks...The bathrooms are all handicap access.

The folks at the powwow highlighted the preservation of a culture that has been pushed to near extinction and has a long history of respecting and including elders, who often experience disability. Vince, a 46-year-old married father attending the powwow with his elementary-aged daughters, talked about his father's involvement in the powwow council and their cultural commitment to elders, which translates to making elder-informed decisions and accommodations.

> they always try to teach them how to make special accommodations for the elderly and disability because in our culture the elders--they're prized possessions because they have all our history. That's pretty much all throughout Indian Country. The elders aren't there--stuff's not done without us talking about it first.

In terms of benefits for herself, Jennifer, a 44-year-old vendor, got straight to the heart of the purpose of the powwow. 'I get a lot out of it. I mean it's in you, it's a part of our culture. I'm a strong, strong advocate for our culture and our ways of the Bitterroot Salish people'. Additional examples of intentional efforts to preserve culture include activities like the stick game and traditional dancing at the powwow. Respondents talked about the accessibility and willingness to make accommodations to include people with disabilities in the programming.

Other events elicited conversations about difficulties balancing the preservation of culture and accommodating people with disabilities. This was especially true at the Ghost Town Celebration. The acceptance in the lack of accessibility is highlighted in the first interview we completed sitting in on the boardwalk in the shade with Ann, a 68-year-old woman with multiple sclerosis. When we ask about accommodations, she describes her satisfaction with the limits placed on her by the environment in order to preserve authenticity:

> But if you want it to stay authentic, there's a limited amount that you can do about that and I'm content to send him off with the camera while I sit and wait and I usually end up having a nice conversation with somebody so you know I learn a little bit from them so it works out either way.

Similarly, Laura, a 25-year-old who grew up not far from the Ghost Town, shared these justifications for not adapting the town to accommodate people with disabilities and instead described informal kinds of personal interventions:

> I mean, it's a ghost town so there are boardwalks and things like that. You're very limited on what you might be able to improve with it, but I think the bathrooms here are really easy to get to and there's no steps or anything. I think for the most part, you can at least peek in if you can't get up the couple steps to get into an old building or something with a wheelchair. They'll have walkers or something, you know, you can just step into most of the cabins so we'll just grab their hands and help them up.

Despite these expectations of foregoing formal accommodations in favour of preserving the integrity of the Ghost Town, we learned from our interview with Roy, a man in his 70s who uses a wheelchair, that the buildings were actually adapted in the 1990s following the passage of the ADA to make them accessible from the back, although most people are still unaware of the features 30 years later. Roy told us:

> the people here at [Ghost Town] wanted to know how to make [Ghost Town] accessible...My wife was in a wheelchair, and we got involved with the [Ghost Town] and making it accessible...getting these ramps around the backsides of that so all of the buildings that have got steps in front like the church...Go all the way around, and they're all flat on the back.

The process of making the Ghost Town accessible brought together the community of people who care about the facilities and the inclusion of Roy and his wife in the modification process indicates that making spaces accessible can be community building, but problems with visibility and awareness still linger.

Finally, the relationship between reproducing culture and efforts to accommodate were most apparent at the rodeo, where some recent controversial changes to the event and venue were perceived as negatively impacting accessibility for people with mobility impairments. This event takes place in a demographically mixed community with both strong American Indian and white settler heritage. The changes to the rodeo appeared to be mostly driven by new white leadership and the lack of attention given to 'elders' was highlighted in our interviews. By far, the discussion about accessibility at the rodeo was the most problematic. The sense of people with and without disabilities was that the seating, walkways, beer garden and general viewing areas were not as accessible as they could have been or even as accessible as they had been in the past. Danny, a married father of four, sums up the lack of accessibility like this:

> For the, like I said, the elders--There should be a spot-- There used to be a spot for the-- This used to be a baseball field... There used to be a dug-out on that end and a dugout on that end. That's where the handicapped people would sit because they could get in there with their chairs.

Although Danny is not native himself, he uses the term elders to indicate a position of reverence that he feels is no longer being honoured by their community.

Rural events create space for culture to be reproduced and in some cases modified. In this study, there is sometimes tension between preserving traditional culture and the physical environment and making adaptations that would be more inclusive. In a few instances, the act of actually creating accommodations for people with disabilities was embraced as a way to build community, either through cultural reproduction or change.

Space for self-improvement in alternative networks

A final theme important to the potential for social justice for people with disabilities in rural places is how rural events can provide alternative routes to empowerment through self-development and networks outside typical power structures. Many people with disabilities are kept outside of mainstream networks both formally and informally. For instance, this happens when children and youth are segregated from mainstream classrooms for special education as well as in traditional paths to employment where expectations for participation are ableist and exclusive. Self-development at these rural events happened through having the opportunity to learn, practice and teach unique skills, and pass along traditional knowledge. These opportunities happen through connecting with supportive and caring people, especially when connecting over special topics like weaving or working on hot rod cars. These events create space for individuals with and without disabilities to be teachers, learners, leaders and followers while also organisationally existing as an economic and social structure outside of traditional business and community.

Events like the ones we attended, especially the arts festival, allow for participants to develop and nurture a sense of camaraderie. We see this type of connection as different from the themes around connecting and re-connecting because it more explicitly privileges special interests, skills and knowledge. Mike, a wool producer in his mid-60s with both hearing and mobility disabilities, emphasised the importance of comradery that comes with meeting up with people who share similar interests and industry. 'Lots of camaraderie with all the other folks, and you build your friendships and your relationships with those who have animals and a lot of time with breeding comes into that...Comradery is big, you know?' Beth, a 32-year-old festival attendee, explains how comradery can help self-development: 'Inspiration... and just reaffirmation of something I enjoy and comradery. Someone else just doesn't understand some of the things that I'm having trouble with... Someone that doesn't spin has no clue what I'm talking about'.

For older adults, events like the arts festival help them stay connected to how things are changing and progressing. Verna, a 70-year-old woman attending the arts festival with Beth, highlighted the importance of staying current and connected to the arts through events like this one. 'For me, it's interesting because I'm 70 years old. So I get to hang around with the younger people and get new ideas and see what's going on. How things have changed and progressed'. Isolation from these kinds of events not only means feeling disconnected from people, but from ideas and progress. For others, it is not just connecting with others and the sense of comradery, but actual building of confidence in a space where they can practice and learn. Barbara, a fibre arts small business owner in her mid-40s, said this about her craft: 'I figured, I can do this. So really, my self-confidence grew'.

While the Arts Festival provided very specific opportunities for networking and skill development, other rural community festivals, like Hometown Days, offered more varied opportunities to engage in different interests, like hot rod cars, the Military Colour Guard or even disability-specific leadership. Matthew, the father of four in his late 20s who we interviewed while he watched his children play in the bouncy castle, shared about making connections among the car enthusiasts and getting a lead on a part he needs for cheap. Don, the man in his 80s with significant disabilities that we caught up with while he was people watching, shared with pride about his participation in the Colour Guard as part of the parade. These types of opportunities contribute to his sense of connectedness and identity as a veteran both honouring and being honoured in the military tradition that is still very important in many rural places in the United States. Teresa, the Navajo woman with 'bad knees' at the powwow, explained how she passes on cultural and institutional knowledge about accessibility by asking other vendors and attendees where they are going next so she can share about her experiences with accessible bathrooms, showers and camping or lodging.

These events not only create space for individual experiential engagement but are themselves alternative economic and social structures where some people who experience marginalisation can participate and be recognised. Barbara, the fibre arts volunteer in her mid-40s, explained how these events create space for women entrepreneurs. 'I like meeting new people, especially people with the same interest…especially in Montana, and with women I really like to make sure we make those connections with other small business women owners'. These types of rural events have the potential to create space for collaboration and empowerment of folks left out of the typical power structures. Teresa, the Navajo Indian in her 60s travelling with her son, explained how powwows provide an alternative to the dominant economic system that has kept many people like her out or on the fringe. It gives her opportunity to teach younger people about the powwow circuit and trusting the system. 'So you're taking the risk of going to these things and sometimes you win, sometimes you break even. You never lose because the environment, the sound, the people'. She goes on to explain why it's important for her to be her own boss and avoid the potential exploitation of working for someone else:

> That's how I look at life. You wake up and you don't need to bend over backwards for somebody, you know. A boss. You are doing your job, and you know that you're doing it to the best of your ability. You don't have to bend over backwards. That's just the way I look at things, you don't just bend over backwards for somebody who will just take advantage of you.

Rural events create a variety of opportunities to engage in special interests and to grow in expertise and connectedness. As entities outside of the typical dominant economic structure, some folks find fulfilling economic homes that are not available to them elsewhere. Having moments to recognise others and to be recognised as a community resource helps keep people with disabilities visible and engaged.

Discussion

How people with disabilities are viewed matters. If community members are either unaware of people with disabilities or if they view them as less than human, there is a potential for feeling apathetic or justified in the lack of accessibility or inclusion. Current ableist cultural beliefs dictate community dialogs and decision-making that tends to exclude people with disabilities. Rural community events are opportunities for connecting, building community and engaging in self-development within an alternative network. These events create cultural spaces where 'there are no strangers' and where participants can more readily interact, observe and be seen as part of the community with strangers, acquaintances, friends and family. Having access to these events also creates opportunities for historical or cultural activities that are less common now than they were in the past, allowing for current rural residents to maintain a connection to a version of a traditional rural culture. Riding horses, panning for gold, listening to bluegrass music and cheering on small children as they do their best to ride a sheep for eight seconds in the rodeo arena provide socialisation opportunities to create or reinforce cultural and individual rural identities, reproducing social structures and expectations. Having access to these periodic events allows people with disabilities to individually experience the process and also contribute to it, shaping how others see their role within the production and reproduction of rural culture. For people with disabilities, participating in meaningful and conventional ways (not being tokenised), whether in organising, vending or attending, enhances a sense of community and integrates community members who might otherwise be excluded and marginalised.

This study highlights the importance of being together in these physically shared spaces in order to create community. For some, making these environments and programming accessible for all people also contributed to community building experience in both formal and informal ways by bringing community members together to ensure that everyone has the opportunity to participate. When this did not happen, such as the case at the rodeo, the breakdown in the sense of community is apparent in our interviews. We turn now back to two important examples in our study to reinforce how inclusion of people with disabilities in rural events can create tension but is also an incredible and welcomed opportunity.

First is the example of Sandra who we met at Hometown Days as she pushed her brother in his large tilted wheelchair down Main Street. Sandra and her family's adaptive behaviours to deal with the inaccessibility of the community event (e.g. showing up over an hour early in hopes of getting an accessible parking spot somewhat close to the festivities) are part of the reproduction of the culture around disabilities. It promotes inclusion while also maintaining patterns of inaccessibility. If this family decides it's just too much work to participate, not only do they miss out on feeling like part of their community, but the rest of the community members miss out on the opportunity to see and be with people with disabilities as part of their community. Her brief interview demonstrates the tug of war that some rural residents feel between their attachment to place and how their personal history intersects with the community history and the need for the event organisers to better address accessibility. If not for the extra effort to be present and seen, Sandra's family and her brother's disability could easily become invisible.

Second, for someone like Roy, these types of events can create powerful opportunities for participation, leadership and empowerment. Although almost everyone we interviewed perceived the venue and much of the programming at the Ghost Town Celebration as inaccessible, because of Roy's involvement in the modifications made in the 1990s, he spoke warmly of the accessible nature of the event and his ability to be heard as well as his perspective being taken seriously by the event organisers. As we talked, he transferred himself with ease from his wheelchair in the fenced front yard of an old homestead onto the open porch at waist height. He was there to play some folk music with his long-time bandmates and friends. As he tunes up his instrument with his bandmates, there is an air of normativity and not of a spectacle. Roy's acceptance by his peers with an important perspective to contribute to the greater good of the community creates space for him to continue to participate in ways that are meaningful and integrated. These scenes made us reflect on how, if this was the actual frontier times, this would be very unlikely. Indeed, even in Roy's 75 years, there has been significant progress in moving people from 'freaks' to part of society. Even so, Roy admits that the lack of signage can be a problem for people who 'are afraid to ask'. Thus, self-advocacy and being vulnerable to rejection when asking about accessibility are still necessary to fully participate in an event like the Ghost Town Celebration.

Recommendations and conclusion

Physical accessibility is a first step to inclusion, but event planning should also be purposeful in avoiding practices that might be reproducing social and cultural patterns of exclusion or exploitation of people with disabilities. As this chapter highlights, the costs of being kept out of rural events in terms of connections, community and self-development are high. Rural community events can create important opportunities for all people to interact in ways outside of the day-to-day patterns of community life. With intention, there is potential for enhancing opportunities for people with disabilities, especially in empowering their voices as was the case for Roy. Inclusive festivals are the result of inclusive planning processes (Jepson & Clarke, 2016). Most existing tools for intentionally inclusive planning lack a rural perspective which we believe needs to be more sensitive to a desire to preserve traditional ways and culture. Thoughtful planning that includes people with disabilities can lead to changing cultural norms, reducing exclusion and opportunities for new connections and self-development. There are a number of 'event planning guides' addressing inclusion of people with disabilities that can assist organisers in being purposeful and direct in their efforts to change the physical environment. However, to go beyond the physical environment to create an inclusive culture around rural events, leaders and organisers need to consider who yields power in the process and be reflexive of motivations, opportunities and abilities to participate within their community context (Jepson, Clarke & Ragsdell, 2014). Additionally, event organisers and participants should be cognisant of the conflicted feelings many have about modifications and promotion of tradition. Again, including people with disabilities in the process, especially around accessibility, will assist organisers in thinking outside the box.

Appendix A: Interview Guides

'In-the-moment' interview guide 1: Festival vendors and organisers

Hello! It looks like you helped organise or put on this event. Is that true? [if yes...]

We are from the University of Montana and we are conducting research about rural community events and would like to ask you a few questions about your experiences with organising these kinds of community events. It take just a few minutes and for participating you will receive a $5 gift card/certificate to a local business.

[upon verbal agreement...]

- How did you get involved in organising/participating this event?
- What do you get out of helping out with/attending the event?
- Do you know anyone who would like to come to this event but doesn't? [if yes] What keeps them from attending?
- What kinds of efforts are made to accommodate people with disabilities at this event? [if they ask what kind of disability, tell them it is up to their interpretation, but it would be helpful if they shared what kind of disability they are envisioning in their answer]
- Now I would like you to think about someone you know who has a disability. If that person wanted to come to this event, what kinds of challenges (if any) do you think they would face? [if they ask what kind of disability, tell them it is up to their interpretation, but it would be helpful if they shared what kind of disability they are envisioning in their answer].
- Almost done – can you tell me how old you are?
- And where do you live?
- And finally, would you answer 'yes' to any of these questions on this board? [display next page]
- Thank respondent and provide them with business card if they have any questions or follow up and $5 gift card/certificate to local business for participating.

'In-the-moment' interview guide 2: Festival attendees

Hello! We are from the University of Montana and we are conducting research about rural community events and would like to ask you a few questions about your experiences here today. It take just a few minutes and for participating you will receive a $5 gift card/certificate to a local business.

[upon verbal agreement...]

- How did you get here today? Did you come with anyone?
- What kinds of events or activities have your or will you participate in?

- Did you plan to meet anyone here? [If yes] Can you tell me about that?
- Did you run into people you know? [If yes] Can you tell me about that?
- Did you meet anyone new here today? If so, can you tell me about that?
- What do you get out of coming to this event?
- Are there any programmes, events or activities here you want to go to or do but can't? [If yes] What and why?
- Now I would like you to think about someone you know who has a disability. If that person wanted to come to this event, what kinds of challenges (if any) do you think they would face? [if they ask what kind of disability, tell them it is up to their interpretation, but it would be helpful if they shared what kind of disability they are envisioning in their answer].
- Almost done – can you tell me how old you are?
- And where do you live?
- And finally, would you answer 'yes' to any of these questions on this board? [display next page]
- Thank respondent and provide them with business card if they have any questions or follow up and $5 gift card/certificate to local business for participating.

'In the Moment' follow-up questions to determine disability status

Would you answer 'yes' to any of the following questions?

1 Are you deaf, or do you have serious difficulty **hearing**?
2 Are you blind, or do you have serious difficulty **seeing** even when wearing glasses?
3 Because of a physical, mental or emotional condition, do you have serious difficulty **concentrating, remembering or making decisions**?
4 Do you have serious difficulty **walking or climbing stairs**?
5 Do you have difficulty **dressing or bathing**?
6 Because of a physical, mental or emotional condition, do you have difficulty **doing errands alone** such as visiting a doctor's office or shopping?

References

Americans with Disabilities Act of 1990, Pub. L. No. Public L. No. 101–336, Stat. 328 (1990) Available from: www.eeoc.gov/eeoc/history/35th/thelaw/ada.html [Accessed 1st October 2017].

Arcodia, C. & Whitford, M. (2006) Festival attendance and the development of social capital. *Journal of Convention & Event Tourism.* 8 (2), 1–18.

Bourdieu, P. (1993) *The field of cultural production.* New York, Columbia University Press.

Chemers, M. M. (2008) *Staging stigma: a critical examination of the American freak show.* New York, Palgrave Macmillan.

Clare, E. (2015) *Exile and pride: disability, queerness, and liberation.* Reissue edition. Durham, NC, Duke University Press.

Clare, E. (2017) *Brilliant imperfection: grappling with cure.* Durham, NC, Duke University Press.

Clarke, A. & Jepson, A. (2011) Power and hegemony within a community festival. *International Journal of Event and Festival Management.* 2 (1), 7–19.

Coleman, J. S. (1988) Social capital in the creation of human capital. *American Journal of Sociology.* 94, S95–S120.

Derrett, R. (2003) Festivals and regional destinations: how festivals demonstrate a sense of community & place. *Rural Society.* 13 (1), 35–53.

Garland Thomson, R. (1997) *Extraordinary bodies: figuring physical disability in American culture and literature.* New York, Columbia University Press.

Getz, D. (2010) The nature and scope of festival studies. *International Journal of Event Management Research.* 5 (1), 1–47.

Habermas, J. (1989) *The structural transformation of the public sphere: an inquiry into a category of bourgeois society.* Cambridge, MA, MIT Press.

Jaeger, K. & Mykletun, R. J. (2013) Festivals, identities, and belonging. *Event Management.* 17 (3), 213–226.

Jepson, A. & Clarke, A. (eds.) (2016) *Managing and developing communities, festivals and events.* Houndmills, Palgrave Macmillan.

Jepson, A., Clarke, A. & Ragsdell, G. (2014) Investigating the application of the motivation–opportunity–ability model to reveal factors which facilitate or inhibit inclusive engagement within local community festivals. *Scandinavian Journal of Hospitality and Tourism.* 14 (3), 331–348.

Lichter, D. T. & Ziliak, J. P. (2017) The rural-urban interface: new patterns of spatial interdependence and inequality in America. *The ANNALS of the American Academy of Political and Social Science.* 672 (1), 6–25.

Olmstead v. L. C., 527 US 581 (US Supreme Court 1999) Available from: www.law.cornell.edu/supct/html/98-536.ZS.html [Accessed 15th July 2018].

Putnam, R. D. (2001) *Bowling alone: the collapse and revival of American community* (1st Touchstone ed.). New York, Touchstone.

Quinn, B. & Wilks, L. (2013) Festival connections: people, place and social capital. In: Richards, G., de Brito, M. P. & Wilks, L. (eds.) *Exploring the social impacts of events.* Abingdon, Routledge, pp. 15–30.

Saldaña, J. (2013) *The coding manual for qualitative researchers* (2nd ed.). Los Angeles, Sage Publications.

Sharpe, E. K. (2008) Festivals and social change: intersections of pleasure and politics at a community music festival. *Leisure Sciences.* 30 (3), 217–234.

Spracklen, K. & Lamond, I. R. (eds.) (2016) *Critical event studies.* London, Routledge.

Taylor, S. (2017) *Beasts of burden: animal and disability liberation.* New York, The New Press.

US Census Bureau (2016, July 1) US Census Bureau QuickFacts selected: Montana. Available from: www.census.gov/quickfacts/MT [Accessed 13th October 2017].

von Reichert, C., Greiman, L. & Myers, A. (2014) The geography of disability in America: on rural-urban differences in impairment rates. *Independent Living and Community Participation.* Available from: http://scholarworks.umt.edu/cgi/viewcontent.cgi?article=1006&context=ruralinst_independent_living_community_participation [Accessed 12th October 2017].

Waterman, S. (1998) Carnivals for elites? The cultural politics of arts festivals. *Progress in Human Geography.* 22 (1), 54–74.

Williams, R. (1974) On high and popular culture. *The New Republic*, 21 November. Available from: https://newrepublic.com/article/79269/high-and-popular-culture [Accessed 1st July 2018].

Ziakas, V. & Costa, C. A. (2010) 'Between theatre and sport' in a rural event: evolving unity and community development from the inside-out. *Journal of Sport & Tourism*. 15 (1), 7–26.

5 'De-marginalising' marginalised communities

The case of participatory arts events and the over 70s in rural Hertfordshire, the United Kingdom

Allan Stewart Jepson

> *Loneliness and the feeling of being unwanted is the most terrible poverty.*
> Mother Teresa (1910–1997)

Introduction

This chapter provides an insight into a much larger longitudinal study into the potential benefits of participatory arts events for the over 70s in rural communities in Hertfordshire, the United Kingdom. In order to achieve this, the chapter gives an overview of literature into how older communities in the United Kingdom (especially in rural areas) are becoming increasingly marginalised. The chapter begins by introducing the reader to the current situation in relation to older people in the United Kingdom. Following this, literature is explored in relation to the particular psychosocial impacts faced by the over 70s, collective bonding and memory creation, and the potential of arts and creative events as critical intervention to degenerative diseases.

Following the review of literature, the chapter explores suitable methodologies and methods to investigate the potential of participatory arts events for the over 70s including using reminiscence interviews and measuring electrodermal activity (EDA). The final sections of the chapter provide some intermediate findings from the case study on participatory arts events in rural areas of Hertfordshire, the United Kingdom; concluding remarks for policymakers in the United Kingdom with respect to the potential of participatory arts events and the over 70s; and a conceptual framework for future projects in this important area of research.

Literature review

It has been well documented that events hold the unique ability to motivate people to come together in order to socialise (Van Zyl & Botha, 2004; Bowen & Daniels, 2005; Li & Petrick, 2006; Syson & Wood, 2006; Kim et al., 2007; Liang,

Illum & Cole, 2008; Pegg & Patterson, 2010; Hixson et al., 2011; Kulczynski, Baxter & Young, 2016; Jaimangal-Jones, Fry & Haven-Tang, 2018) and share cultural understanding which bonds and enhances their relationships. Yet in many communities especially in relation to older generations this ability remains largely underutilised. There is currently a paucity of research into how planned festivals and events can potentially enhance the lives of older people – particularly those who have retired from employment and are aged over 70.

Gratton and Scott (2016) concluded that in the developed world, people are living longer than ever before. And furthermore, that over the last two centuries, life expectancy has increased by two years every decade, meaning that half of the people being born in the West today can expect to live to 100 years old. Naturally this will present a notable impact on requirements for public-sector spending, which is especially relevant with respect to the United Kingdom, if one considers that National Health Service (NHS) trusts that care for patients in England are now expected to end 2018–2019 around £900m in deficit (Campbell, 2018). As well as the direct increase in public health spending in hospitals there are also much wider psychosocial issues within our communities which are being exacerbated by longevity. The recent Holt-Lunstad et al.'s (2015) study for example found that actual and perceived loneliness and isolation can both be associated with early mortality, particularly for those living alone and with reduced mobility.

Whilst many older people still lead culturally enriched and satisfied lives, as we get older our health is determined by income and by previous educational experience (Morris et al., 2007). Our attained educational level predicts our life expectancy (Marmot, 2015), and older people living in deprived neighbourhoods are much more likely to experience mobility difficulties than those in less deprived neighbourhoods (Lang et al., 2008). Marmot's (2015) study found that on average higher-economic status people experience the vitality of people 15 years younger than themselves. A recent report commissioned by the All-Party Parliamentary Group, UK Government (2017) found that 'a lack of mobility exacerbates social isolation has a negative impact upon health and diminishes participation in leisure activities' (p. 123).

Defining the creative arts in the United Kingdom

Although many definitions of the creative arts exist most remain, according to Leckey (2011), elusive and vague. In this chapter, we advocate Leckey's (2011) research approach and suggest the adoption of the Arts Council England (2007: p. 5) definition of creative arts as encompassing 'literature and writing, theatre and drama, dance, music and visual arts, which include crafts, new media, moving image and combined arts'. Research by Hackling et al. (2006), White (2009) and Holt (2008) found that the highest participation rates in creative arts were within the visual arts, which took various forms, including drawing and painting (77 percent), crafts (60 percent), writing (59 percent), visiting exhibitions (55 percent) and photography (53 percent).

Their studies also concluded that most activities included more than one creative activity. More recently dance has recognised physical health benefits, including improvements in balance, strength, gait, posture and reaction time, with the latter being an important prerequisite to preventing falls. The alertness required for dancing has been proven to increase mental acuity, and the social aspects of dancing are preventative for loneliness and isolation, which results in an increase in one's subjective well-being (The Centre for Policy on Ageing, 2011).

Other studies have focussed on the benefits of singing and specifically choral singing. Livesey et al.'s (2012) large-scale survey of choral singers in England, Austria and Germany confirmed the notion that singing enhanced the well-being of participants. A further study by Clift and Hancox (2010) concluded that singing was very good to focus attention and control breathing which offset anxiety and stress. They also found that the group offered each other social support outside of the group which helped to overcome isolation and loneliness. Furthermore, it promoted learning to counteract cognitive decline and provided a regular social commitment which kept people active, raised their spirits and made them happy. So, although the arts are often perceived as an individual journey, the creative arts clearly provide great scope for events where like-minded people with shared interests can come together, create and learn in a social situation.

Psychosocial impacts and the benefits of participatory arts events for the over 70s

Within published literature, terms such as loneliness, social isolation, self-worth, quality of life and well-being are often used interchangeably and generalised without appreciation of their meaning and appropriateness within research. As a result, there is a clear lack of understanding and consistency in these terminology and definitions which has resulted in a lack of detailed analysis especially with regards to the potential of arts events to reduce negative psychosocial impacts associated with growing older. Figure 5.1 is an adapted version of our previous conceptual framework; it illustrates the role that critical gerontology can play in understanding the potential lasting personal benefits that participatory arts events can have, and in particular for people over 70 years old.

A brief review of the potential lasting benefits of participatory arts events in relation to loneliness, isolation, inclusion, belonging, self-esteem and self-worth are presented in the following.

Loneliness

Loneliness is the result of the perception of having too few social contacts and/or poor-quality contacts (Peplau & Perlman, 1982). Social and psychological issues such as loneliness or the propensity to feel lonely are likely

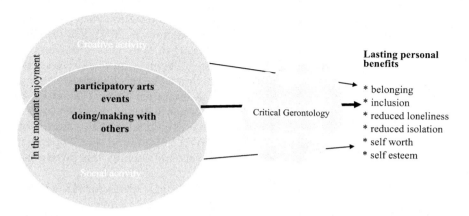

Figure 5.1 The potential lasting personal benefits of participatory arts events.
Adapted from: Wood, Jepson & Stadler (in press).

to increase as we get beyond 50 years old, and although loneliness has been shown to decline with age it begins to rise again from age 70 onwards (Tornstram, 2011). In the United Kingdom, nearly half (49 percent) of all people aged 75 and over live alone (DEFRA, 2011).

A report by Taylor Nelson Sofres (TNS) (2014) found that as a direct consequence a million older people (over 65+) in the United Kingdom said that they were always or often feel lonely, and within this sample nearly half said that television or pets are their main form of company. Following this a study by Age UK (2016) estimated that 1.2 million older people living in the United Kingdom could therefore be defined as chronically lonely. Tornstram's (2011) study found that although loneliness ebbs and flows naturally it tends to rise from age 70 onwards. Further research in the United States by Holt-Lunstad, Smith and Layton (2010) concluded that weak social networks could potentially carry a health risk that is more harmful than not exercising, twice as harmful as obesity and comparable to smoking 15 cigarettes a day or being an alcoholic.

Social isolation

Social isolation has been defined as 'the distancing of an individual, psychologically, physically or both from his or her network of desired or needed relationships with other people' (Biordi & Nicholson, 2011: p. 98). It has also been defined by Cutler (2009) as less than weekly contact with either family, friends or neighbours. Cutler's (2009) research estimates that more than two million people over 60 in the United Kingdom are affected by social isolation; his and Lang et al.'s (2008) work concludes that those on low incomes are twice as likely to feel trapped and lonely than their more affluent counterparts. Isolation, which accounts for up to a third of UK GP visits, is associated with poor physical and mental health and significantly increases the risk of dementia (Cutler, 2009; Biordi & Nicholson, 2011). While isolation could be a positive choice (i.e. in a seeking of apartness, aloneness or solitude), when imposed by others or society it becomes more akin to social exclusion and clearly has negative implications. Research suggests that a great number of older people feel trapped in their own homes (Davidson & Rossall, 2014), leaving them feeling out of touch with the pace of modern life or cut off from society (TNS, 2014). In the United Kingdom, a survey by the Department for Work and Pensions (DWP, 2014) found that 24 percent of pensioners (those over 65 years of age) went out socially less often than once a month.

Holt-Lunstad, Smith and Layton's (2010) study reviewed 148 articles (308,849 respondents) and found that socially isolated people are 3.4 times more likely to suffer depression, 1.9 times more likely to develop dementia in the following 15 years and 2–3 times more likely to be physically inactive, which may result in a 7 percent increased likelihood of developing diabetes, an 8 percent increased likelihood of suffering a stroke and a 14 percent likelihood of developing coronary heart disease. A study by Machielse (2015) found that any intervention, such as a participatory arts event, aimed at reducing social isolation will need to be tailored to the individual (or at least the type) as one size will not fit all. The wide range of activity types and levels available within participatory arts events allows for individualisation whilst also maintaining the all-important social setting.

Social inclusion

There is some evidence (see Thomas et al., 2011) that arts engagement helps the socially excluded or marginalised to participate in their community and therefore to move towards being socially included (as well as encouraging the forming of more positive identities). In considering the potential effects of participatory arts events upon older adults, the potential to affect broader social inclusion is less likely than the potential to reduce loneliness and social isolation. Wood et al. (in press) advocate that assessing the value of creative arts activities on felt loneliness appears to be a more useful focus of event research which they include within their conceptual framework (Figure 5.1).

Belonging

Krause (2007) found that art and craft activities for elderly women connected them with others and allowed them to continue contributing to family and community. Liddle, Parkinson and Sibbritt (2013) found that taking part in creative events enabled one to help others and feel valued as well as a multitude of personal benefits not least of which was the experience of pleasure. Feelings of belonging in social groups can give life meaning in various ways, such as providing stability, helping individuals create a shared social identity and allowing them to pursue higher order collective goals (Baumeister, Finkenauer & Vohs, 2001; Haslam et al., 2008; Tajfel, 1972 cited in Lambert et al., 2013).

In order for us to feel we belong within society we must experience weak and strong social ties, with both being of equal importance. Sandstrom and Dunn's (2014) research, for example, tested whether subjective well-being was related not only to interactions with strong ties (i.e. family and close friends) but also to interactions with weak social ties (i.e. acquaintances). They concluded that we should not underestimate the value of our acquaintances as interactions with weak ties are related to our subjective well-being and feelings of belonging. These results are consistent with the idea that the more peripheral members of our social network shape our day-to-day happiness. For example, a chat with the coffee barista, postman, yoga classmate or fellow dog owner may contribute meaningfully to our happiness, above and beyond the contribution of interactions with our close friends and family.

It is argued in this chapter that the process of making and creating together inherent within a participatory arts event can play a crucial role in developing these all important 'ties' and foster a strong sense of belonging. Creativity is an important aspect within participatory arts events; there is evidence to show that socialising within a group setting is just as important to older attendees as the activity itself (Bedding & Sadlo, 2008). The being together and the 'doing' create a sense of belonging closely related to social identity and self-worth.

Self-esteem and self-worth

Self-esteem and self-worth are the final two potential personal benefits of participatory arts events for the over 70s. Seen as important psychosocial well-being concepts, self-worth and self-esteem are often used interchangeably and constitute the key building blocks of self-concept (along with self-image and ideal self). Studies have shown that self-esteem follows a specific pattern as we age, increasing in young and middle adulthood, peaking at about 60 and then declining in older age. This decline in old age is thought to be largely due to changes in one's socio-economic status and physical health (Orth, Trzesniewski & Robins, 2010). Meira et al. (2017) found that both educational level and the quality of interpersonal relationships are significant protective factors for high self-esteem in older people. These studies suggest that although self-esteem is affected by background and health, it is also strongly related to our social connections and our ability to maintain them and make new ones in later life. Participatory arts events therefore would appear to provide the opportunity for self-esteem maintenance and/or strengthening in older age.

Self-worth relates more specifically to how we value ourselves and our role in society (albeit this is also based on how we perceive the extent to which others value us) (Meira et al., 2017). The act of doing or making within a supportive social environment is likely to positively affect self-worth and the sharing of this experience to enhance self-esteem. There is also growing evidence to suggest that creativity and social activities can reduce loneliness, enhance feelings of belonging and build self-worth and esteem. What is still lacking is an understanding of the process through which these benefits are accrued by the older individual. Participatory arts events provide an ideal context in which to study these phenomena.

Methods for investigating the marginalisation of older people in the community

The methods employed here sit within a constructivist approach and therefore need to be more 'natural' or 'humanistic' for the participants and the context (Denzin & Lincoln, 2000). Humanist approaches to research have been associated more recently with the concept of 'hopeful tourism scholarship'. Ateljevic, Morgan and Pritchard (2007) and Tribe (2009) present this as an emergent network of tourism enquiry with a fundamental aim to enrol people within ideas and inscriptions. Ren, Pritchard and Morgan (2010) maintain that this type of inquiry is a value-led 'bottom up' approach built on partnership and reciprocity. This should be considered vitally important for research settings investigating marginalisation as builds and maintains trust amongst everyone involved within the research. When trust is established and maintained a transformation of relationships occurs between the researcher and the researched, and it is through this transformation that co-creation of research can occur (Richards, Pritchard & Morgan, 2010; Sedgley, Pritchard & Morgan, 2011) leading to an honest and open account of marginalisation.

Methods similar to autobiographical memory interviews aim to discover issues and responses by asking about specific memories or 're-interpreted versions of the original experience' (Kirkegaard Thomsen & Brinkmann, 2009: p. 294). A further advantage of this technique is that it recognises that specific memories are not representative of experiences more generally, but they capture the novel, emotionally intense and/or important aspects of the experience, such as the peak experiences that live events aim to create.

Additionally, participant focus groups and semi-structured interviews could also be incorporated into methodological design to build up a holistic picture of how, when and where marginalisation is occurring within communities. The original study by Stadler, Jepson and Wood (2018), which investigated collective memory and experience at arts events for the over 70s, incorporated events observation, photography (using a digital autographer device), capturing EDA data, reminiscence interviews and the simplified Warwick-Edinburgh mental well-being scale. This chapter presents excerpts and findings from qualitative (audio recorded) reminiscence interviews conducted in rural villages in Hertfordshire, the United Kingdom.

Sample size and methods

This chapter is focussed upon the samples gathered in rural Hertfordshire. Across five locations (Pirton, Codicote, Whitwell, Stanstead Abbotts and Royston), 30 women over the age of 70 took part in the research facilitated by Age UK within either sheltered housing or community centres. Each group participated in a number of different art activities (e.g. bag making, glass painting, model making, origami) over a three-week period with the data gathering taking place weekly over a total of eight months from November 2017 to June 2018 (Figures 5.2 and 5.3).

Participants in the study were advised of the purpose of the research through an initial consultation and given a handout detailing all the information. Following this, respondents signed consent forms and were advised of the right to withdraw at any time.

After the second week of arts activities respondents were interviewed to find out their views on the previous art activity they participated in, what they enjoyed and their happiest memories from the activity, how they felt before, during and after the activity, the significance of the activities they participated in and also to talk more generally about being over 70 and living in a rural location post-retirement. It is this breadth and depth of data gathered through the more general qualitative accounts during Weeks Two

Figure 5.2 'Plant pot painting' with over 70s in Whitwell, Hertfordshire.
Source: Author.

Figure 5.3 'Canvas shopping bag' design and make with over 70s in Stanstead
        Abbotts, Hertfordshire.
Source: Author.

and Three (three one-hour discussions for each of the 30 participants) which
are used to form the findings and conclusions presented in this chapter.

Findings and discussion

The following coding is applied to participants in the following discussions:
R = respondent, number = number in the sample, followed by rural area
code: C = Codicote, W = Whitwell, SA = Stanstead Abbotts, R = Royston.
For example, R1R = respondent 1, Royston.

The over 70s in rural Hertfordshire as marginalised communities

The potential lasting benefits that accrue to those who wish to participate in creative arts events have been discussed previously, but of course
the other side to this narrative is that a great many older people living in
our communities are marginalised. The marginalisation of older people in
our communities happens due to a number of contributing factors which
will now be considered in relation to the previous literature discussions

surrounding loneliness, isolation, inclusion, belonging, self-esteem and self-worth, with a particular focus upon mobility, loss of independence and autonomy.

Initial findings from our study suggest first that a major challenge to the over 70s in four out the five rural areas investigated (Codicote, Whitwell, Stanstead Abbotts and Royston) was poor mobility. This was caused by either a lack of public transport in rural areas (cited by 16 respondents); a lack of disposable income (being able to afford taxis); the unavailability of friends or relatives to give lifts to clubs, community centres or sheltered housing; or the unwillingness of respondents to ask for help in getting to venues to participate in clubs or societies as they felt either uncomfortable or embarrassed:

> R4C: .... 'well now that I'm you know getting along a bit I don't like to bother my daughter Nancy as she has two children and she's got enough on running around after them, it's just down the hill and I used to walk it but my husband is ill so I have to get back to look after him so I tend not to stay as along at the meadow as I used to......'

> R2W: ... 'I don't live in the village anymore, I used to but now I have to get a bus here (Whitwell) and they only run once an hour and are always late so sometimes I don't bother I just stay at home and watch the television......after all there's only so much cleaning and housework you can do and my flat is small.'

There is a clear need for arts intervention within the groups we visited in rural Hertfordshire, and as one can see from the respondent interviews there is a clear relationship with having poor mobility and feeling lonely and isolated (Holt-Lunstad et al., 2015) especially as the majority of respondents interviewed lived alone and therefore are at risk with regard to early mortality.

Many respondents talked about the difficulty in attending their favourite groups and many were upset that they could not attend every week, and they felt their relationships with others in the group suffered as a result. A number of respondents commented on how they felt with regard to the lack of attendance at their local groups:

> R3W: .... 'I suppose since I moved out my house after my husband died I felt a bit lonely and on my own, at first, I sort of hid myself away, but I realised ......I needed to meet other people and share my grief or just talk about the news or the weather anything really, I just didn't want to feel alone anymore so these clubs are important, and I've made good friends I feel lonely if I don't go.'

> R2SA: .... 'I don't really get out much, so I like to go to the ten to three club it gives me something to look forward to I had a fall about 6 weeks ago and I couldn't walk well so I just stayed in, and I got depressed and felt quite anxious about being on my own.'

The findings from the groups also hold true with the All-Party Parliamentary Group, UK Government (2017) report, which found that 'a lack of mobility exacerbates social isolation has a negative impact upon health and diminishes participation in leisure activities' (p. 123).

A lack of mobility (caused by poor public transport, lack of disposable income, unwillingness/unavailability to get lifts by car to venues) in the over 70s in the areas of rural Hertfordshire therefore had increased people's loneliness and isolation, and in some cases, it had also lowered a person's self-worth and self-esteem as a result. This combination of factors resulted in older people in four out of five of the areas sampled (Codicote, Whitwell, Stanstead Abbotts and Royston) not feeling part of the local community and thus being marginalised as a result.

The second finding in our Hertfordshire sample was a loss of independence. Many of the older people interviewed had suffered a loss of independence as a result of having to give up driving:

> R4R: …. 'I used to drive the minibus to bring people to this club, and I had a little car up until recently but my Doctor told me I could no longer drive… it's my eyes you see I've had a cataract removed from this one and now I only have partial sight….and now I'm getting cloudy in this eye as well, it makes me sad …….because…………… I used to do everything on my own and now I struggle to watch the tele go shopping and sometimes cooking is difficult, and I burnt myself on the grill …so I just…well now I just order these meals that come twice a day and put them in the microwave…'

Other respondents had suffered as a result of ill health or a fall at home, which resulted in them moving into warden-managed accommodation or sheltered housing communities:

> R6W:… 'I don't really like it here, I mean the people are nice enough but it doesn't feel like my house used to, it feels you know like a surgery it's all clean everywhere and smells of bleach in the toilets….people always knocking at the door are you alright and then the next hour are you alright…well I would be if you leave me alone [laughs]….….'

> R4SA:….. 'I had a four bedroom house, but after the kids moved on….my son's in London and my daughter works in the hospital at Stevenage …then my husband had a stroke and after him being assessed we had to move into a bungalow in Stevenage, but I didn't like it I missed my garden and my friends and I didn't go out as much…'

It can be seen from the respondents' views presented here that the loss of independence and autonomy has had a detrimental impact upon the quality and meaningfulness of respondents' social relationships, and unless some level of autonomy or independence is realised this will continue to have a negative impact on an older person's perceived quality of life (WHO Centre for Health Development, 2004).

A loss of independence in a period of change, such as adjusting to retirement, grieving for partners, relatives or close friends, or suffering ill health, can be very detrimental to one's psychological as well as physiological health and it could be argued that this is underestimated by care givers and at local, regional and national government level. As such a case-by-case option is not always applied as a result of a lack of carers in the local community or a lack of nearby suitable sheltered housing options. Perhaps the major concern though is the pace at which this change happens which is potentially the most damaging to older people psychologically. From the sample in Hertfordshire there were examples of older people that had been relocated and were living in rural communities that were previously unknown to them resulting in them feeling isolated, lonely and apprehensive about meeting new people and making friends as well as missing friends from their previous social networks.

Many of the over 70s were angry that there was not enough going on within walking distance and transport/mobility became an issue: where as some of the older people interviewed were either unhappy with being 'Nannied over' (R3C) or they had become institutionalised and bored very quickly as a result of not getting out or engaging in the clubs or activities that they did previously:

> R2SA:..... 'As soon as I get here it's the same old same old, I don't know why I come, people moaning.....it's boring...I could tell you now what we will do next Monday because it's the same, we should go on trips... but I suppose coaches are expensive.....there's another club in Hitchin that's supposed to be good but I can't get there I don't have anybody to take me and I don't want to go on my own........'

Conclusion: over 70s arts events as critical intervention: de-marginalising the marginalised

Our sample of rural villages in Hertfordshire demonstrates that there is a clear need for critical intervention in rural communities to reduce the negative and potentially damaging psychosocial and physiological impacts faced and felt more consciously by older generations.

There is clear evidence from this research that engaging older generations in creative arts activities is vital, as it often involves social interaction which helps older people form new relationships and networks to supplement the ones that may have gone, which further helps them to feel included (Thomas et al., 2011). Social interaction with the arts can work on many different levels, and even if a participant is engaged in an individual activity there is still interaction with regard to the creative decisions made and then comparative discourse on what the individual has produced as an artefact. Put another way, participatory arts activities are co-creative and they create thick sociality, bonding and 'we-relationships' through the personal and collective experience, which once shared becomes very powerful for one's self-esteem. And the more this memory is discussed the stronger the bonds will exist between members; it matters not if the narrative of the memory changes or distorts over time; it is the sociality of the memory that is important.

Participatory arts events therefore have a unique ability to de-marginalise marginalised older communities particularly within rural areas where opportunities to engage in arts activities might be far and few between. There is a great need for further research in this area especially with regard to over 70 males and their engagement with the arts as so far this has been very limited. There is also a clear need to assess the potential of different forms of participatory arts events (i.e. dance, drama, painting, music, choral/singing groups, museums and concerts) as critical intervention to reduce loneliness, isolation and delay the onset of degenerative disease and forms of dementia. It is estimated that 850,000 older people in the United Kingdom have been diagnosed with dementia, a number which is predicted to rise to one million by 2021 and two million by 2051, and with it treatment costs are estimated to rise from £26.3 billion (2017) to £50 billion by 2047 (All-Party Parliamentary Group, UK Government, 2017).

The most commonly diagnosed form of dementia in the United Kingdom is Alzheimer's (62 percent of dementias in the United Kingdom). The Department of Health (2015) reported that if the onset of Alzheimer's disease could be delayed by five years, then a person's longevity and quality of life savings to the NHS in the United Kingdom between 2020 and 2035 could be as high as £100 billion. The Alzheimer's Society (2017) further concluded in its report that for every person with dementia living at home rather than in a residential care home, savings of £941 per month (or £11,296 per year) could be made; if five percent of admissions could be delayed by a year, £55 million would be saved (Department of Health, 2015).

Finally, there is an untapped research opportunity to bring all of the popular art forms mentioned here and connect them under the foci of a community festival for the benefit of older people. One project that has achieved this with some success is the 'Here and Now Festival', which is run over seven months in Northern Ireland. The festival's goal is to enhance the well-being and quality of life of people over 60 through participatory arts workshops, which include music composition and singing, contemporary/modern dance, visual art, drama, film-making/photography and creative writing. For example, in 2014 the Here and Now Festival delivered 343 workshops over seven months and across 84 host organisations, with a focus on health, social care and community well-being. The intention was to increase arts access to older people in rural areas to reduce isolation and improve their quality of life and levels of social interaction (Arts Care, 2015).

It is well known that arts engagement can boost brain function and improve the recall of personal memories, yet the potential of arts-based community festivals remains underutilised; there are numerous opportunities to give older people the opportunity to learn and build new creative skills. Community arts festivals aimed at older people could also highlight the issues faced by older people, such as loneliness, isolation, belonging or self-esteem, to younger generations within the community; they could also be used to inform the community that older people suffer from many different forms of dementia and to promote understanding into how the community can be more dementia friendly. Arts-based community festivals can also foster social integration, reduce loneliness, increase self-esteem and give older people a sense of belonging; they can give older people the opportunity to engage with a wide range of arts activities and introduce them to new ones, allow older people to learn about their community and connect to arts groups or social clubs nearby.

The current and future challenge is for local governments to be brave and take the initiative to lead and develop partnerships with public, private and voluntary stakeholders within their communities so that the documented physiological, psychosocial and socio-economic benefits that arts events and community festivals offer can be realised.

References

Age UK (2016) *Combating loneliness: a guide for local authorities*. London, Age UK.

All-Party Parliamentary Group, UK Government (2017) *Arts, health and wellbeing inquiry report – creative health: the arts for health and wellbeing*. Available from: www.artshealthandwellbeing.org.uk/appg-inquiry/ [Accessed 12th July 2018].

Arts Care (2015) Arts Care online. Available from: www.artscare.co.uk [Accessed 2nd June 2018].

Arts Council England (2007) *The arts health and wellbeing*. Liverpool, Research Directorate, Centre for Public Health, Liverpool John Moores University.

Ateljevic, I., Morgan, N. & Pritchard, A. (2007) Editors' introduction: promoting an academy of hope in tourism enquiry. In: Ateljevic, I., Pritchard, A. & Morgan, N. (eds.) *The critical turn in tourism studies: innovative research methodologies*. Oxford, Elsevier, pp. 1–10.

Baumeister, R. F., Finkenauer, C. & Vohs, K. D. (2001) Bad is stronger than good. *Review of General Psychology*. 5 (4), 323–370.

Bedding, S. & Sadlo, G. (2008) Retired people's experience of participation in art classes. *British Journal of Occupational Therapy*. 71 (9), 371–378.

Biordi, D. L. & Nicholson, N. R. (2011) Social isolation. In: Lubkin, I. M. & Larsen, P. D. (eds.) *Chronic illness: impact and interventions* (8th ed.). Burlington, MA, Jones & Bartlett Learning, pp. 97–124.

Bowen, H. & Daniels, M. (2005) Does the music matter? Motivations for attending a music festival. *Event Management*. 9 (3), 155–164.

Campbell, D. (2018) NHS deficit and staff shortage data 'held up' by government. *The Guardian*, 21 February. Available from: https://www.theguardian.com/society/2018/feb/21/nhs-deficit-and-staff-shortage-data-held-up-by-government [Accessed 10th July 2018].

Clift, S. & Hancox, G. (2010) The significance of choral singing for sustaining psychological wellbeing: findings from a survey of choristers in England, Australia and Germany. *Music Performance Research*. 3 (1), 79–96.

Cutler, D. (2009) *Ageing artfully: older people and professional participatory arts in the UK*. London, The Baring Foundation.

Davidson, S. & Rossall, P. (2014) *Age UK loneliness evidence review*. Available from: www.ageuk.org.uk/Documents/EN-GB/For-55%202014.pdf?dtrk=true [Accessed 2nd May 2018]

Denzin, N. K. & Lincoln, Y. (2000) *Qualitative research*. Thousand Oaks, Sage Publications.

Department for Environment, Food and Rural Affairs (DEFRA) (2011) *Survey of public attitudes and behaviours towards the environment*. Available from: http://webarchive.nationalarchives.gov.uk/20110704135447/http://archive.defra.gov.uk/evidence/statistics/environment/pubatt/index.htm [Accessed 10th June 2018]

Department for Work and Pensions (DWP) (2014) *Households below average income: an analysis of the income distribution 1994/95–2012/13*. London, Department for Work and Pensions. Available from: www.gov.uk/government/collections/households-below-average-income-hbai--2 [Accessed 8th June 2018]

Department of Health (2015) *Prime Minister's challenge on dementia 2020*. London, Department of Health. Available from: https://assets.publishing.service.gov.uk/government/uploads/system/uploads/attachment_data/file/414344/pm-dementia2020.pdf [Accessed 15th May 2018]

Gratton, L. & Scott, A. (2016) *The 100-Year Life*. London and New York, Bloomsbury.

Hackling, S., Secker, J., Kent, L., Shenton, J. & Spandler, H. (2006) Mental health and arts participation: the state of the art in England. *The Journal of the Royal Society of the Promotion of Health*, 126, 121–127.

Haslam, S. A., Jetten, J., Postmes, T. & Haslam, C. (2008) Social identity, health and wellbeing: an emerging agenda for applied psychology. *Applied Psychology: An International Review*. 58 (1), 1–23.

Hixson, E. J., Vivienne, S., McCabe, V. S. & Brown, G. (2011) Event attendance motivation and place attachment: an exploratory study of young residents in Adelaide, South Australia. *Event Management*. 15 (3), 233–243.

Holt, J. (2008) A space for creativity and healing. In: Kaye, C. & Howlett, M. (eds.) *The Path to Recovery? Mental Health Today and Tomorrow*. Oxford, Radcliffe Press, pp. 149–162.

Holt-Lunstad, J., Smith, T. B. & Layton, J. B. (2010) Social relationships and mortality risk: a meta-analytic review. *PLoS Medicine*. 7 (7), 1–20.

Holt-Lunstad, J., Smith, T. B., Barker, M., Harris, T. & Stephenson, D. (2015) Loneliness and social isolation as risk factors for mortality: a meta-analytic review. *Perspectives on Psychological Science*. 10 (2), 227–237.

Jaimangal-Jones, D., Fry, J. & Haven-Tang, C. (2018) Exploring industry priorities regarding customer satisfaction and implications for event evaluation. *International Journal of Event and Festival Management*. 9 (1), 51–66.

Kim, K., Sun, J., Jogaratnam, G. & Oh, I. (2007) Market segmentation by activity preferences: validation of cultural festival participants. *Event Management*. 10 (4), 221–229.

Kirkegaard Thomsen, D. & Brinkmann, S. (2009) An interviewer's guide to autobiographical memory: ways to elicit concrete experiences and to avoid pitfalls in interpreting them. *Qualitative Research in Psychology*. 6 (64), 294–312.

Krause, N. (2007) Longitudinal study of social support and meaning in life. *Psychology and Aging*. 22 (3), 456–469.

Kulczynski, A., Baxter, S. & Young, T. (2016) Measuring motivations for popular music concert attendance. *Event Management*. 20, 239–254.

Lambert, N. M., Stillman, T. F., Hicks, J. A., Kamble, S., Baumeister, R. F. & Fincham, F. D. (2013) To belong is to matter: sense of belonging enhances meaning in life. *Personality and Social Psychology Bulletin*. 39 (11), 1418–1427.

Lang, I. A., Llewellyn, D. J., Langa, K. M., Wallace, R. B. & Melzer, D. (2008) Neighbourhood deprivation and incident mobility disability in older adults. *Age and Ageing*. 37, 403–411.

Leckey, J. (2011) The therapeutic effectiveness of creative activities on mental well-being: a systematic review of the literature. *Journal of Psychiatric and Mental Health Nursing*. 18 (6), 501–509.

Li, R. & Petrick, J. (2006) A review of festival and event motivation studies. *Event Management*. 9 (4), 239–245.

Liang, Y., Illum, S. & Cole, S. (2008) Benefits received and behavioural intentions of festival visitors in relation to distance travelled and their origin. *International Journal of Event Management Research*. 41, 12–23.

Liddle, J. L., Parkinson, L. & Sibbritt, D. W. (2013) Purpose and pleasure in late life: conceptualising older women's participation in art and craft activities. *Journal of Aging Studies*. 27 (4), 330–338.

Livesey, L., Morrison, I., Clift, S. & Camic, P. M. (2012) Perceived benefits of choral singing on health: a comparison of singers with high and low psychological well-being. *Journal of Public Mental Health*. 11 (1), 10–12.

Machielse, A. (2015) The heterogeneity of socially isolated older adults: a social isolation typology. *Journal of Gerontological Social Work*. 58 (4), 338–356.

Marmot, M. (2015) *The health gap: the challenge of an unequal world*. London, Bloomsbury.

Meira, S. S., Alves Vilela, A. B., Casotti, C. A. & da Silva, D. M. (2017) Self-esteem and factors associated with social conditions in the elderly. *Revista de Pesquisa: Cuidado é Fundamental Online*. 9 (3), 738–744.

Morris, J., Wilkinson, P., Dangour, A. D., Deeming, C. & Fletcher, A. (2007) Defining a minimum income for healthy living (MIHL): older age, England. *International Journal of Epidemiology*. 36 (6), 1300–1307.

Orth, U., Trzesniewski, K. H. & Robins, R. W. (2010) Self-esteem development from young adulthood to old age: a cohort-sequential longitudinal study. *Journal of Personality and Social Psychology*. 98 (4), 645–658.

Pegg, S. & Patterson, I. (2010) Rethinking music festivals as a staged event: gaining insights from understanding visitor motivations and the experiences they seek. *Journal of Convention and Event Tourism*. 11 (2), 85–99.

Peplau, L. A. & Perlman, D. (1982) *Loneliness: a sourcebook of current theory, research, and therapy*. New York, John Wiley & Sons Inc.

Ren, C., Pritchard, A. & Morgan, N. (2010) Constructing tourism research: a critical enquiry. *Annals of Tourism Research*. 37 (4), 885–904.

Richards, V., Pritchard, A. & Morgan, N. (2010) (Re)Envisioning tourism and visual impairment. *Annals of Tourism Research*. 37 (4), 1097–1116.

Sandstrom, G. M. & Dunn, E. W. (2014) Social interactions and wellbeing: the surprising power of weak ties. *Personality and Social Psychology Bulletin*. 40 (7) 910–922.

Sedgley, D., Pritchard, A. & Morgan, N. (2011) Tourism and ageing: a transformative research agenda. *Annals of Tourism Research.* 38 (2), 422–436.

Stadler, R., Jepson, A. & Wood, E. (2018) Electrodermal activity measurement within a qualitative methodology: Exploring emotion in leisure experiences. *International Journal of Contemporary Hospitality Management.* 30(8).doi:10.1108/IJCHM-11-2017-0781

Syson, F. & Wood, E. (2006) Local authority arts events and the South Asian community: unmet needs – a UK case study. *Managing Leisure.* 11 (4), 245–258.

Taylor Nelson Sofres (TNS) (2014) *Loneliness omnibus survey.* London, Age UK.

Teresa, M. (1997) *Mother Teresa: in my own words.* Bexley, OH, Gramercy Books.

The Alzheimer's Society (2017) In: All-Party Parliamentary Group, UK Government (2017) *Arts, health and wellbeing inquiry report – creative health: the arts for health and wellbeing.* Available from: www.artshealthandwellbeing.org.uk/appg-inquiry/ [Accessed 9th June 2018]

The Centre for Policy on Ageing (2011) *Keep dancing: the health and well-being benefits of dance for older people.* London, BUPA.

Thomas, Y., Gray, M., McGinty, S. & Ebringer, S. (2011) Homeless adults' engagement in art: first steps towards identity, recovery and social inclusion. *Australian Occupational Therapy Journal.* 58 (6), 429–436.

Tornstram, L. (2011) Maturing into gerotranscendence. *Journal of Transpersonal Psychology.* 43 (2), 166–180.

Tribe, J. (2009) Tribes, territories and networks in the tourism academy. *Annals of Tourism Research.* 37 (1), 7–33.

Van Zyl, C. & Botha, C. (2004) Motivational factors of local residents to attend the Aardklop National Arts Festival. *Event Management.* 8 (4), 213–222.

White, M. (2009) A 'homecoming' for arts in mental health. *A Life in the Day.* 13, 37–40.

WHO Centre for Health Development (2004) *A Glossary of Terms for Community Healthcare and Services for Older Persons.* Geneva, World Health Organisation.

Wood, E., Jepson, A. & Stadler, S. (2018) Making new memories; the potential benefits of creative arts events for the over 70s, and the impact upon their psychosocial wellbeing. *Event Management.* doi:10.3727/152599518X15346132863283

Part II

Empowerment, resistance and transformation

6 The FAFSWAG ball

Event spaces, counter-marginal narratives and walking queer bodies into the centre

Jared Mackley-Crump and Kirsten Zemke

Introduction: going to the library

> There's no neutral space where you can just enter and our gender politics is never an issue; it's always an issue.
>
> Tanu Gago (FAFSWAG co-founder)

This paper uses the framework of marginalisation to contextualise how a queer arts collective use events to recentre narratives and reclaim excluded stories and creative practices. FAFSWAG are an Auckland, New Zealand-based collective who, inspired by the gay black and Latinx ball culture of New York, explore their own Pacific backgrounds and gendered identities in a range of spaces for a range of audiences. Their name is a portmanteau of the words *fa'afafine* and 'swag'. *Fa'afafine* is a Samoan word literally meaning 'in the manner of a woman' and refers to a complex trans-gendered third gender common throughout the Pacific but beyond the scope of this discussion (however see Besnier & Alexeyeff, 2014). 'Swag', a common slang form of the word swagger, has been self-defined by FAFSWAG co-founder Tanu Gago as 'your demeanour, your attitude, your cool' (in Olds, 2015).

FAFSWAG run vogue nights at gay clubs, collaborate with visual and music artists, curate exhibitions at galleries, compose and perform theatrical shows, and have released an interactive documentary (meticulously archived at https://fafswag.com). FAFSWAG's queer artistic activism incorporates influences from ball culture and indigenous *whakapapa* (genealogy), bringing their life stories and counter-narratives not only into the Euro-centred New Zealand mainstream but also from the periphery of both the Pacific and (white) queer communities. For example, the collective more recently staged a vogue ball at the Auckland War Memorial Museum as part of an evening called 'Explicit Inclusion Identity', in support of the world's first ever transsexual mayor, Georgina Beyer. Inserting their disruptive practices into central city events, FAFSWAG are conscious of, and intentional with, creating uniquely queer Pacific spaces that not only explore and celebrate their complex layers of identity (ethnicity, gender, sexuality, diaspora) but also provide safety and inclusion for a community often subject to violence, trauma and rejection. FAFSWAG expertly utilise their markers of difference as cultural capital, selling and hustling their salient deviance in order to develop their practise and collaborators, yet are conscious of their role in having to educate outsiders in order to mitigate racism and homophobia.

FAFSWAG members are considered and self-reflexive; they run blogs, do countless media interviews, have featured in two online documentaries and are very active on multiple social media platforms, as this chapter demonstrates. As such, the researchers did not request interviews to repeat interrogations they have been asked time and again; instead, we have watched and read their progress online and at live shows over four years. Their creative projects are the members' most undeniable and willing means of discourse, evocatively expressing their unique queer Pacific struggles, trauma, joys, alliances and identities.

Events and marginalisation: giving you life

The application of marginalisation in our research, as an analytical tool, is concerned with how socio-spatial inequalities create dynamics of centre and periphery, and how these dynamics generate event-led responses. In ethnomusicology, the native discipline of the researchers, notions of centre and periphery have long been a theoretical framework through which to interrogate the interplay between music and concepts such as migration and diaspora, power, race and gender (e.g. Chambers, 1993; Raykoff & Tobin, 2007). Growing global inequalities has led to a recent resurgence of interest in how peripheries are produced, and how marginalisation occurs (e.g. Kühn, 2015); indeed, this book can be read as a contribution to these debates.

As an approach to marginalisation, we are informed by theorising of peripheralisation as a multidimensional concept. Kühn (2015) proposes five factors through which peripheralisation can be understood. Peripheralisation is: relational, and linked to a complementary process of centralisation; process-centred, concerned with spatial dynamics and not just geographic remoteness; multidimensional, comprising social, economic and political dimensions; multi-scalar, concerned with contexts ranging from local to global; and temporal, allowing for change over time. We focus on the first three factors, as we are concerned with the dynamics between centre and periphery that generate FAFSWAG's counter-narratives, and the broader contextual dimensions that influence these processes.

In terms of event studies, there are two dominant perspectives: how events can marginalise and how marginalised people can use events to (re)centre their narratives. The literature provides a wealth of examples that reflect these themes across a range of contexts and event types, with a common theme that these events are often planned at the governmental level to achieve particular sociopolitical outcomes. Silk (2015), for example, explores narratives of Britishness produced during the London 2012 Olympics Opening Ceremony. He argues that it presented a display of selective silencing, a multi-ethnic contemporaneity that ignored a multi-ethnic past and in which divisions were disregarded in place of an Anglicised, simple, stable and safe display of fantastical fantasy. Here peripheralisation is centred around race and rooted in a centre-periphery discourse of London as the centre of empire. As he argues, the display 'positioned minority communities within new hierarchies of be(long)ing that replay aspects of colonial racism', where whiteness makes a claim to automatic belonging, while the 'Other' is tolerated so long as it does not disrupt the hierarchy (Silk, 2015: p. 79).

Other aforementioned axes are also visible in the literature. Boland (2010), for example, focusses on class as a peripheralising force at the 2008 European Capital of Culture, staged in Liverpool. He challenges the official hyperbole, with its triumphant evaluations of urban regeneration, and instead highlights how its events centred certain narratives while marginalising others. For those of the investment, tourist and professional classes, *Liverpool08* provided 'flash apartments and pleasure spaces for those with surplus income and cultured tastes' (Boland, 2010: p. 640). By contrast, for a not insignificant number of other residents, the city became 'a distant place upon which they gaze' for, 'although several events were free, the real beneficiaries were salaried groups able to enjoy the cultural spectacle on offer' (ibid). In a queer context, the global celebration of Pride festivals, which began as overtly political events, has been criticised as devolving into commercialised, spectator-centred spectacles that are used in tourism marketing (e.g. Ammaturo, 2016; Taylor, 2016). Johnston (2005) goes as far as to suggest that the professionalisation of parades creates physical barriers that reinforce the marginalisation of gay bodies: a space where non-queer folks can 'consume the Other' without threat of being consumed by the Other (p. 58).

Conversely, though, regarding Toronto's Pride Parade, Hoxsey (2010) makes a pertinent observation: 'Essentially, it has not been just "our" Parade for a long time' (p. 189). The increasing popularity and interest in events necessitate that, once they achieve a certain scale, a new set of relationships are required to achieve sustainability, and concessions are sometimes necessary as the social conditions that created the event have irrevocably changed. This reflects how contemporary cities no longer comprise an amalgamation of stages; cities are now staged. Urban public spaces have been increasingly 'eventised' and, in doing so, processes of inclusion and exclusion can take place: events can be used to make public spaces more accessible at the same time as less accessible (spatially, economically and so forth) (Smith, 2015). Here, Waitt (2008) is compelling. He positions the turn towards urban festivity as offering geographies of hype, hope and helplessness. The political interest in events as panaceas for the challenges of achieving urban and economic development alongside social outcomes represents hype. A reading of this as merely a mechanism for social and political elites to maintain normative power structures, disadvantaging marginalised groups in the process, represents helplessness. As a way of synthesising these two positions, geographies of hope approach events as containing both the possibility of disempowering while simultaneously opening up spaces for local resistance.

This raises the notion that events celebrating the margins can also be emancipatory. Mackley-Crump (2015) has shown how diasporic Pacific communities in New Zealand, long marginalised along axes of class and race, have used festivals as a creative response. The festivals create highly public statements about nation and belonging, allowing communities a degree of control over festival content and narratives, and providing opportunities for community development and capacity building. Slater (2009) argues that festivals can be used by indigenous peoples to assert a belonging to a particular sociopolitical body while also reaffirming commitment to shared nationhood. Indigenous festivals are spaces of multiple and contradictory performances, challenging narrow perceptions of 'authentic' Indigenous culture and creating opportunities for those who feel marginalised by the cult of the authentic. This sort of strategic essentialism can be utilised as cultural capital for communities and peoples without material capital who may have on offer a 'salient blackness' (Basu & Werbner, 2001).

Gender and the diasporic Pacific context: sissy that walk

For those outside queer and/or Pacific spaces, a brief note regarding gender, queerness and Pacific cultures is important. To begin with, gender and sexuality are two different things. This can be perplexing, as trans is not a sexuality while other letters in the LGBTQ+ appellation are (L=lesbian, G=gay, B=bisexual). Trans, broadly, represents people who perform a gender other than that which they were assigned at birth. This includes those who have undergone or wish to have gender reassignment surgery; those who associate with neither gender (genderqueer, nonbinary); or, simply, those who feel like or perform a different gender but have no desire to alter their biology. Trans is important in this chapter because the FAFSWAG collective perform a range of non-mainstream gender types, completely blurring any lines between male and female, and problematising the gender binary altogether. Acceptance of diverse gender identities and sexualities has undergone considerable revolution in recent decades. There has been a dismantling of gender binaries, with the understanding that human sexual and gendered expression does not conform to dualities (male/female, homo/hetero) (Butler, 2002; Halberstam, 2012). Notions of fluidity, spectrums and multiplicities (even within one person) have now been recognised as a truth of human lived experience. This is further complicated by the fact that gender and sexual identities are lived in racialised bodies and subject to a number of other factors, such as class and culture (e.g. hooks, 1992; Crenshaw, 1993).

In the pre-missionary Pacific, more fluid conceptions of gender existed; furthermore, in the contemporary Pacific (and its diaspora), blurred boundaries between gender and sexuality can still be more fluid than Western conceptions allow (Besnier & Alexeyeff, 2014). Bartlett and Vasey (2006: p. 660), for example, discuss the Samoan gender construct, *fa'afafine*, which literally means 'in the manner of a woman'. The gender has historically been assigned to those born male but who show signs of nonconformity with conventional notions of prescribed masculinity. Raised as *fa'afafine* they may perform a range of mannerisms considered both masculine and feminine, and traditionally undertake women's roles in society, including in dance and the arts. Poasa (1992) says *fa'afafine* can be defined as effeminate or trans, but the word 'gay' does not fit into Samoan thought. This is echoed in Tonga where *fakaleiti* translates as 'men who behave in the fashion of women' and describes a gender construct defined by specifically Tongan relationships, social transactions and hierarchies (Besnier, 1997). This fluidity, however, is at odds with the conservative Christian doctrines that remain dominant across the region. Schmidt (2003: p. 418) calls the precarious situation of queer Pacific people a 'paradox of apparent cultural acceptance and very real social marginalisation', due to their sometimes-public acceptance and inclusion, but as individuals they can suffer familial expulsion, religious damnation, shunning and violence (Farran, 2010). Feu'u (2014) says colonisation, Westernisation, global trends and medical advancements have seen indigenous Pacific concepts and acceptance of queerness subject to confusion and change. This puts FAFSWAG members in a precarious position of feeling both within and outside of their Pacific cultures. Furthermore, these gender constructs show how Western thinking around gender and sexuality does not adequately provide for all the queer expressions and alliances of the FAFSWAG crew.

The collective: spilling the tea

FAFSWAG have their roots in a photography project that co-founder Tanu Gago was completing as part of his arts degree. Capturing young Pacific men in the midst of developing their personal identities while negotiating their understandings of masculinity and cultural traditions, at the project's end a close circle of friends had formed and they decided to continue working together. Starting slowly, the collective soon started attracting attention and started staging their own events. Throughout, the collective have maintained meticulous control over their image by utilising the full potential of digital platforms, blogs[1] and their website – fafswag.com – to disseminate their work and contribute to dialogues around queerness in Pacific communities.

This desire to control narratives is rooted in FAFSWAG's mission to reframe these dialogues away from (outsider) deficit perspectives to ones that centre the voices of queer Pacific people. Gago has commented that, we decided at a really early stage that we wanted to shift the way the conversation about our community was happening and the way it was being articulated ... So we did a lot of things around the idea of it being cool to be a queer person of colour, and not apologising, ever, for that.

(in Olds, 2015)

Furthermore, on their use of digital spaces,

the internet wasn't a thing for some of us when we were kids, so it was harder to access visible imagery of a proud queer person of colour ... We didn't have maps of our own. We're creating a map.

(in Olds, 2015)

In this sense, FAFSWAG's online dissemination is a crucial part of their advocacy, providing young queer people with freely available information, imagery and representation. This desire for representation manifests in the FAFSWAG ball, a localised adaptation of ball culture.

The immediate precedent for the FAFSWAG balls is the ball culture that developed out of 1960s and 1970s New York, where 'houses' would compete against each other in elaborate competitive events based around 'walking' (Lawrence, 2011). Here, competitors would walk a runway in drag, competing in various categories, many of which were based around 'realness', meaning to appear passably as female. These houses and events became safe spaces for young queer black and Latinx men who were often estranged from their biological families. By the 1980s ball culture had expanded to include a range of categories (now including masculine performance drag) and had morphed into a specific language and dance styles, chief among them voguing (Lawrence, 2011). It was at this time that a documentary was made about ball culture (*Paris is Burning*) and Madonna appropriated voguing for her hit song 'Vogue'. This circulation beyond the ball community allowed the culture to disseminate, inspire and replicate across and eventually outside of America.

The documentation of ball culture in *Paris is Burning*, and its themes of inclusiveness, participation and belonging became the reference point for FAFSWAG to recreate but localise the concept in Auckland; Gago has noted that 'I thought those themes were really transferable to a Maori and Pacific audience, so I thought the perfect solution was to put on a ball **for** ourselves' (in *Fresh*, 2014). This was an event created for its community as opposed to an external audience:

We wanted to provide people with an opportunity where you didn't have to fight so hard. It's good to see examples and reflections of self that are positive ... They can own this floor and they can make this space their own.

(in *Fresh*, 2014)

Fellow FAFSWAG artist, Pati Solomona Tyrell, made the same observation when he noted that

> as Pacific queer people, I feel like we don't always have the opportunity to express ourselves in life in general. When we do get the opportunities that Fafswag gives it's important, because where else can we tell our stories? We need to be the authors of our own stories.
>
> (in Olds, 2015)

This again reinforces the notion that FAFSWAG, as a collective, are utilising event spaces as a medium to shift the centre, to deny narratives that continue to marginalise. The first FAFSWAG ball was held in South Auckland in 2013 and continued there for two more years. From 2016, however, FAFSWAG started staging events in central Auckland, creating queer Pacific spaces at the centre of both queer and art worlds in the city. Most recently, and perhaps prominently, in early 2018 FAFSWAG were invited into the Auckland Art Gallery, where a ball was staged to coincide with the launch of their interactive documentary, during the city's Pride festival.

Counter-narratives: throwing shade

Many of the FAFSWAG collective were raised in the Pacific communities of South Auckland. These communities arose in the mid-twentieth century, as New Zealand's post-WWII economy expanded and citizens from a range of other South Pacific nations were invited to migrate in order to meet labour shortages. As a result, the suburbs from which FAFSWAG come are inherently multicultural and diverse, with a dominant Pacific flavour (Stevenson & Stevenson, 2006). These migrant communities worked, were educated and socialised together and increasingly inter-married (and with other ethnicities, albeit to a lesser degree), resulting in a unique 'Southside' identity and culture (e.g. Borrell, 2005). Mackley-Crump (2015) has shown how this particular history and unique identity resulted in marginalisation – economic, sociopolitical, sociocultural – and that these challenges remain. However, he also argues that these challenges resulted in creative responses through festivals and increasing visibility in the arts. This dualism can be seen in representations of South Auckland, where media have consistently stereotyped its communities from a range of deficit perspectives (Allen & Bruce, 2017). In response, a broad range of Pacific-owned and/or -centred media try to present counter-narratives (Neilson, 2015). The small amount of positive coverage appearing in mainstream media often centres on creative or sporting pursuits (Allen & Bruce, 2017).

By contrast, central Auckland and its picturesque harbour, bustling waterfront and (multi)million-dollar homes are dominant in national (and international) narratives about Auckland's recent prosperity. Arts and culture have been identified as integral to the city's continued development, but the need to diversify access for residents, and what kinds of arts and culture are supported, is noted in Auckland Council's strategic plan (2015):

> while Aucklanders value arts and culture in all their forms, many do not engage with them, and access and participation are not equitable across the region … We need to recognise the impact of Auckland's geographical diversity and spread on access and participation.
>
> (pp. 24–27)

Furthermore, it notes that, by 2021, Māori, Pacific and Asian peoples will comprise over half the city's population; the way arts operate must change to reflect this diversity. Reading between these bureaucratic lines, the writing is clearly on the wall: the way arts and culture operate across Auckland is dominated by an Auckland Central-centric view; further, what is supported continues to reflect dominant *Pākehā* (European New Zealander) perspectives. The strategic plan is an attempt to stem the socio-spatial process of peripheralisation that has occurred in Auckland across geographic, social, political and economic lines.

FAFSWAG's activities act as a counter to this peripheralisation, which posits that the greatest social, economic and artistic wealth emanates from the urban centre. In fact, initially FAFSWAG worked against the existence of this marginalisation, purposefully situating their art and activities within their communities, and not explicitly seeking out approval from any urban centre. This aligns strongly with the collective's *kaupapa*, or guiding ethos, something that can be read against the temporal characteristic of peripheralisation, where 'the role of a periphery may change in long-term perspective and a "de-peripheralisation" (or "re-centralisation") is possible' (Kühn, 2015: p. 374). FAFSWAG ultimately seek to counter a marginalising centre-periphery binary, instead recentring their events as the centre in a queer, Pacific Auckland dialogue. Their more recent takeover of central Auckland spaces reinforces the denial of this centre-periphery narrative, reversing the flow and bringing the so-called margins into the centre. This makes their events richly and symbolically powerful. They are akin to Bakhtin's ideas about the subversive potential of carnival to transgress social norms, reverse power dynamics and challenge ownership of space, ideas now widely applied to events (e.g. Matheson & Tinsley, 2016). However, FAFSWAG's subversive potential is not limited to transgressing socio-spatial peripheralisation; their events also radically confront both the queer and Pacific cultures that marginalise them.

As noted, the acceptance of non-mainstream genders and sexualities has undergone a radical shift in recent decades. However, these advances had a predominantly Eurocentric focus and often failed to consider the voices and experiences of black or Latinx queerness, for example (Spargo, 2000). The result is a homonormative centre and a process of queer 'othering', marginalising along race, class and gender lines. This centre privileges educated, middle-class, white, masculine-performing, gay males as idealised representations of queerness, and with growing mainstream acceptance, the gravitational force of this centre increased. This was also a result of the considerable consumptive power of the so-called 'pink dollar' and the types of queer identities and bodies made acceptable by processes of gentrification and urban development (e.g. Kanai & Kenttamaa-Squires, 2015; Mattson, 2015). Increasing mainstream acceptance of queerness has thus been wed to urban and civic pride, and this has, in turn, led to the exclusion of 'shameful' queer identities in the normalisation of globalised gay villages (Bell & Binnie, 2004).

Furthermore, in New Zealand, the so-called 'Pacific voice' has historically positioned the communities as having a unified, heavily religious and socially conservative voice. However, as Salesa (2018) points out, this belief misguidedly assumes that a particular category of older Pacific people, who have undoubtedly been more prominent in the public sphere, are the sole voice. FAFSWAG co-founder Tanu Gago has reflected on this. He believes that queer Pacific spaces and the continued role of the church can coexist within the same landscape:

> Our young people are embedded in religious frameworks; it's part of their culture and their identity and just because they identify this way [queer] doesn't mean they've abandoned those values. It's still very much a part of their life and I feel that's reflected in the landscape, these two things coexist geographically the same way they do within our young people.
>
> (in Moata-Cox, 2014)

However, as elsewhere, queer Pacific people still occupy precarious positions: while there are safe spaces within their communities, there remains much stigmatisation.

Spaces of safety and liberation: shante you stay

The ways in which FAFSAWG experience peripheralisation – socio-spatially and socioculturally – lead us to read the FAFSAWG balls as events that purposefully create counter-narratives to marginalisation, in order to provide spaces of safety, liberation and transformation. In interviews and reflective commentary, members have been explicit about their desire to control and own the events they create, creating multiple forms of space. For example, Pati Tyrell (in Olds, 2015), explained that

> for me personally, when I came out, I felt like there was nothing, no presence of a Pacific queer community ... When you're coming out and trying to navigate that space, that's really difficult when there's no one to look up to or look to for help.

The FAFSWAG balls are an explicit action to create safe queer Pacific spaces, both for themselves and for others within the broader queer and Pacific communities. As Olds (2015) notes, 'their idea is that if someone who is coming to terms with their sexuality jumps online to find help ... they'd come across this proud, empowered group of people'.

Creating spaces in which queer Pacific people can safely explore and negotiate their gender and cultural identities provides them with a medium to tell their own stories. Artist Jonathan Selu (n.d.) eloquently calls this 'Poly rainbow space'. Attending a pre-ball event, held at a community centre built in the style of a traditional Samoan meeting house and used extensively by the Samoan community, Selu notes that 'I felt like two of my worlds had come crashing together', something that was initially discomforting (Selu, n.d.). However, realising that the meeting house is often used by the community as a space of *talanoa* (storytelling; discussing issues), he realised that they were, in effect, doing the same thing: 'Isn't that exactly what our voguers were doing? Were they not telling their stories, highlighting issues that the outside world don't even know exist?' (Selu, n.d.). His answer to that was a resounding yes:

> The Pre-Ball was a space for our Poly Rainbows to share their voice with the world ... Better than that, they were supported, encouraged and celebrated ... So I started thinking Yass! Where else would you hold an event like this? Let's take back our cultural spaces and tell the world, and our communities, just how much we matter. That we don't have to be Poly and Rainbow but actually we can be Poly Rainbows.

In this respect, the FAFSWAG balls are unapologetically creating spaces in which people who are Pacific and queer are able to tell their stories and construct narratives, in a safe and supportive environment, that counter Pacific narratives and queer narratives, neither of which adequately reflect who they are. For co-founder Tanu Gago, this opens up the possibility of true transformation:

> it's the one opportunity for them [walkers] to really feel connected to a space, a physical space that feels safe for them, to be able to take ownership of their identity and their diverseness ... that this was a really transformative space, and that we had a responsibility to continue nurturing this space and giving people that freedom.
>
> (in Olds, 2015)

Thus, in defiance of forces that attempt to marginalise and exclude them, the FAFSAWG balls provide spaces in which queerness and Pacificness are not mutually exclusive, but, in fact, can be resolved into a singular, holistic performance of identity. Their Pacificness is centred in a space that is overtly queer; their queerness is centred in a space that is overtly Pacific.

Selling culture: you better werk

One thing that previous theorising around events has not emphasised, but is important here, is the complexities around histories of racism and colonisation which have rendered the marginalised as marketable due to exoticism and fetishisation. There is a conflict between the notion of 'hustle', understanding and marketing one's creativity and uniqueness in a competitive marketplace, and 'selling out' by reiterating historical tropes of selling race as exotic spectacle. bell hooks (1992) calls the entertainment value of black bodies 'imperialist nostalgia', which, she argues, re-enacts 'the imperialist colonising journey' as a 'narrative fantasy of power and desire' (p. 369). Yousman (2003), for example, calls the white obsession with hip-hop 'Blackophilia', which does not reveal an understanding or humanising but rather is a mask for 'Blackophobia' (p. 371). Said (1978) famously called this process 'Orientalism', imagining the Other as simultaneously an alluring exotic figure of intrigue and dangerous sexuality while at the same time primitive, inferior and uncivilised. This was echoed in the European colonisation of the Pacific, with brown bodies simultaneously coded as beautiful and savage (Suaalii, 2000; Tengan, 2002). The FAFSWAG members are fully aware of these histories and conflicts, as well as their need to survive in a country with little opportunity and funding for the Arts. On this paradox, Gago has noted that, 'they want the fa'afafine to catwalk her way through the nightclub so all the patrons can have a good laugh. It's super gross' (in Olds, 2015). And so,

> there is definitely parts of it that are quite voyeuristic, and we can't avoid those people attending and coming in to see if there's a circus show that's going to happen, or who are just super curious and don't know what it is.
>
> (Gago, in Radio New Zealand, 2017)

FAFSWAG try to mitigate this by making sure their projects are community-driven and always prioritise performers' voices and needs (Radio New Zealand, 2017). Gago articulates that any exotica-derived voyeurism is 'rendered powerless' because they themselves have reflexively crafted and curated their own images: 'I know my identity so well and so thoroughly, when it's presented on the wall, it feels really bulletproof to me' (in Prior, 2017). In addition, some members have reflected that the sexual nature of their work marks a reconnection with their Pacific histories. Selu (n.d.), for example, has noted that 'I started to think about the *po siva* in Samoa before European contact. It was a celebration of sexuality and the beauty of the body. It was a space to dance and express yourself'.

Basu and Werbner (2001), in reference to hip-hop, give the name 'bootstrap capitalism' and 'ethnic entrepreneurship' to a process where marginalised communities utilise non-material resources they have access to, the 'specialised cultural goods which are uniquely theirs', and turn them into capital (p. 242). This can be applied to FAFSWAG, who also draw upon their 'unique experiences' and 'deploy their cultural knowledge' to create a saleable product which they manage and own. FAFSWAG members are fully aware of their position in both selling and protecting their work and identities, and this is grounded in a very real need to pay the bills: 'nor is money ever the motivation for our art, but somehow I feel torn cus for me money is very much on my mind, and a bitch needs to get her life shit together' (Fisiinaua, in Matagi, 2018). Thus, even though they are now positioned firmly within the worlds that might seek to continue to marginalise them, and even though they do so at risk of festishisation of their queer Pacific bodies, they do so from a position of empowerment: they enter event spaces and make them their own; they control the narratives, the representations, the gaze of their audiences.

Conclusion: the realness

FAFSWAG are astute and self-aware, and have eloquently considered some of the same discourses around events that we have contextualised here regarding centre and periphery:

> Fafswag has always been trying to decentralise power ... which is why our ball culture was cultivated in the suburbs ... We realised that the challenge of inclusion and participation and diversity is actually to come into the centre, and to operate in a way that is still authentic and meaningful to [our] cultural space, but has the visibility to reach a wider audience.
>
> (Gago, in Byrt, 2017)

Their work is a constant counter-narrative to exclusion, racism and heterocentricity, and they are using the immediate resource they have on offer, their bodies:

> When we have a vogue ball, it's a chance for them to put their bodies on the line, and really unpack these politics. And they do. Every time, it's so transformative ... We've realised that our bodies are the only thing we have control over. Because outside of our bodies, the world is constantly trying to manoeuvre us and position us.
>
> (Gago, in Byrt, 2017)

FAFSWAG's sexualities, gender presentations and ethnicities give them a cultural capital which they can manoeuvre into funding and interest. Revisioning and reworking the historical tropes of selling racialised bodies as exotic spectacle, their practice is a prime example of emancipatory events that celebrate the margins from a position of empowerment and authenticity. Their muse of ball culture, which also projected and expressed dynamic queer identities, is enhanced by their unique Pacific narratives. The artists' personae and subjectivities do not conform to the usual binaries of gay OR straight, male OR female or even cis OR trans. Their events disrupt urban space, and FAFSWAG transgress the multiple oppressions, exclusions and limitations the various centres try to impose upon them.

Note

1 Gago's pre-FAFSWAG blog remains active at http://jerrythefaafafine.blogspot. co.ns/ [Accessed 2nd May 2018].

References

Allen, J. & Bruce, T. (2017) Constructing the other: news media representations of a predominantly 'brown' community in New Zealand. *Pacific Journalism Review.* 23 (1), 225–244.

Ammaturo, F. (2016) Spaces of pride: a visual ethnography of gay pride parades in Italy and the United Kingdom. *Social Movement Studies.* 15 (1), 19–40.

Auckland Council. (2015) *Toi Whītiki: Auckland's Art and Culture Strategic Action Plan.* Available from: www.aucklandcouncil.govt.ns/plans-projects-policies-reports-bylaws/our-plans-strategies/topic-based-plans-strategies/community-social-development-plans/Documents/toi-whitiki-strategic-action-plan.pdf [Accessed 30th April 2018].

Bartlett, N. & Vasey, P. (2006) A retrospective study of childhood gender-atypical behavior in Samoan fa'afafine. *Archives of Sexual Behavior.* 35 (6), 659–666.

Basu, D. & Werbner, P. (2001) Bootstrap capitalism and the culture industries: a critique of invidious comparisons in the study of ethnic entrepreneurship. *Ethnic and Racial Studies.* 24 (2), 236–262.

Bell, D. & Binnie, J. (2004) Authenticating queer space: citizenship, urbanism and governance. *Urban Studies.* 41 (9), 1807–1820.

Besnier, N. (1997) Sluts and superwomen: the politics of gender liminality in urban Tonga. *Ethnos.* 62 (1–2), 5–31.

Besnier, N. & Alexeyeff, K. (2014) *Gender on the edge: transgender, gay and other Pacific Islanders.* Honolulu, University of Hawai'i Press.

Boland, P. (2010) 'Capital of Culture—you must be having a laugh!' Challenging the official rhetoric of Liverpool as the 2008 European cultural capital. *Social and Cultural Geography.* 1 (7), 627–645.

Borrell, B. (2005) Living in the city ain't so bad: cultural identity for young Māori in South Auckland. In: Liu, J. H., McCreanor, T., McIntosh, T. & Teaiwa, T. (eds.) *New Zealand identities: departures and destinations.* Wellington, Victoria University Press, pp. 191–206.

Butler, J. (2002) *Gender trouble.* London and New York, Routledge.

Byrt, A. (2017) Art of disruption: Fafswag's alternative look at the Pacific body. *Metro.* Available from: www.noted.co.ns/culture/arts/art-of-disruption-fafswags-alternative-look-at-the-pacific-body/ [Accessed 24th May 2018].

Chambers, I. (1993) Travelling sounds: Whose centre, whose periphery? In: Naficy, H. & Gabriel, T. (eds.) *Otherness and the media: the ethnography of the imagined and the imaged.* London and New York, Routledge, pp. 205–220.

Crenshaw, K. (1993) Beyond racism and misogyny: Black feminism and 2 Live Crew. In: Matsuda, M., Lawrence, C., Delgado, R. & Crenshaw, K (eds.) *Words that wound*. Boulder, CO, Westview Press, pp. 111–131.

Farran, S. (2010) Pacific perspectives: Fa'afafine and Fakaleiti in Samoa and Tonga: people between worlds. *Liverpool Law Review*. 31 (1), 13–28.

Feu'u, P. (2014) *a e Ola Malamalama I Iou Fa'asinomaga: a comparative study of the fa'afafine of Samoa and the whakawahine of Aotearoa/New Zealand*. Unpublished Master's dissertation. Wellington, Victoria University.

Fresh. (2014) *Television New Zealand*. Available from: www.youtube.com/watch?v=hB8sjPsESs0 [Accessed 2nd May 2018].

Halberstam, J. (2012) *Gaga feminism: sex, gender, and the end of normal* (Vol. 7). Boston, MA, Beacon Press.

hooks, b. (1992) *Black looks: race and representation*. Boston, South East Press.

Hoxsey, D. (2010) *Whose Pride? An institutional ethnography on participating in Toronto's Pride Parade*. Master's thesis, Victoria, University of Victoria.

Johnston, L. (2005) *Queering tourism: paradoxical performances at gay pride parades*. New York, Routledge.

Kanai, J. & Kenttamaa-Squires, K. (2015) Remaking South Beach: metropolitan gayborhood trajectories under homonormative entrepreneurialism. *Urban Geography*. 36 (3), 385–402.

Kühn, M. (2015) Peripheralization: theoretical concepts explaining socio-spatial inequalities. *European Planning Studies*. 23 (2), 367–378.

Lawrence, T. (2011) 'Listen, and you will hear all the houses that walked there before': a history of drag balls, houses and the culture of voguing. In: Baker, S. (ed.) *Voguing and the House Ballroom Scene of New York 1989–92*. London, SJR Publishing, pp. 3–10.

Mackley-Crump, J. (2015) *Negotiating place and identity in a new homeland: the Pacific festivals of Aotearoa New Zealand*. Honolulu, University of Hawai'i Press.

Matagi, E. (2018) FAFSWAG's Akashi Fisi'inaua: 'institutions need us. And not the other way round'. *The Spinoff*, 7 February. Available from: https://thespinoff.co.ns/music/07-02-2018/fafswags-akashi-fisiinaua-institutions-need-us-and-not-the-other-way-round/ [Accessed 24th May 2018].

Matheson, C. & Tinsley, R. (2016) The carnivalesque and event evolution: a study of the Beltane Fire Festival. *Leisure Studies*. 35 (1), 1–27.

Mattson, G. (2015) Style and the value of gay nightlife: homonormative placemaking in San Francisco. *Urban Studies*. 52 (6), 3144–3159.

Moata-Cox, D. (2014) Gays in leis. *Radio New Zealand*, 21 December. Available from: www.radions.co.ns/national/programmes/spiritualoutlook/audio/20159962/spiritual-outlook-for-21-december-2014-gays-in-leis [Accessed 2nd May 2018].

Neilson, M. (2015) *Pacific Way: Auckland's Pacific community diaspora media*. Auckland, Pacific Media Centre.

Olds, J. (2015) Fafswag: The artists telling queer Pacific stories. *Sunday Star Times*, 9 August. Available from: www.stuff.co.ns/entertainment/arts/70898666/fafswag-the-artists-telling-queer-pacific-stories [Accessed 2nd May 2018].

Poasa, K. (1992) The Samoan fa'afafine: one case study and discussion of transsexualism. *Journal of Psychology and Human Sexuality*. 5 (3), 39–51.

Prior, K. (2017) We're Here, We're Queer, We're Going Nowhere: FAFSWAG at The Basement in 2017. Available from: http://pantograph-punch.com/post/fafswag-at-the-basement [Accessed 24th May 2018].

Radio New Zealand. (2017) Tanu Gago: decolonisation and queer activism. *Saturday Morning.* Available from: www.radions.co.ns/national/programmes/saturday/audio/201833730/tanu-gago-decolonisation-and-queer-activism [Accessed 2nd May 2018].

Raykoff, I. & Tobin, R. (2007) *A song for Europe: popular music and politics in the Eurovision Song Contest.* Hampshire and Burlington, Ashgate.

Said, E. (1978) *Orientalism: Western representations of the Orient.* New York, Pantheon.

Salesa, D. (2018) *Island time: New Zealand's Pacific futures.* Wellington, BWB.

Schmidt, J. (2003) Paradise lost? Social change and fa'afafine in Samoa. *Current Sociology.* 51 (3–4), 417–432.

Selu, J. (n.d.) Bitch! Why you mad? Cause my pussy pops severely, and yours don't? *FAFswag.com.* Weblog. Available from: https://fafswag.com/blog/jono/ [Accessed 21st May 2018].

Silk, M. (2015) 'Isles of Wonder': performing the mythopoeia of utopic multi-ethnic Britain. *Media, Culture and Society.* 37 (1), 68–84.

Slater, L. (2009) Beyond celebration: Australian Indigenous festivals, politics and ethics. In: Boyd, S., Gil, A. & Wong, B. (eds.) *Culture, politics, ethics: interdisciplinary perspectives.* Oxford, Inter-Disciplinary Press, pp. 171–179.

Smith, A. (2015) *Events in the city: using public spaces as event venues.* London and New York, Routledge.

Spargo, T. (2000) *Foucault and queer theory.* Sydney, Allen and Unwin.

Stevenson, B. & Stevenson, M. (2006) *Pacific: a study of island communities in the Southwest Pacific.* Auckland, Pearson Longman.

Suaalii, T. (2000) Deconstructing the 'exotic' female beauty of the Pacific Islands. In: Jones, A., Herda, P. & Suaalii, T (eds.) *Bitter sweet: indigenous women in the Pacific.* Dunedin, University of Otago Press, pp. 93–108.

Taylor, J. (2016) Festivalising sexualities: discourses of 'Pride', counter-discourses of 'shame'. In: Taylor, J. & Woodward, I. (eds.) *The festivalisation of culture.* London and New York, Routledge, pp. 27–48.

Tengan, T. (2002) (En)gendering colonialism: masculinities in Hawai'i and Aotearoa. *Cultural Values.* 6 (3), 239–256.

Waitt, G. (2008) Urban festivals: geographies of hype, helplessness and hope. *Geography Compass.* 2, 513–537.

Yousman, B. (2003) Blackophilia and blackophobia: white youth, the consumption of rap music, and white supremacy. *Communication Theory.* 13 (4), 366–391.

7   Transformative effects of hip-hop events in Khayelitsha, South Africa

Sudiipta Shamalii Dowsett

Afternoon park jams are one of the biggest avenues hip-hop exists in, in Cape Town. Hip-hop heads will never run out of places to go to in order to experience the culture in its rawest form: beats, rhymes, and the omnipresent rap cipher.

(Mkhabela, 2014)

Introduction

Much of the scholarship on global hip-hop neglects the live performance context of hip-hop culture in favour of lyrical analysis. This is in part due to a tendency to conflate rap music with hip-hop (Forman, 2002; Chang, 2006). Hip-hop, though difficult to define (see Allen, 2006), encompasses a key set of practices (emceeing, breaking, turntablism and graffiti), and is based on a live performance culture.[1] Rap music need not be tied to any local live performance traditions, while 'hip-hop' implies a connection to the broader culture of hip-hop (Pough, 2004). While analysis of rap lyrics is crucial for understanding the textual production of emceeing it can only tell part of the story of what hip-hop is doing and enabling worldwide. As hip-hop spread globally, youth all over the world began organising their own live hip-hop events such as Park Jams and informal cyphers. Yet this live performance context – the backbone of underground hip-hop scenes the world over – is rarely mentioned in the literature. This chapter addresses this gap through description and analysis of live hip-hop events in Khayelitsha – an isiXhosa-speaking township on the outskirts of Cape Town, South Africa. I argue that the regularity of events of a particular spatial, sonic, embodied structure – such as outdoor parties in everyday community spaces – provides youth with a means of transforming belonging, identity and locality.

Ethnographic fieldwork conducted from 2008 to 2013 in Khayelitsha revealed how youth remake locality in diverse ways through hip-hop. Hip-hop culture in Khayelitsha consists of regular, artist-initiated, live performance events that produce community and foster collective participation. In the spatial context of the township, hip-hop functions as an organic form of youth work and includes sharing stories among groups of peers and fostering a community of practice and participation but also demonstrates to the next generation a distinct collective mode of storytelling and way of being in and of the township. Importantly, hip-hop in Khayelitsha brings bodies together in a life-affirming feel-good activity that is most often open to the community as events are held on the street, in empty lots and in shacks and houses in densely populated areas. It provides a means through which youth can rework their relationship to place – a particularly crucial and complex project in the post-apartheid era.

In this chapter I argue that reframing hip-hop as an events-based culture allows for a deeper understanding of what hip-hop is doing in a given context. What effects do hip-hop events have on the lives of participants? This chapter first provides a brief history of hip-hop events and their global spread, including to Cape Town in the 1980s. Hip-hop events in Khayelitsha are then described in terms of their social and physical context. The impact of these events is analysed in terms of two key effects – community capacity building and identity and belonging amongst hip-hop artists – in order to understand what such events enable. In doing so, this chapter contributes to a shift in the anthropology of events as outlined by Kapferer and Meinert (2010) away from event as anecdote or symbolic of larger social forces and towards a closer examination of events themselves.

Hip-hop as events-based culture

Live performance events are crucial for the maintenance of a local hip-hop 'scene'. Yet most of the focus in hip-hop scholarship has been on rap lyrics (Chang, 2006). Aspects of live performance events are widely acknowledged, such as the call and response between emcees and the audience (such as Dimitriadis, 1996; Perry, 2004), but rarely are events themselves examined in detail. Descriptions of live events and performances are present in the literature on hip-hop, yet these often take the form of anecdotes to open up discussion about broader social issues. Rose (1996) looks at the policing of rap concerts at large venues in the United States as demonstrative of pervasive racist public discourses that 'construct ... black youth ... as a permanent threat to social order' (p. 245). Rose also examines the broader societal meaning and impact of hip-hop as a whole in relation to access to public space. Spady, Alim and Meghelli (2006) develop the cypher (or cipha) as a conceptual space. A cypher can refer to an organised or spontaneous 'battle' where two or more emcees or b-boys/b-girls engage in a contest of skill and style against each other. As soon as this type of interaction begins, people gather forming a circle closely around the artists in the centre. The spatial, social and ethical structure of hip-hop events shape other types of spaces hip-hop artists, heads and scholars engage in.

Williams and Stroud (2010) analyse live events in terms of their productive capacities and how live events frame lyrics produced during freestyle battles or cyphers. Johnson's (2009) PhD dissertation provides in-depth analysis of b-boy cyphers as embodied events. Gupta-Carlson (2010) writes about the 'community building' work of b-girls in Seattle but, while she mentions hip-hop events, the focus is on the efforts of key hip-hop artists networking and creating female spaces within hip-hop. Kline (2007: p. 214) notes that during cypher performances the audience is *expected* to respond and to 'participate kinetically'. In the specific context of the cypher, kinetic motion is not only physical and multisensory but also intellectual as the lyrics are followed closely (Kline, 2007: p. 214) and in fact determine the outcome of the cypher. Maxwell (2003) found hip-hop heads in the early scene in Sydney, Australia claimed authenticity through their performance and practice of hip-hop arts in the context of live events. Maxwell's (2003) work is crucial for recognising the meaning produced by and experienced during events themselves. Such detailed accounts of live performance events are crucial for understanding the interactive nature and embodied experience of events such as cyphers.

Dowdy's (2007) approach looks at how live hip-hop shows function as a form of political action that:

> create a collective agency, wherein the audience members are at least momentarily empowered to enact change, to practice subversive action, and to speak out about injustice and current political issues.
>
> (p. 75)

Dowdy (2007: p. 76) argues that 'hip hop artists utilise alternative channels for community building and participatory political engagement'. The activism of individual artists and crews has been widely explored in the literature (for example see Rose, 1996; Gupta-Carlson, 2010) along with the use of hip-hop art forms in community projects (such as in 'hood work' see Forman, 2013). In this chapter I am rather concerned with the ways in which hip-hop organically functions as a form of community capacity building (self-organising, working together to create events and produce collectivity, theorising about social, class conditions). Akom, Ginwright and Cammarota (2008) argue that contexts such as hip-hop cyphers 'ultimately lay the foundation for community empowerment and social change' (p. 3), though they do not examine cyphers in detail. Dowdy (2007) argues: '[t]he otherwise lost experience of the political – citizens acting together in a public space with coordinated effort – is a distinctive characteristic of the hip-hop show' (p. 76). This supports Ginwright's (2010) argument for the importance of youth self-organising as a form of political engagement. In this sense, hip-hop can be understood as an organic form of community work in the terms Ginwright (2010) models:

> By rebuilding collective identities (racial, gendered, youth), exposing youth to critical thinking about social conditions and building activism, black youth heal by removing self-blame and act to confront pressing school and community problems.
>
> (p. 86)

This is precisely what many hip-hop artists in Khayelitsha were doing in the period I undertook fieldwork. What is crucial to my argument in this chapter is the informal modelling that youth are presenting and embodying to the next generation who watch, follow and mimic at hip-hop events in the township. That is, modelling a creative productive interactive form of expression through which local issues can be addressed, satirised and critiqued.

However, understanding the impact of hip-hop in a specific area requires an inclusion of the context that events take place in. To this end, Alim (2006) argues that a shift in hip-hop scholarship is necessary to account for hip-hop as a cultural practice through considering the 'very sites of Hip Hop cultural activity' (p. 972). Spady's (in Spady, Alim & Meghelli, 2006) development of 'Hiphopography' – a method for researching hip-hop – recognises that hip-hop must be understood as 'embedded in the lived experiences of Hip Hop conscious beings existing in [specific places]' (p. 29). In other words, hip-hop artists must be considered as situated subjects and hip-hop events as *situated* events.

Hip-hop, as it emerged in the specific context of the Bronx in the 1970s, was a deliberate effort to overcome the rupture of the ghetto – the ongoing and irresolvable rupture of living in the destructive wake of the construction of the cross-city expressway through the South Bronx, the rupture of neglect by city services and the state, the rupture of slavery and colonialism. By creating a new set of creative, social and collective practices, it channelled the experience of the ghetto into something that shifted that very experience of the ghetto. It radically transformed the locality of the Bronx.

The importance of hip-hop events as a form of civic engagement is demonstrated in the role of hip-hop pioneers in creating collective spaces for creative cultural production. Civic engagement can be defined as 'the ways in which citizens participate in the life of a community in order to improve conditions for others or to help shape the community's future' (Adler & Goggin, 2005: p. 236). This is evident in Grandmaster Flash's recall in an interview,

> At this time, the Bronx [in New York] was ruled by street gangs – Black Spades, Savage Skulls, Ghetto Brothers and Casanovas. These gangs would call a truce at Kool Herc's parties. Afrika Bambaataa formed the Universal Zulu Nation as a peaceful alternative to fighting. Breakdancing battles developed as a way to diss rivals without anyone getting hurt. 'Bambaataa played a major part,' Flash says. 'He took all the different cliques and transformed fighting against each other into a more positive energy. Kool Herc had his way of doing it and I had my way. If people had beef and started something, I would shut the music down. The block party thing caused peace in the neighbourhood'.
>
> (Purcell, 2009)

Hip-hop channelled gang affiliation, rivalry, hostility into a creative outlet. It also provided an avenue, through the development of 'crews',[2] for the sense of family that gangs had created. Ginwright (2010) argues for recognising the establishment of youth crews, posses and street organisations as important examples of youth 'civic engagement'. Breaking and rap crews provided a productive, life-affirming, creative alternative to the pervasive gang culture (Chalfant, 2006). The structured battle format was a different way of bringing bodies together – it produced new and productive forms of collectivity. Skott-Myhre (2012) argues that 'what becomes the necessary political act' in the war zone-like situation of the ghetto is the maintenance of 'spaces in which dwelling can occur', that is, 'to refuse alienation in favour of bodies creating together' (pp. 41–43). It is precisely dwelling in public spaces and 'bodies creating together' that hip-hop events have enabled amongst marginalised communities the world over.[3]

Globally hip-hop culture – often referred to as underground hip-hop[4] – remains dependent on regular, low-key, live performance events (see Chang, 2006). At the core of the underground are people coming together in live hip-hop scenes based on emcee, b-boy/b-girl and turntable battles, and performances held at bars, clubs, empty allotments, parks, basketball courts, abandoned buildings, street corners or community halls. Turner (2010) argues that the reduction of hip-hop to rap music 'serves utterly to mask the grassroots hip-hop cultural nexus and its powerfully pervasive collective ethos' (p. 45). Dowdy (2007) also argues that collective identity is central to live hip-hop shows. Hip-hop began as a powerful youth-initiated response to local issues grounded in creative, productive forms of collectivity where, in Chang's (2007) words, 'competition and community feed each other' (p. 65). In this chapter, I argue that hip-hop continues to organically encourage youth to initiate their own events and build their own capacities to maintain a live performance culture. The value that hip-hop artists and community members place on maintaining a local hip-hop scene based on regular live performance events is absolutely central to hip-hop culture on the ground.

Methods

This chapter is based on ethnographic fieldwork conducted between 2008 and 2013. The main focus of my research was confined to the lived experience of diverse artists from a single township in order to investigate the relationship between embodiment, performance and place. At any event there often coexists a diversity of lyrical styles and types of content that engage in a common embodied practice of storytelling. A key question driving the research was: what does emceeing as an embodied mode of storytelling enable within the broader historical context of colonisation, apartheid and cultural change? The methodology utilised necessarily combined phenomenological ethnography and decolonial research. Methods used included participant observation, attendance and performance at events, jamming with other emcees, in-depth interviews with 40 hip-hop artists and collective discussions. Collaborative methods were developed with research participants in the field in order to decentre the researcher in the production and analysis of knowledge and included collaboration on rap songs, documenting hip-hop through photography and film, and events organisation.

During the period of fieldwork, there were regular hip-hop events in key areas of Cape Town. Regular open sessions I attended and performed at on Long Street – the main entertainment strip in the centre of Cape Town – included Verses at Zula Sound Bar (this included spoken word, poetry, rap and song), Kool Out Lounge at The Waiting Room (from late 2008) and Lyric District at Ragazzi Live Bar. Open sessions in Khayelitsha included a street session organised by Sound Masters Crew in Site B and Struggle and Poetry sessions organised by Soundz of the South at Look Out Hill. Hip-hop heads from Khayelitsha would often also attend AllNYz Park Jam in Gugulethu (running since 2006), Heads n' Raps outside Philippi Library and a session at Mlamli's in Gugulethu.[5] In addition to this there were irregular events, such as Park Jam's in I Section, organised by Intellectual Seeds movement; Park Jams in Kuyasa, organised by PM Productions; and other sessions on occasions, such as Youth Day. At many of these sessions there were often spontaneous cyphers.

Hip-hop events in Cape Town and Khayelitsha

The complex matrix of issues affecting access to media under apartheid contributed to the fact that hip-hop was first taken up by 'coloured' youths on the Cape Flats of Cape Town in the mid-1980s. Only later was it taken up by youth in isiXhosa-speaking townships such as Khayelitsha and Gugulethu. Access to hip-hop in South Africa in the 1980s was difficult under apartheid due to segregated media, cultural sanctions and censorship laws. Access was even more difficult for more economically and geographically marginalised isiXhosa-speaking people. The *Natives (Urban Areas) Act* (1923) required all 'Africans' in urban areas to carry a pass and largely confined 'Africans' without passes to designated deliberately impoverished reserves called 'Bantustans'. In 1955 Cape Town was declared a 'Coloured Labour Preference Area' (Ndegwa, Horner & Esau, 2004) which further restricted Africans from working in the city.

Key members of this initial phase were instrumental in shaping hip-hop in Cape Town. This was not only through their maintenance of b-boy culture, and the influence of lyrical content and use of vernacular language (see Haupt, 2004 on Prophets of da City), but also through their active role in organising live events, such as early dance competitions, hip-hop nights uptown, Park Jams and Emile YX?'s Annual Hip-hop Indaba (running since 2000). Early hip-hop performances also took place at school political rallies to entertain youth while waiting for political speeches (Emile YX?, 2014). Haupt (2004) argues that hip-hop parties in the late 1980s in Cape Town 'went a long way toward constituting a creative community away from the watchful eye of the apartheid state ... constituting new forms of publics that had not existed before' (p. 87). However, descriptions of these early events along with reflections on the experience of participants are needed to examine their impact.

With the end of apartheid in 1994, formerly white and 'coloured' schools were de-segregated. Youth from Khayelitsha who were among the first black students to attend such schools interacted with people outside of the township and were exposed to and gained access to hip-hop. MC Steel went to Cape Town High School in the city centre. He started going to hip-hop gigs in the city with friends from high school and introduced this to friends from the township:

> There were events in Khayelitsha but I was more based in the suburban areas because I had coloured and white friends ... and I ended up meeting up with Scrooge [MC Indigenous] and Metabs [MC Metabolism] ... and they would perform at the mall in Khayelitsha ... and I was like 'why don't we go up town to this club called Angels?' So, I took them uptown ... we'd catch a train uptown ... 'cause I'd always get 10 Rand a day so I'd save up and have 50 Rand by the end of the week ... and I would save it for the rest of the soldiers ... the end of the jam would be around 4[am] and we would wait until the first train at 5[am] and catch it back home.
>
> (Interview, 2008)

The first generation of hip-hop artists from Khayelitsha began organising their own Park Jams based on what they had experienced in 'coloured' townships. This generation straddled the nexus between the city, broader Cape Town and Khayelitsha and made the township their own through hip-hop. MC Metabolism and Intellectual Seeds Movement started organising Park Jams in the year 2000 modelled on Park Jams they had been to in the 'coloured' areas like Mitchell's Plain and Grassy Park. Around the same time Rattex (a pioneer of 'Spaza' – rap in isiXhosa) and MC Mafiyana also organised Jams in different areas of Khayelitsha. The effect of events organised by first-generation hip-hop heads was to inspire the next generation to create their own crews and community events.

Hip-hop events in the township

There is a distinct difference between hip-hop events in the city and the township. This partly stems from the different social and architectural context of commercial versus residential zones. In the city centre, live performances are staged inside, at a venue, usually a nightclub or bar. These venues are surrounded by other commercial and entertainment businesses populated by international tourists and people from mostly middle-class backgrounds. In different areas of Khayelitsha regular open sessions are held outside in public spaces. In Site B they are held on the street. In I Section, they are held on a run-down basketball court. In Kuyasa, they are held in an empty sandy field behind rows of government housing. Lookout Hill is a venue that is sometimes used for hip-hop events which is further away from homes. All of these spaces, with the exception of Lookout Hill, are in the middle of densely populated residential areas of houses or shacks. They are deeply embedded within the everyday street life of the township.

The high-density population living in close quarters, such as in Khayelitsha, means that there is little distinction between private and public[6] with a sense of people being everywhere all the time – high visibility, high sociality. This was made clearer to me when driving with Argo, an MC from Khayelitsha (still in high school when I met him), through Muizenberg, the area of Cape Town I was living in at the time. Muizenberg is known for being a racially mixed and vibrant community, specifically in comparison to other formerly designated White Areas of Cape Town. Yet Argo was visibly shocked at the seemingly desolate, 'empty' streets and asked, 'where are all the people?' Hip-hop events that occur in the township in outdoor places enter into and take place in highly visible, highly social in-between private-public spaces. They are physically deeply communal.

At such events, there was an interweaving of audience members specifically in attendance to watch performances; passers-by; residents of all ages from nearby homes coming by to watch performances, dance or interact with participants; and always a small crowd of young children. Organisers setting up equipment would be closely watched by young children keeping a respectful distance of less than a foot at all times, a spontaneous cypher would be replayed through mimicry by a group of littles aged around four to ten years, gestures and movements of emcees, dancers and audience members would be acted out by young children. After a Park Jam in I Section that I had collaborated with iSM in organising, MC Metabolism informed me that several local parents had dropped their children off at the Park Jam for the day – such events are seen as safe and entertaining places for young children. The constant community presence was demonstrated by a comment from MC Axo: although inspired by Eminem's style he said emphatically, 'we can't rap like that! We can't use that kind of language! What would our mothers say?!' (Interview, 2011). That is, there are necessary contextual limitations placed on hip-hop in the township because of the close-up and enmeshed nature of its performances within the broader community. Hip-hop events in densely populated neighbourhoods – townships, ghettoes – do not in this sense simply spill over into the neighbourhood. They are of it and from it, inseparably.

In Khayelitsha the population is 96 percent isiXhosa speaking (Brown University, 2006). The audiences at street-based events are usually known to the performers. They often include friends, extended family, people from the neighbourhood and regular faces in the hip-hop community. Events outdoors in the townships speak to a public that is much broader and includes passers-by, neighbours, parents and children. Performances in the city centre are to a certain age group – over eighteen and mostly young adults. Audiences in the city centre are also of mixed background, unlike those in the (formerly officially) segregated isiXhosa-speaking or 'coloured' townships, where the audience is mostly people from that area, or from other townships speaking the same language(s).

Performing to a largely known audience who share cultural and life experiences means emcees can speak directly to peers and youth facing common issues. Most emcees in or from Khayelitsha compose exclusively in isiXhosa[7] which is called Spaza after the informal township 'spaza' shop. MC Rhamncwa explains one reason for his choice to do this: 'I wanna reach my people and tell my stories, and tell their stories. And talk about the way we live ... from the little ones to the older people' (Interview, 2011). MC Lemzin states that 'most of the time I want to rap in Xhosa so that people around me can understand what I'm saying' (Interview, 2011). At AllNYz Park Jam, MC Korianda frequently emphasised the importance of having a message in one's lyrics whilst he moderated the open sessions. Examples of this can be seen in the lyrics of Mic Substance, Lemzin, Undecided Crew, Uzwi Kantu, Sound Masters Crew and Maxhoseni, among others. Audience members that I conversed with at hip-hop events in Khayelitsha explained to me that they loved spaza music because, 'they are always encouraging us', 'they are coming with a positive message', 'they advise us on what to do'.[8] Many emcees, such as Styles from Undecided, Emage, Zanzolo and Mfura, also had stories of audience members coming up to them to thank them for the encouraging messages in their lyrics and telling stories they could relate to their own lives. Mic Substance stated that 'the main important thing of spaza is education ... *with* entertainment' (Interview, 2011). The physical presence of the intended audience shapes the types of narratives and content in rap. Hip-hop, in this sense, is (on the ground) a direct embodied linguistic encounter, exchange and interaction with others.

Within the post-apartheid context, Haupt (2004) hints at the role of hip-hop events in providing a form of civic engagement:

Conscious' hip-hop has ... constituted a public in which young subjects can congregate in which to make sense of the reality of post-apartheid South Africa as well as to develop key creative and critical skills in ways not afforded to them by the formal education system ... these communities form parallel discursive arenas in which to regroup, educate themselves and formulate their interpretation of how oppressive discursive formations interpellate them.

(p. 88)

Yet Haupt does not explore this further in terms of embodied interactions and limits this potential to one 'genre' of rap. The effects on the next generation of the combination of being open to the community and the presence of politically and socially conscious raps at events can be demonstrated in an example from my fieldnotes. I was at a regular informal hip-hop workshop at Luyanda's grandmother's place in Harare, Khayelitsha. The group called Afrikana had just finished rehearsing. A younger group of nine to twelve-year-olds wanted to perform a track they had prepared;

> The younger kids know the words to Afrikana's songs and they rap along with them. Then it is their turn. They call themselves the Flamingoes. There are five of them. Their rap is all in isiXhosa. The only thing I can make out is 'viva ANC'. So, I step back outside and ask Black Vision what they are saying. He tells me they are rapping about Hector Peterson (a young boy made famous by a photograph after he had been shot by police during the Soweto uprising of June 16, 1976) and how people used to sing 'viva ANC' even when they were sick with fever, they sang it till they rotted their liver, but now 'we have freedom' but what is the ANC doing?
>
> 'Whoa!! That's maaaaaad! And they came up with that themselves?!' I ask
>
> 'Yeah we didn't have anything to do with it. They just went away and wrote it and came back and showed us. We were surprised too!' Black Vision explains.

Through the active presence of hip-hop in their local area this group of youth had learnt, through observation and mimicry, a rhythmic embodied mode of voicing that allowed them to express their own perspectives about things that matter. This demonstrates an effect of hip-hop events in organically enabling the development of Haupt's (2004: p. 88) 'creative and critical skills' and in forming collective 'parallel discursive arenas'.

Belonging, identity and habit

Hip-hop events provide a format and context for taking up a specific embodied stance through which performers can express themselves, act out different roles and 'subvert the public, dominant transcript' (Rose, 1994: p. 101). This is a crucial point for, 'individuals exploring different ways of being in collective contexts is the prelude and precursor to all important social political action' (Dimitriadis, 1996: p. 181). Lipsitz (1994) argues that 'cultural production plays a vital role in nurturing and sustaining self-activity on the part of aggrieved peoples ... [and] ... enables people to rehearse identities, stances, and social relations not yet permissible in politics' (p. 137). The identity-effects of hip-hop are tied to its basis in public, live events where people can and do literally 'act' out distinctive forms of embodiment in front of an audience. This acting out is first learnt through mimicry. To paraphrase Biddle (1993) we learn how to be in the world through other bodies for, as she quotes Merleau-Ponty, '[t]he very first of all cultural objects, and the one by which all the rest exist, is the body of the other person as the vehicle of a form of behaviour' (p. 189). Hip-hop has provided marginalised youth all over the world with a new way of being in and from 'the ghetto' complete with a set of practices to shift locality.

To understand the situated nature of hip-hop events in Khayelitsha it is necessary to understand the relationship between place, space, embodiment and locality. Khayelitsha was built in 1984 on the outskirts of Cape Town (35 km from the city centre) as a part of the racially segregated apartheid town planning under the Group Areas Act (1950). amaXhosa were forcibly relocated from other parts of Cape Town. The relaxing of pass laws in the lead up to the 1994 elections saw an influx of migrants from the deeply impoverished rural areas (former 'Bantustans') of the Eastern Cape. Post-1994 this has continued to increase. This is not a one-way movement, as many of the hip-hop artists in Khayelitsha go back to the Eastern Cape for cultural and family reasons. Khayelitsha has a number of negative stereotypes attached to it due to such rural connections. According to emcees I interviewed Khayelitsha is seen by amaXhosa from other areas, such as Gugulethu, as rural, ignorant and backwards.

This is demonstrated in the controversial lyrics of a track by MC DAT – an influential pioneer of Spaza hip-hop. MC DAT's track is about how people from the rural areas in the city are called 'i-junkies' because they walk around the city as if in a drug-induced daze.[9] Khayelitsha is also seen as 'not hip' as the well-respected spaza producer, Mashonisa, explained to me. Khayelitsha is depicted in the media as heavily violent, lawless and poverty stricken – an image demonstrated to me by white South African people's reactions to the idea of a single white female regularly going there. Countering these negative stereotypes and redefining the meaning and experience of the space of Khayelitsha have been important projects and an effect of hip-hop in Khayelitsha.

In order to understand how youth remake the space of Khayelitsha through hip-hop, we need to understand the relationship between place, space, identity and vocality. de Certeau's (1984) definition of 'space as a practiced place' suggests that place is made meaningful through what we do there. Locality is about how people relate to a specific place, but also the structure of feeling that such relating – as practices, habits, movements, social relations – enables as specific to that place. This is a fragile thing as it changes over time, buildings crumble, different social assemblages manifest, the landscape shifts. Locality as defined by Appadurai (1996) is a 'structure of feeling that is produced by particular forms of intentional activity' (p. 182). Activity in place shapes space and makes locality. It also makes and remakes identity. This is a crucial point as much has been written about hip-hop and identity but not from a phenomenological perspective; the relationship between bodies, and between bodies and place and space, shapes identity.

Wise (2000) makes a case for understanding the subject, and identity, as constituted in our embodied relationality with space. He does this through the concept of home – this is not just where we live but how we make spaces familiar. As Wise (2000) argues:

> our identity ... is comprised of habits ... it is through habits that we are brought into culture ... We live our cultures not only through discourse, signs and meaning, but through the movements of our bodies.
>
> (p. 303)

Hip-hop begins a home through sound, through the voice, but also, it does this through particular habits of occupying space in specific ways – through regular live performance jams in community. In this way – where hip-hop becomes a regular collective practice open to the public, open to children already playing in the street, open to the everyday space of the township – it facilitates a way of making order out of the chaos of the township. It provides a way of making a new kind of sense out of the chaotic and traumatic effects of colonialisation and apartheid – a particularly unhomely experience. Order emerges or is produced through habits. As Wise (2000) argues, 'Our habits are not necessarily our own. Most are created through continuous interaction with the external world' (p. 303). Habit organises space in meaningful ways, or makes space meaningful in organised ways, through repetition. As Janz (2001), argues, 'my subjectivity lies in the set of rhythms and repetitions I have found to be useful' (p. 395). This is crucial for opening up how we think about 'identity' and subjectivity in relation to hip-hop. We possess, or accumulate, ways of inhabiting the world. Wise (2000) argues that, 'we are who we are, not through an essence that underlies all our motions and thoughts, but through the habitual repetition of those motions and thoughts' (p. 303). Hip-hop is more than just a way of youth stating 'I am', of negotiating identity. While the body-schema expresses 'identity' proper in the sense of 'representing' hip-hop it also provides a way of being in the world that transforms our experience of that world. Hip-hop created a different way of inhabiting the rupture of the ghetto, through new habits, practices, styles – Park Jams, rap and breaking battles, emceeing as a rhythmic mode of storytelling.

Hip-hop provided a particular stance towards the material and discursive space of the 'hood and township. It provided, to use Merleau-Ponty's (1964) words, youth in Khayelitsha with a specific 'way of grasping the natural and cultural world surrounding' (p. 117) them. This entailed both a conceptual affective stance towards discourse and a bodily stance through the physical practice of emceeing in place: in the city centre at hip-hop events and in the township during live performances at park jams that they organised themselves. Hip-hop provided a way of being in the world that was applicable both to the spaces of the city centre and that of the township – (reframed as a global ghetto space) – transforming identity and their relationships to place at the same time.

The first generation of hip-hop heads from Khayelitsha that I interviewed expressed a sense of alienation from the township due to their attendance at schools outside. MC Metabolism explains the effects of his schooling on his voice – where he spent the majority of his time, first through boarding school and later traversing the spaces of a white school and the black township. It was precisely his accent that further alienated him from the township and marked his difference. For MC's Metabolism, Steel, Indigenous and others of their generation, hip-hop, and specifically Black American English, provided a way into English that was not white – that validates the vernacular and provides, as Alim (2006) argues, a 'Black Language Space' (p. 69). I asked Metabolism what it was about hip-hop that he initially liked. He explained that it was the beats but also the sound of the lyrics:

> I was into English at the time, you know, because of the school that I was at, so the main reason why I paid attention to the lyrics a lot ... I was still trying to be like articulate in English ... and the beats as well you know ... it was something completely different because out here [Khayelitsha] people aren't into hip-hop, you know like in Khayelitsha it's your house vibe, your kwaito vibe and this was something different ... That's what I felt the most you know? Everybody's into that garbage music that they listen to, it was like, well try this, listen to some Snoop Dogg and you'll actually feel cool afterwards ... I started writing down the lyrics and I would rap along with the track.
>
> (Interview, 2008)

Hip-hop provided a way of making sense of, and being in, the township in a different way than the dominant youth cultures in the township at the time.[10] It connected the experience of the township with the global experience of historically oppressed Black folk and marginalised youth in ghettoes around the world.

The importance of hip-hop in providing youth with a sense of global belonging is crucial when there is a disrupted and alienated sense of belonging and emplacement. The postcolonial condition is one of having no place – of fitting neither with a precolonial archaic definition of 'traditional', nor with the Western ideal imposed on the colonised. Hip-hop does this through its ability to remix and to represent. Amongst the first generation of hip-hop heads, a sense of belonging through hip-hop was further solidified through their efforts at self-organising community hip-hop events.

Conclusion

From its inception, hip-hop culture has been dependent upon live performance events. Despite the fact that hip-hop music became separable from the live performance context, hip-hop culture has been taken up globally in the form of live performance events and practices. Whilst much scholarship has importantly examined lyrical production; hip-hop discourse; and the community minded, social justice activism of hip-hop artists, analysis of events themselves within their own cultural, social and physical context has been largely neglected. This chapter has demonstrated some of the key effects and processes enabled through hip-hop events in the township of Khayelitsha. Hip-hop events in Khayelitsha are deeply embedded in the everyday – a situation that shapes the effects of the events themselves. Self-organised hip-hop events reconfigure the relationships between bodies, space and sound. In doing so they transform the experience of the township and redefine the symbolic place of the township within the global Black experience. Through maintaining a local hip-hop scene, artists from Khayelitsha create physical spaces in which a specific form of embodied habit can be taken up by local youth. This type of embodied habit provides identity-forming possibilities for practitioners. Hip-hop artists involved in events create change in their communities by changing what happens there, providing a physical interactive context for storytelling, social commentary and the exchange of ideas. I have argued in this chapter that community building through events is a *core* tenet of hip-hop.

Notes

1 Though graffiti is often necessarily executed in private it has been historically and contemporarily linked to live performance culture. Hip-hop also involves a key set of ethics, aesthetics and philosophies.
2 In hip-hop a 'crew' is a small group of artists, usually tied to a specific neighbourhood, who in any element work together and compete in battles against other crews (see Rose, 1994, pp. 10–11).
3 Hip-hop was taken up in less marginalised spaces but in different contexts it has different effects.
4 See Perry (2004) for more on underground hip-hop.
5 Events occurred in 'coloured' areas of the Cape Flats but I restricted my attendance to isiXhosa-speaking areas.
6 This is key to Bhabha's (1994) definition of the 'unhomely' in postcolonial contexts and is also utilised by Erlmann (1996) specifically in relation to South Africa and migrant labour.
7 Spaza emcees often say they compose 'strictly in Xhosa'; this does not mean to the absolute exclusion of words from other languages but that the majority of their lyrics are in isiXhosa.
8 There were also some emcees that produce fun party tracks, satirical, comic or gangsta raps and some that rap about things they don't have, such as expensive clothes and cars. The most popular artists all had conscious messages in their raps. Part of hip-hop's power is the creation of 'open discourse' (Perry, 2004) spaces of public performance.
9 This track can be viewed along with commentary, and critique by MC Indigenous, at: www.youtube.com/watch?v=8xEA-80M5So. [Accessed 3rd November 2018]
10 The second generation of hip-hop artists in Khayelitsha was largely born and raised, in their younger childhood, in the rural areas of the Eastern Cape and

maintain more cultural connections. Hip-hop also provides a means of reworking the place of the rural in the city and experimenting with traditional modes of storytelling. This is explored in depth in my PhD dissertation (Dowsett, 2017) but is beyond the scope of this chapter.

References

Adler, R. P. & Goggin, J. (2005) What do we mean by 'civic engagement'? *Journal of Transformative Education*. 3 (3), 236–253.

Akom, A. A., Ginwright, S. & Cammarota, J. (2008) Youthtopias: towards a new paradigm of critical youth studies. *Youth Media Reporter*. 2 (4), 1–30.

Alim, H. S. (2006) *Roc the mic right: the language of hip hop culture*. New York, Routledge.

Allen, H. (2006) Dreams of a final theory. In: Chang, J. (ed.) *Total chaos: the art and aesthetics of hip-hop*. New York, Basic Civitas, pp. 7–9.

Appadurai, A. (1996) *Modernity at large: cultural dimensions of globalisation*. Minneapolis, University of Minnesota Press.

Bhabha, H. K. (1994) *The location of culture*. London and New York, Routledge.

Biddle, J. L. (1993) The anthropologist's body or what it means to break your neck in the field. *The Australian Journal of Anthropology*. 4 (3), 184–197.

Brown University. (2006) Community reports: Khayelitsha. Available from: https://s4.ad.brown.edu/Projects/southafrica?Reports/CapeTown/Khayelitsha. pdf [Accessed 21st July 2009].

Chalfant, H. (Writer) (2006) *From mambo to hip hop: a South Bronx tale* [Documentary]. City Lore Inc. and Public Art Films.

Chang, J. (2006) Introduction. Hip-hop arts: our expanding universe. In: Chang, J. (ed.) *Total chaos: the art and aesthetics of hip-hop*. New York, Basic Civitas, pp. ix–xv.

Chang, J. (2007) It's a hip-hop world. *Foreign Policy*. 163 (Nov–Dec), 58–65.

de Certeau, M. (1984) *The practice of everyday life*. Berkeley and Los Angeles, University of California Press.

Dimitriadis, G. (1996) Hip hop: from live performance to mediated narrative. *Popular Music*, 15 (2), 179–194.

Dowdy, M. (2007) Live hip hop, collective agency, and 'acting in concert'. *Popular Music and Society*. 30 (1), 75–91.

Dowsett, S. S. (2017) *'Revolutionary but gangsta': hip-hop in Khayelitsha, South Africa*, Unpublished PhD dissertation. Sydney, University of New South Wales.

Emile YX? (2014) The B-Boy element. Paper presented at the Heal The Hood Lecture Series, Centre for Multilingualism and Diversities Research, University of the Western Cape, August. Available from: www.youtube.com/watch?v=ujlkxV FUe-w [Accessed 25th November 2014].

Erlmann, V. (1996) *Nightsong: performance, power, and practice in South Africa*. Chicago and London, University of Chicago Press.

Forman, M. (2002) *The 'hood comes first': race, space, and place in rap and hip-hop*. Middletown, Wesleyan University Press.

Forman, M. (2013) Doing their own thing: hip-hop youth activism in the twenty-first century. *Cultural Politics*. 9 (3), 371–376.

Ginwright, S. A. (2010) Peace out revolution! Activism among African American youth: an argument for radical healing. *Young: Nordic Journal of Youth Research.* 18 (1), 77–96.

Gupta-Carlson, H. (2010) Planet-B-Girl: community building and feminism in hip-hop. *New Political Science.* 32 (4), 515–529.

Haupt, A. (2004) Counterpublics, noise and ten years of democracy. *New Coin Poetry.* 40 (2), 76–90.

Janz, B. B. (2001) The territory is not the map: place, Deleuze and Guattari, and African Philosophy. *Philosophy Today.* Winter, 392–404.

Johnson, I. K. (2009) *Dark matter in B-Boying cyphers: race and global connection in hip hop,* Unpublished PhD dissertation. Los Angeles, University of Southern California. Available from: http://digitallibrary.usc.edu/cdm/ref/collection/p15799coll127/id/265317 [Accessed 18th July 2012].

Kapferer, B. & Meinert, L. (2010) In the event: towards an anthropology of generic moments. *Social Analysis.* 54 (3), 1–30.

Kline, C. (2007) *Represent!: hip-hop and the self-aesthetic relation.* Unpublished PhD dissertation. Bloomington, Indiana University. Available from: https://scholar-works.iu.edu/dspace/handle/2022/7659 [Accessed 10th July 2018].

Lipsitz, G. (1994) *Dangerous crossroads: popular music, postmodernism and the poetics of place.* London and New York, Verso.

Maxwell, I. (2003) *Phat beats, dope rhymes: hip hop down under comin' upper.* Middletown, Wesleyan University Press.

Merleau-Ponty, M. (1964) *The primacy of perception.* Evanston, Northwestern University Press.

Mkhabela, S. (2014) Cape Town segregation and hip hop. Africa is a Country. Weblog, 9 December. Available from: https://storybuilder.jumpstart.ge/ka/south-african-hip-hop-series-cape-town-segregation-and-hip-hop [Accessed 5th February 2015].

Ndegwa, D., Horner, D. & Esau, F. (2004) *The links between migration, poverty and health: evidence from Khayelitsha and Mitchell's Plain.* Cape Town, University of Cape Town.

Perry, I. (2004) *Prophets of the hood: politics and poetics in hip hop.* Durham, Duke University Press.

Pough, G. D. (2004) Seeds and legacies: tapping the potential in hip hop. In: Forman, M. & Anthony Neal, M. (eds.) *That's the joint! The hip-hop studies reader.* New York, Routledge.

Purcell, A. (2009). All hands on deck. *The Guardian,* 27 February. Available from: www.theguardian.com/music/2009/feb/27/grandmaster-flash-interview [Accessed 8th April 2011].

Rose, T. (1994) *Black noise: rap music and black culture in contemporary America.* Middletown, Wesleyan University Press.

Rose, T. (1996) Hidden politics: discursive and institutional policing of rap music. In: Perkins, W. E. (ed.) *Droppin' science: critical essays on rap music and hip hop culture.* Philadelphia, Temple University Press.

Skott-Myhre, H. A. (2012) Resistance to the present: dead Prez. In: Richardson, C. & Skott-Myhre, H. A. (eds.) *Habitus of the hood.* Bristol and Chicago, Intellect Ltd.

Spady, J. G., Alim, H. S. & Meghelli, S. (2006) *Tha global cipha: hip hop culture and consciousness.* Philadelphia, Black History Museum Press.

Turner, P. (2010) *Hip hop versus rap: an ethnography of the cultural politics of new hip hop practices.* Unpublished PhD dissertation. London, University of London.

Williams, Q. E. & Stroud, C. (2010) Performing rap ciphas in late-modern Cape Town: extreme locality and multilingual citizenship. *Afrika Focus.* 23 (2), 39–59.

Wise, J. M. (2000) Home: territory and identity. *Cultural Studies.* 14 (2), 295–310.

8 Assessing the potential of the European Capital of Culture to integrate refugees

The case of Matera 2019

Nicholas Wise

Introduction

Mass migration and the influx of refugees into Europe have received much attention in the media in recent years. It is estimated that 180,000 refugees currently reside in Italy (DeMarco, 2018). A pressing issue is that refugees who do manage to enter Europe become marginalised and struggle to assimilate. African and Middle Eastern migrants entering Europe seek to escape struggles of war, famine and political instability. Current debates are at the forefront of academic inquiry and have a direct impact on public policymaking, urban/regional planning and business practice. Critical discussions brought forward in this chapter relate to geographical, demographic, economic and cultural understandings of how refugees are integrated and what they can contribute to events and the wider creative industries. Given the current situation, there is a need to also look at this from an event studies perspective to position how research impacts policy, planning and business decisions, concerning assimilation and enabling futures for migrants. One side of the policy debate positions how to handle mass numbers of migrants whilst managing negative perceptions of fear and dependency which threaten local qualities of life.

From a social policy perspective, there are debates over how migrants are treated and managed when they settle in a new place (see Eugster, 2018), and little academic work has considered how events can be used to help assimilate migrants. Therefore, this study will consider elements of cultural integration and enterprise opportunities for migrant refugees based on what is happening in the south of Italy ahead of the 2019 European Capital of Culture (ECoC). Given discussions and considerations around what refugees can contribute to events is an underexplored area in the academic literature, this chapter is an attempt to start this discussion because it is an important topic when we consider the assimilation of marginalised groups. It must be noted that work does exist in the sport studies literature concerning sports participation and initiatives for refugees (e.g. Jeanes, O'Connor & Alfrey, 2015; Spaaij, 2015; Doidge & Sandri, 2018). To help achieve this from an event studies perspective, this chapter will address wider issues concerning refugee isolation (exclusion) and contestations surrounding their presence (in place such as Italy) from the literature. From the conceptual stances and evidence of what is happening locally, this is an attempt to reconsider policy debates concerning how to manage migrants locally in an attempt to create more inclusive futures using events so that migrants can build self-sustaining futures and contribute to their new local economy (by making cultural contributions to support social and economic integration).

Consideration of refugees is also important in the context of the ECoC, discussed in the next section, especially as migration and demographic change are resulting in new place identities. This has been a point of focus underexplored in the academic literature. Refugees do not always get positive media coverage (see Triandafyllidou, 2018), so catalysing culture can be a challenge for them in destinations where they may initially find it difficult to gain acceptance among local residents – but given that events are mass gatherings to showcase culture and ideas it can be argued that events can help people assimilate. This is where inclusive policies that support social and economic integration can bring forth change so that refugees can get involved in events and showcase their culture alongside the local traditional culture. Therefore, this chapter offers a discussion of how refugees can assimilate in a new place by contributing to a cultural event, and the case of Matera is an ideal case to conceptualise this given the mass migration of refugees to the south of Italy in recent years and the ECoC in 2019.

From the work on social impacts of events, much attention is placed on the support and employability skills that local residents acquire before, during and after events. The same holds true for refugees who now reside in an area – they too have much to gain from the event including skills acquisition, educational opportunities and the chance to start a new enterprise to help display their culture in line with an event that celebrates (European) culture. This is important because given the refugee crisis, these migrants are Europe's newest residents and they can now contribute to the new cultural demographics of an area. This chapter takes insight and debate from the academic literature and initiatives presented in the media to begin this discussion. This conceptual chapter is organised primarily around points of discussion from the academic literature, with some context from Matera and the south of Italy (as presented in recent media articles). This will provide a basis of discussion that will build into directions concerning the need for future work on refugees, events and assimilation, to present a framework for future research.

Place, identity and refugees: foreseen pressures and the new role of events

An influx of refugees can put social pressures on host countries as large groups of people coming from outside a place, region or area are not culturally related (Edwards, 2017). In today's world, social and/or cultural phenomena have become mediators through which to connect people based on their (different) identities – bounded exclusively through the shared association of living in the same place. The culture of a place is a social construction of everyday life, and embeds significant meaning aiding how people unite (Anderson, 1991; Shobe, 2008). At times, this becomes contested when people from different cultural backgrounds attempt to make their presence known (see Gruffudd, 1999; Wise, 2011). This can occur through the presence of an influx of outsiders, when local residents may see their own semblance of identity is threatened (Howard, 2001).

Sentiment towards how local residents view an influx of refugees can best be understood through discussions of the literature on national identity. Smith (1991) suggests that nations are bounded entities, but in a nascent era of transnational movements, the nation is no longer bounded geographically, per se, but is fluid. Other scholars have referred to this as the interconnectedness of national societies across borders (Cronin & Mayall, 1998; Grainger, 2006; Lepp & Harris, 2008; Langellier, 2010), and such an understanding is ever present during the hosting of large-scale events where people from different backgrounds often unite to celebrate or consume what is on offer. However, it is important to look beyond the consumption of events to assess new local production of events where cultural differences are also important, as migrants not only shape the current demographics of a place but also the future construction, production and staging of culture (Edensor, 2002). In relation to transnational migrations and their contribution to a new local identity, coinciding with the rapid advances of globalisation, it is still impressions and imaginations of 'the nation [which] remains one of the significant (if not the most significant) markers of identity in the post-modern age' (Lepp & Harris, 2008: p. 525).

Refugees have been forced from their homes due to war or violence. When people move they try and forge a new sense of home and identity, and in many instances they are met with prejudices and pressures to assimilate socially and culturally (Eggenhofer-Rehart et al., 2018; Gericke et al., 2018; Wehrle et al., 2018; Yalcinkaya et al., 2018). The media does not always help with constructing a positive image of refugees, instead showing desperate people living in poor conditions departing refugee camps, from countries succumbed to violence and (terrorist) attacks (Triandafyllidou, 2018). If a supposed 'terror' attack or violent situation happens, or if an imminent threat is perceived, this can make host communities (especially in Europe) feel unease towards people coming from (what are perceived as dangerous countries) and want to isolate them (Triandafyllidou, 2018). With the increasing pressure to assimilate, change or adapt, local societal pressures sometimes mean failing to do so results in an 'othering' of outside groups if they are not accepted or do not 'change their ways' (Korac, 2003; Vincenza Desiderio, 2016). This 'othering' creates clear divisions, concerning who is in place and who is out of place (Wise, 2011; Cresswell, 2014).

Despite living in a new place, migrants do use their culture as a way of establishing a sense of belonging as a way of connecting the home they know with their current (new) home. However, migrants often perform and celebrate their culture in isolation if they do not conform to their new social and cultural surroundings (see Spaaij, 2015). This was observed in Wise's (2015) work on Haitians living in the Dominican Republic. Haitians resided in more remote locales away from Dominicans, living separately due to negative sentiment and contestations between the two groups (see also Wise, 2011, 2014). Cultural events can represent a way for migrants to educate local residents about their culture, while at the same time helping them integrate locally. This will help local residents become familiar with how migrants perform and celebrate their sense of identity. Given the fluidity of transnational migration today, people are continually seeking ways to present positive features of culture in their new surroundings to ease tensions and help create awareness. This is also a chance to socialise and learn a new business system, another way for migrants to integrate. When culture is performed, and potential enterprise opportunities are present, this can help shape a new awareness of a group's culture and identity, as a way to overcome negative stereotypes, fearful associations and notions of otherness – helping them feel in place (Edensor, 2002; Cresswell, 2014).

The previous paragraphs address some of the pressures migrants face to offer a reference point from the literature that is useful in conceptualising how events can help us understand opportunities for marginalised migrant groups living in the south of Italy. It seeks to address if a future event can help mitigate marginalisation from geographical and sociological perspectives. The following sections look beyond discussions of fear and separation, which are often based on differences in identity and culture. Instead, they offer a discussion of directions to consider when addressing what exposure migrants have when it comes to cultural integration and business opportunities, to help remove barriers, mitigate tensions and reduce prejudices. It is important to consider how an event such as the ECoC 2019 in Matera can act as a driver to help migrants assimilate and showcase their new culture within an existing culture and the contributions they can make to a (perhaps repositioned) new European (multi)cultural event. The upcoming 2019 ECoC is in a position to place, highlight and celebrate elements of culture that transcend traditional (Italian, Southern Italy, Basilicata, Matera) culture. Thus, there is a need to acknowledge a new way of understanding how/what migrants contribute to cultural capital as opposed to their being marginalised based on being (distinctly) different culturally, ethnically or racially. An emphasis on the (multi)cultural blending of identities in such an event that celebrates the culture of a place is needed in the events management/studies literature to recognise nascent meanings of place and identity. Therefore, recognising skills, supporting involvement and seeking creative ways to increase employability, by contributing to events, can help minimise marginalisation and promote integration.

Cultural events and Matera 2019 ECoC

Cities and regions across Europe are increasingly using events to catalyse culture and aid social and economic development (Richards & Palmer, 2010; Keofoed, 2013; Richards, de Brito & Wilks, 2013; Wise & Harris, 2017; Wise, Aquilino & Armenski, 2018). The ECoC promotes urban management and economic production, using culture to drive the restructuring of social legacies, job creation and civic repositioning (Richards & Wilson, 2007; Richards & Palmer, 2010; Spirou, 2011; Liu, 2016). It is essential that ECoC host cities have long-term competitive strategies in place, aimed at strengthening the capacity of their cities to deliver diverse cultural programmes and placemaking locally for their own citizens – including those who may have only recently arrived. Hosting the ECoC may define a destination for years to come, as has been shown in research from the cities of, for example, Glasgow 1990 (Mooney, 2004; García, 2005), Rotterdam 2001 (Richards & Wilson, 2007), Liverpool 2008 (Spirou, 2011), Cork 2005 (O'Callaghan & Linehan, 2007) or Guimarães 2012 (Keofoed, 2013).

The ECoC is a display of the local and/or traditional culture associated with a place (Richards & Palmer, 2010). In 2019, Matera, Italy will host the ECoC. Matera is already internationally renowned for its UNESCO World Heritage Status (designated in 1993). The ECoC represents an opportunity for Matera to highlight the city and Basilicata Region beyond the city's *Sassi* (Matera's main tourist attraction: ancient cave dwellings). Plans put emphasis on Italian culture in this southern region of Italy and the *Sassi* as the city and region are seeing increased investments in urban regeneration and infrastructure in preparation for ECoC 2019 (Matera 2019, 2015). However, there is another story running in parallel with the intended successes and promotions of the 2019 ECoC and that is the extensive migration into the Basilicata region, in and around greater Matera. Many voice concerns of future social instability with increased numbers of migrants and refugees arriving in the southern regions of Italy from Africa and Middle East (DeMarco, 2018). This increase in migration will likely change the demographics of the Basilicata Region and likewise the adjacent regions in the coming decades (ISTAT, 2015). Therefore, the groups of migrants and refugees who sit on the periphery of Italian culture have a unique opportunity to showcase their culture (aligned with the increasingly diverse demographics in this region). The timeliness here is that, while the ECoC is about displaying the culture of a place, more and more migrants and refugees are playing a role in cultural event activities – thus contributing to the creative heterogeneity of Matera and Basilicata. Some media content is beginning to focus on displays of migrant culture in the lead-up to Matera 2019, and these examples will be discussed later. The chapter will incorporate critical notions of inclusion and exclusion, escapism and in place/out of place to critically frame interpretations when making sense of local initiatives and challenges concerning migrants/refugees, events and involvement in the 2019 ECoC.

For researchers it is important to get a sense of how local planners and policymakers perceive policies aimed at including under-represented groups and whether what they have to offer is considered part of the event (and tourism) offering. Given the increasing racial and ethnic heterogeneity in many destinations, hosts of the ECoC could consider a multicultural approach to embracing different cultures beyond the vernacular – as an attempt to promote integration. This is a chance to showcase the culture of more recent arrivals amid European diversity in contemporary times – including migrant refugees who seek to make a new start. After all, it is local residents (meaning both those originally from a place *and* the migrants who are just getting established) who will be the ones participating in, contributing to and therefore affected by event planning and change (Wise, Aquilino & Armenski, 2018). This is always a challenge in events research as tangible impacts can be measured, whereas intangible impacts (including initiatives that generate ideas and new skills) are often just proposed (Pappalepore, 2016; Wise & Harris, 2017). This is common across research findings composed by scholars who critically evaluate projected (or intended) legacies of future events (see Evans & Van Huer, 2013) or prospective planning for social impacts (Hixson, 2013; Wise & Perić, 2017; Wise, Aquilino & Armenski, 2018).

Similarly, this chapter is concerned with what migrants can contribute, which relates to both social and economic impacts, but considers assimilation among a different group of people which is underexplored in academic discussion in events studies (as addressed earlier in this chapter). Nonetheless, and as Wise and Perić (2017) argue, more research concerning the social impacts and opportunities of events is needed. Researchers need to further explore social conditions, and understand contested notions of place and identity by non-local groups, before we can consider opportunities and how migrants can be involved in the process of producing culture.

Towards assimilation and enabling opportunities

Refugees are a vulnerable marginalised group that struggle to assimilate. Marginalisation occurs due to social and cultural ignorance, and this can result in exclusion and isolation among refugee migrants who seek new opportunities elsewhere (in Europe). Refugees may lack skills or relevant education that can limit job prospects, and a lack of employment opportunities puts pressures on supporting refugees. This can then result in negative sentiment among local residents who (sometimes) see migrants as a burden economically amid other various cultural sensitivities. Refugees in more remote peripheral areas see increased difficulty, compared to more urban locales where there is generally more diversity. With regard to Matera 2019, the event is being hosted in a more peripheral city in a region that has seen an influx of refugee migrants. As academics, there is a need to link what is referred to as the refugee crisis alongside considerations of events and what benefits may arise to assist with assimilating refugees.

Therefore, discussions of assimilation are important and part of contemporary debate, especially when discussing refugees entering Europe where a strong sense of local and national identity exists. This section frames the ways refugees can be helped to assimilate ahead of (and during) a cultural event such as the ECoC. Here, some content supported by news stories on refugees currently in Matera and Basilicata will be used to guide the development and discussions in this section. There are three key considerations here based on insight and direction offered by the Migration Policy Institute (see Vincenza Desiderio, 2016), which focus on issues facing migrants. Recognising skills, supporting involvement and seeking creative ways to increase employability involve a number of considerations and are discussed from an events perspective to identify how events can lead to social and economic impacts concerning assimilation, integration and enabling opportunities, and these lead into the next section in proposing a research agenda going forward with research on events and refugee assimilation.

Mendoza (2016) mentions that in Matera and Basilicata 'some locals are reluctant to open their doors to refugees'. However there is a strategy in Basilicata, where they are 'using the arrival of asylum seekers as a means of developing its labour force and to boost services' (Mendoza, 2016). Mendoza (2016) later adds:

> At the heart of the Basilicata reception model is the idea of having smaller groups of asylum seekers spread across the different local communities in order to prevent segregation and facilitate integration.

Here we see the aspiration to integrate the asylum seekers (refugees) to extend opportunities for more individuals so that they have the chance to integrate in smaller communities. Segregation is common when large masses of migrants move to a particular area, and this sometimes limits opportunities to a selected few. This is a strategic plan ahead of the ECoC, as the region of Basilicata is expected to see expanded opportunities before, during and after the event, as projected increased tourism is making the city and region more competitive (see Wise, Aquilino & Armenski, 2018; Aquilino, Armenski & Wise, 2018). Geographically spreading refugees across the region is both an attempt to enable opportunities for them and an opportunity for local residents to get to know them personally as opposed to seeing them as a collective group – thereby attempting to remove the process of 'othering'.

Because migrants relocate their culture, this is a starting base when it comes to addressing what refugees can contribute to nascent cultural place promotion. Amidst the negative press and sometimes fearful images that marginalise refugees, it is useful for places to position the cultural opportunities of the traditional host and see what corresponding cultural elements exist that can run in parallel so to showcase traditional and new cultural values simultaneously. This can be difficult to overcome given symbolic interactions, as a sociological construct, place people at odds. This goes back to negative associations that can lead to prejudices against groups of people, based on sociopolitical contexts of image perceptions, framed on meanings subjectively constructed on bias and difference, where people deduct others by excluding them (Nimmo, 1976). Linking to the significance of refugees as a marginalised group, the creative and cultural industries can seek unique solutions because they position specific contributions and distinctive elements of culture to recognise the positives of difference. Staging and performing identity lead to a more interactive symbolic interaction that allows people to highlight themselves based on their skills and to contribute their interests to promote social cohesion as opposed to their being seen as socially constructed media images based on negative persuasion and subjective bias towards a group of people. Some initiatives, which are widely accepted around the world, see sport being used to unite different groups of people with local residents (DeMarco, 2018).

In the south of Italy, Einashe (2017) found some are using theatre as part of an initiative to connect young Italians and migrants from Africa. It is especially important to involve both local resident and refugee youths when attempting to unite people. Mitigating negative sentiment by connecting young people and getting them to collaborate means that the 'young Italian generation is ready to be connected to the migrant culture [and] they can use theatre to connect migrants' (Einashe, 2017), to help assess and recognise skills through shared interests. Connecting through culture then becomes a performance, and staging culture with a mix of local and migrant performers helps to showcase not only skills through the arts but also how collaboration promotes coexistence off the stage and away from the performances. The symbolic display of theatre can be used to motivate people to interact locally, uniting people through shared interests and association.

Bratti and Conti (2018: p. 934) note that 'cultural and language differences raise communication costs; reduce trust, cooperation and social capital; and increase social conflict'. This helps confirm what needs to happen in the south of Italy, to go beyond difference to use the upcoming ECoC to help support, train and educate refugees – thus promoting integration as opposed to segregation. Indeed, DeMarco (2018) notes the emphasis of the Italian government, whereby 'Fixing the economy rather than blaming refugees can help to strengthen bonds' as marginalised groups are easily blamed during times of economic hardship. However, assimilating marginalised groups such as refugees involves support (through Italian government and European Funds) to train and educate refugees so that they can contribute to economic growth as opposed to being seen as a financial drain on the economy (DeMarco, 2018). Some of the plans involve training refugees through work initiatives to learn manual labour or a new trade. The refugees are not paid but are supported with food and shelter, with the hope that they can start a future business or seek employment. Such training for lower-wage or undesired jobs may be seen as a start, and an attempt to fulfil certain types of jobs, but there is still a need to educate refugees with skills that will allow them to participate in the creative event industries with the opportunities that may/will emerge before, during and after the 2019 ECoC. Labour jobs can be isolating and thus may limit interactions or chances to become immersed in the community. Acquiring new skills in the creative and cultural industries, the arts and events brings migrants into the community as resident members as opposed to their just being regarded as outsiders or 'others'. While refugees have the opportunity to gain from new skills acquisition, they can emphasise their culture strengths and contributions in this regard by bringing forward particular elements of culture to promote symbolic interactions that overcome negative associations (addressed earlier). It is unlikely that interactions with refugees will lead to cultural appropriation, given the dominant local traditional culture in the south of Italy in this more peripheral locale.

Building on the discussions thus far in this section, an initial step perhaps is to focus on language, which is key to integration initially in more peripheral homogenous regions (Edwards, 2017) where another language may not be regularly spoken, nor accepted by local residents. Language support and training can lead to a greater sense of belonging and help establish connections more efficiently. Training and educating are often viewed as economic drivers, but can also have sociological implications among refugees who seek to use and express their skills in the same way as local residents (see O'Neill & Spybey, 2003; Spaaij, 2015). The events industry requires socialisation, and this means effective communication between stakeholders and business operators. If refugees are going to integrate as business owners and active participants, they will require active training enabling them to gain the skills necessary to start a business or have the initial confidence by speaking the local language (to integrate with local residents) and learning English (for the purpose of business and communicating with tourists – as the business language). What is needed is training and educational support to guide refugees in the lead-up to the event so that they are better equipped to socialise and actively engage. Here again, social policies are necessary to help assimilate refugees so that they can actively take part as opposed to having only peripheral status. Refugees need to be considered active stakeholders as opposed to how the media positions them as part of the wider European migrant crisis. Playing an active role, therefore, is not just a chance to integrate with local residents but also a chance to change perceptions surrounding what and how they contribute to outside audiences. Some may see Matera as an event host with a migrant problem. However, it is about how the south of Italy has found ways to display heterogeneous culture, linking both the traditional and new.

Cultural entrepreneurship responds to changing economies in places that have seen extensive manufacturing to service sector restructuring, and events are seen as current sustainable economic bases. Vincenza Desiderio (2016) suggests that inclusive policy is key, but for employability to rise among migrants, the points outlined in the previous paragraphs are important prerequisites. Social enterprises are initiatives where a society profits

(Dwivedia & Weerawardena, 2018), and for migrants it is about profiting by collaborating with local residents and local business owners. Events are about value creation, and training refugees to gain adequate skills to start a new business that align with the ECoC will showcase refugee success in a different light. The events industry is reliant on various operations, and while we see youths getting involved in theatre and the arts, seeking ways to train on the delivery of performances can expand an individual's possibilities to engage with the supply side of events. This involves a range of operational considerations beyond just performance, to the staging side of events. Various opportunities are emerging as preparations for Matera 2019 draw near. It is not just events specifically but the entire visitor economy that will rely on suppliers and operators to support the staging of the event as well as innovative individuals (be they local residents, refugees or these in partnership); there are currently different possibilities that can support this bourgeoning industry in the south of Italy.

A framework for future research

Refugees are a vulnerable group of people; therefore future research needs to consider their lived experiences, opportunities (or lack thereof) and stories (Wise, 2011, 2014). While inclusive policies can help mitigate marginalisation, it is the practical delivery and changing attitudes locally that is essential. But with the right policies and altered perspectives of local residents, events can help implement and move towards achieving assimilation. This study addresses and starts a discussion by looking at the case of Matera, Italy ahead of the 2019 ECoC. Future ECoC events will be hosted in cities across southern and eastern Europe directly impacted by the refugee crisis. This is a consideration for subsequent ECoC hosts between 2017 and 2023, for example: Pafos, Cyprus 2017; Valletta, Malta 2018; Plovdiv, Bulgaria 2019; Rijeka, Croatia 2020; Timişoara, Romania 2021; Elefsina, Greece 2021; Novi Sad, Serbia, 2021; and Hungary's 2023 designated host city. Such contestations surrounding migrants and the right to relocate are at the forefront of discussions in many of these countries, and local policymakers, event planners and managers can seek alternative ways to try and assimilate and showcase multiculturalism as opposed to marginalising those who are different or perceived as outsiders.

In proposing a research agenda going forward, what is needed is in-depth research to initially frame existing issues to produce new understandings, so to position critical evaluations of existing policies, situations and circumstances. Such academic insight is needed to inform and influence policy (connecting the research-policy nexus) to raise awareness and how to realise new opportunities in practice. Deductive research here is not relevant initially as the topic needs more inductive research given each region and local residents differ vastly in terms of location, opportunities and attitudes towards migrant refugees depending on the ongoing situations, which transcend scales across the European, national, subregional and local level. This will help locally shape social and economic impact, which needs to be considered on a case-by-case basis. A prescriptive approach might not be useful with marginalised groups such as refugees. While refugees are (often) viewed as a collective group, people are attracted to different areas and they are culturally diverse, so one approach or policy is not appropriate given the social and cultural differences of the refugees, and the places where they settle are distinctly different, with some countries being much more welcoming and other places/regions not so much.

A more enabling research agenda, therefore, and arguably, involves an inductive qualitative research approach, where academics collaborate with and for a range of different stakeholders, most notably the refugees themselves directly, local residents and then policymakers. The sociological nexus joining insight and perspective across refugee and event studies needs to drive the development of understanding from the bottom-up to determine perceptions and thought processes at the grass-roots level, which is impacted by much larger political, economic and social forces putting people into the situations they are in to begin with. Nevertheless, while we are aware of the wider issues, researchers are missing the stories that develop locally based on the desire to assimilate, get involved, gain new skills or learn a new trade. Where we observe a cultural event occurring in a city and region impacted by an influx of refugees, it is easy to position one as a celebration of local and regional culture, and the other as a group of people forced from their homes. However, an event represents a chance, an opportunity, as argued in this chapter, for newly arriving migrants to display their traditional culture alongside the dominant local (traditional) culture. Through events, research can help tell the story of contemporary Europe and local multiculturalism in more remote locales amid a larger sociopolitical crisis. Demographics may change, but events can adapt to promote, inform and embrace change, and as researchers we need to look for ways to merge different ideas, such as refugee studies with events studies, to consider deeper and more personalised meanings at the surface and in the very places where interactions are occurring. Future ECoC host cities are now situated between these areas of research, and there is a need to bring the gap between these areas to build new conceptual approaches and inform new understandings in events research to evaluate how perceived marginalisation can lend insight on inclusive policies to promote assimilation.

Social science researchers (those who guide theoretical development and offer critique and evaluation) can assess critical conceptual issues including inclusion and exclusion, staging and performing identity and consider social/intangible impacts going forward. By developing a sociological basis of understanding, regional planners, tourism/events managers and policymakers (those who can implement change) have a basis for which to inform social developments, guide practice and make enabling decisions for how to best utilise people's social capital, skills and abilities. This represents an attempt to help guide assimilation and enable inclusive futures for refugees in the new places they call home. Future research needs to not only conceptualise but also identify practical solutions going forward. Matera 2019 is about creating opportunities for the region beyond the city (Matera 2019, 2015), and careful consideration on how to include the range of traditional and new displays and performances of cultures is necessary. A focus on the refugee 'crisis' positions the need for such research in event studies. There appear to be attempts to get migrants in cultural entrepreneurial activities, and this links well with the upcoming ECoC in Matera, based on some of the insight earlier (ideally to showcase traditional culture alongside migrant culture). Multiculturalism is evident across Europe, and whilst the ECoC designation tends to emphasise the traditional (or founded dominant) culture, we are living in an increasingly mobile world which is transcending what we might deem as local place meanings, perceptions and imaginations.

Concluding remarks

For migrants, entering Europe is perceived as opportunity to escape the struggles of war, famine and political instability in countries across Africa and the Middle East as conflicts escalate. The point of concern here is migration and mobility, and how this impacts place identities, but it seems that assimilation strategies are in place. Events are mass gatherings and displays of local culture and identity. While culture may be consumed, and assumed, as based on the traditional culture, migrants who relocate have the opportunity to contribute their culture to showcase the social transformations of places in a fluid and interdependent world.

Refugees are a marginalised community, and they can struggle to assimilate and integrate into a new home country. But in the south of Italy, with Matera as the 2019 ECoC host city, this represents a unique opportunity for migrant refugees to showcase their culture and identity in a way that highlights the fluidity of culture in this part of the world. Italy is a gateway for refugees, and in some cases sentiment towards refugees is not always positive as they may be seen as outsiders socially and culturally or people who are dependent. As we have seen from this case, opportunities exist for refugees to earn from their creativity, as a way of assimilating and working with (and for) the promotion of cultural capital. The host of the ECoC helps reinforce the local, regional and national culture of a place, but an increased influx of refugees in recent years is shifting local demographics. Going forward, much work is needed to build on some of the initial examples and conceptual understandings brought forward in this chapter. This chapter begins a discussion on the need to focus on the place of migrants, their role and possible contribution to events. Research is needed at events and in the field to observe and conduct inductive qualitative research in migrant communities and in events where refugees are contributing their social and cultural capital to position themselves in their new home.

References

Anderson, B. (1991) *Imagined communities*. London, Verso.

Aquilino, L., Armenski, T. & Wise, N. (2018) Assessing the competitiveness of Matera and the Basilicata Region (Italy) ahead of the 2019 European Capital of Culture. *Tourism and Hospitality Research*. doi:10.1177/1467358418787360

Bratti, M. & Conti, C. (2018) The effect of immigration on innovation in Italy. *Regional Studies*. 52 (7), 934–947.

Cresswell, T. (2014) *Place: a short introduction*. Oxford, Blackwell.

Cronin, M. & Mayall, D. (eds.) (1998) *Sporting nationalisms: identity, ethnicity, immigration and assimilation*. London, Frank Cass.

DeMarco, N. (2018) Government plan promotes refugee integration in Italy. Borgen Magazine, 2 April. Available from: www.borgenmagazine.com/refugee-integration-in-italy/ [Accessed 21st May 2018].

Doidge, M. & Sandri, E. (2018) 'Friends that last a lifetime': the importance of emotions amongst volunteers working with refugees in Calais. *British Journal of Sociology*. ISSN 0007-1315.

Dwivedia, A. & Weerawardena, J. (2018) Conceptualizing and operationalizing the social entrepreneurship construct. *Journal of Business Research*. 86, 32–40.

Edensor, T. (2002) *National identity, popular culture and everyday life*. Oxford, Berg.

Edwards, C. (2017) Italy launches first official migrant integration plan: five things you need to know. *The Local*, 27 September. Available from: www.thelocal. it/20170927/italy-launches-first-official-migrant-integration-plan-five-things-you-need-to-know [Accessed 21st May 2018].

Eggenhofer-Rehart, P. M., Latzke, M., Pernkopf, K., Zellhofer, D., Mayrhofer, W. & Steyrer, J. (2018) Refugees' career capital welcome? Afghan and Syrian refugee job seekers in Austria. *Journal of Vocational Behavior*. 105, 31–45.

Einashe, I. (2017) How theatre is bringing young African migrants and Italians together. *The National*, 1 June. Available from: www.thenational.ae/arts-culture/ how-theatre-is-bringing-young-african-migrants-and-italians-together-1.85040 [Accessed 21st May2018].

Eugster, B. (2018) Immigrants and poverty, and conditionality of immigrants' social rights. *Journal of European Social Policy*. doi:10.1177/0958928717753580.

Evans G. & Van Huer, B. (2013) European Capital of Culture – emancipatory practices and Euregional strategies: the case of Maastricht via 2018. In: Richards, G., de Brito, M. P. & Wilks, L. (eds.) *Exploring the social impacts of events*. London, Routledge, pp. 73–83.

García, B. (2005) Deconstructing the city of culture: the long-term cultural legacies of Glasgow 1990. *Urban Studies*. 42 (5/6), 841–868.

Gericke, D., Burmeister, A., Löwe, J., Deller, J. & Pundt, L. (2018) How do refugees use their social capital for successful labor market integration? An exploratory analysis in Germany. *Journal of Vocational Behavior*. 105, 46–61.

Grainger, A. (2006) From immigrant to overstayer: Samoan identity, rugby, and cultural politics of race and nation in Aotearoa/New Zealand. *Journal of Sport & Social Issues*. 30 (1), 45–61.

Gruffudd, P. (1999) Nationalism. In: Cloke, P., Crang, P. & Goodwin, M. (eds.) *Introducing human geographies*. London, Arnold, pp. 199–206.

Hixson, E. (2013) Achieving significant event impacts for youth residents of the host community: the Adelaide Fringe Festival. In: Richards, G., de Brito, M. P. & Wilks, L. (eds.) *Exploring the social impacts of events*. London, Routledge, pp. 203–216.

Howard, D. (2001) *Coloring the nation: race and ethnicity in the Dominican Republic.* Oxford, Signal Books.

ISTAT (2015) Rapporto annuale 2015: la situazione del Paese. Available from: www.istat.it/it/files/2015/05/Rapporto-Annuale-2015.pdf [Accessed 5th July 2018].

Jeanes, R., O'Connor, J. & Alfrey. L. (2015) Sport and the resettlement of young people from refugee backgrounds in Australia. *Journal of Sport and Social Issues.* 39 (6), 480–500.

Keofoed, O. (2013) European Capitals of Culture and cultures of sustainability – the case of Guimaraes 2012. *City, Culture and Society.* 4 (3), 153–162.

Korac, M. (2003) Integration and how we facilitate it: a comparative study of the settlement experiences of refugees in Italy and the Netherlands. *Sociology.* 37 (1), 51–68.

Langellier, K. M. (2010) Performing Somali identity in the diaspora. *Cultural Studies.* 24 (1), 66–94.

Lepp, A. & Harris, J. (2008) Tourism and national identity in Uganda. *International Journal of Tourism Research.* 10 (6), 525–536.

Liu, Y-D. (2016) Cultural event and urban regeneration: lessons from Liverpool as the 2008 European Capital of Culture. *European Review.* 24 (1), 159–176.

Matera 2019 (2015) Post-designation progress report. Available from: www.matera-basilicata2019.it/it/ [Accessed 21st May 2018].

Mendoza, N. (2016) Italy's rural south welcomes refugees with open arms. *France24,* 15 May. Available from: www.france24.com/en/20161205-focus-italy-basilicata-rural-depopulation-asylym-seekers-schools-public-services-economy [Accessed 21st May 2018].

Mooney, G. (2004) Cultural policy as urban transformation? Critical reflections on Glasgow, European city of culture 1990. *Local Economy.* 19 (4), 327–340.

Nimmo, D. (1976) Political image makers and the mass media. *The Annals of the American Academy of Political and Social Science.* 427, 33–44.

O'Callaghan, C. & Linehan, D. (2007) Identity, politics and conflict in dockland development in Cork, Ireland: European Capital of Culture 2005. *Cities.* 24 (4), 311–323.

O'Neill, M. & Spybey, T. (2003) Global refugees, exile, displacement and belonging. *Sociology.* 31 (1), 7–12.

Pappalepore, I. (2016) Exploring the intangible impacts of cultural events on the creative sector: experiences from the Cultural Olympiad programmes of Torino 2006 and London 2012. *European Urban and Regional Studies.* 23 (3), 441–454.

Richards, G., de Brito, M. P. & Wilks, L. (eds.) (2013) *Exploring the social impacts of events.* London, Routledge.

Richards, G. & Palmer, R. (2010) *Eventful cities: cultural management and urban revitalization.* London, Elsevier.

Richards, G. & Wilson, J. (2007) The impact of cultural events on city image: Rotterdam, cultural capital of Europe 2001. *Urban Studies.* 41 (10), 1931–1951.

Shobe, H. (2008) Place, identity and football: Catalonia, Catalanisme and Football Club Barcelona, 1899–1975. *National Identities.* 10 (3), 329–343.

Smith, A. (1991) *National identity.* London, Penguin.

Spaaij, R. (2015) Refugee youth, belonging and community sport. *Leisure Studies.* 34 (3), 303–318.

Spirou, C. (2011) *Urban tourism and urban change.* London, Routledge.

Triandafyllidou, A. (2018) A 'refugee crisis' unfolding: 'real' events and their interpretation in media and political debates. *Journal of Immigrant and Refugee Studies.* 16 (1/2), 198–216.

Vincenza Desiderio, M. (2016) *Integrating refugees into host country labour markets: challenges and policy options.* Washington, DC, Transatlantic Council on Migration, Migration Policy Institute.

Wehrle, K., Klehe, U-C., Kira, M. & Zikic, J. (2018) Can I come as I am? Refugees' vocational identity threats, coping, and growth. *Journal of Vocational Behavior.* 105, 83–101.

Wise, N. (2011) Transcending imaginations through football participation and narratives of the *other*: Haitian national identity in the Dominican Republic. *Journal of Sport and Tourism.* 16 (3), 259–275.

Wise, N. (2014) Layers of the landscape: representation and perceptions of an ordinary (shared) sport landscape in a Haitian and Dominican community. *Geographical Research.* 52 (2), 212–222.

Wise, N. (2015) Football on the weekend: rural events and the Haitian imagined community in the Dominican Republic. In: Jepson, A. & Clarke, A. (eds.) *Exploring community festivals and events.* London, Routledge, pp. 106–117.

Wise, N. & Harris, J. (eds.) (2017) *Sport, events, tourism and regeneration.* London, Routledge.

Wise, N. & Perić, M. (2017) Sports tourism, regeneration and social impacts: new opportunities and directions for research, the case of Medulin, Croatia. In: Bellini, N. & Pasquinelli, C. (eds.) *Tourism in the city: towards and integrative agenda on urban tourism.* Berlin, Springer, pp. 311–320.

Wise, N., Aquilino, L. & Armenski, T. (2018) Preparing for Matera 2019: local resident participation in research and perceptions of destination competitiveness. In: Clark, J. & Wise, N. (eds.) *Urban renewal, community and participation: theory, policy and practice.* Berlin, Springer, pp. 161–180.

Yalcinkaya, N. S., Branscombe, N. R., Gebauer, F., Niedlich, C. & Hakim, N. H. (2018) Can they ever be one of us? Perceived cultural malleability of refugees and policy support in host nations. *Journal of Experimental Social Psychology.* 78, 125–133.

9   Claiming space through events

The tension of homelessness in the world's most liveable city

*Amanda Ford, Jennifer Laing
and Warwick Frost*

Introduction

The Australian Open takes place over two weeks during the height of summer and this first of four Grand Slam tournaments attracts tennis fans and media attention from across the globe. The world's top players compete within the festive atmosphere of Melbourne Park, just a few minutes' walk from the Victorian capital city's centre. The Open is afforded significant support from state government with the venue recently receiving AUD$975 million for redevelopment, while Melbourne's residents are overwhelmingly proud of the image it portrays of their city (Deery & Jago, 2010). The Australian Open enjoys the position of being one of the most beloved and prized events in a city that has built its reputation around them.

Lacking the attractions of other Australian states, successive Victorian governments have worked to position Melbourne as the events capital of Australia over the last 30 years. In a strategy that can be recognised as 'eventful', events are not only utilised for economic gains but also as 'a means of improving the city and making it more attractive and liveable' (Richards & Palmer, 2010: p. 4). Underpinning this strategy is a programme or portfolio of diverse events designed to maximise policy objectives while spreading risk (Ziakas, 2013). For eventful cities, the staging of events is central to their differentiation in a competitive global environment, for identity development and ongoing economic and social outcomes (Richards, 2017).

Both state and local government and the tourism industry closely collaborate to support Melbourne's well-established portfolio of annual hallmark and major events (Frost, 2012). The Australian Open is one such event within this events suite that delivers economic windfalls to the state, contributes to the development of the city's brand identity and offers opportunities for increased quality of life for residents. However, in the days leading up to the 2017 Australian Open, aspects of the city's attractiveness and liveability were being questioned within the media. This occurred at a time when Melbourne was enjoying an uninterrupted six-year reign as The Economist Intelligence Unit's world's most liveable city (Wright, 2016).

On 11 January 2017, less than a week before the Australian Open commenced, local government workers from the City of Melbourne (CoM) accompanied by police ordered around a dozen homeless people who had formed a camp along an external wall of Flinders Street Station to move along. With its domed roof and French Renaissance architecture, the Station is an iconic emblem of Melbourne for residents and tourists alike. Occupying a prominent position at the cross-roads of the central business district (CBD) and the city's sporting, cultural and casino precincts, Flinders Street Station is a central thoroughfare for those attending the Open. Following the order to move, the group left the station, however, then returned with their belongings a few hours later. They remained in position until they were forcibly removed in a violent confrontation between police and protestors on 1 February 2017, three days after the final game of the tournament had been played.

In the months before the Open, homeless people had become more noticeable in Melbourne's CBD (CoM, 2016). This was during a time when real estate prices across the metropolitan area were growing at an unprecedented rate. Greater numbers of people were sleeping rough on its streets and in safe public spaces such as train stations. Owing to the timing of the move-along order, in the days before the commencement of one of the city's leading events, and with the conspicuous location of the camp, accusations were widely made in the media that the city was being 'cleaned-up' for the Open (e.g. Dow, 2017; Wahlquist, 2017). While police and the CoM strongly denied these claims, this premier sporting event, with its attendant tourism and destination branding benefits, became embroiled in a serious social issue within a city that prided itself as the world's most liveable.

This chapter will consider the intersection of homelessness and events within the context of an eventful city. A qualitative case study has been used to present a snapshot of homelessness within Melbourne during a peak time in the city's events calendar. In early 2017, two of the city's portfolio events, the Australian Open and White Night, took place amidst a backdrop of increasing homelessness. Analysis of the representations of homelessness through these events has highlighted ways that a marginalised group may affect and be affected by events and how the quality of eventfulness may have an influence upon serious social issues such as homelessness.

Literature review

Cities pursue event-led strategies for their potential to realise multiple and enduring outcomes, otherwise known as legacies (Preuss, 2014). These outcomes frequently align with economic goals through urban revitalisation and place marketing (Hiller, 2006). While city developers may justify the hosting of costly, publicly funded events for the positive legacies they can create, research suggests that such outcomes often fail to materialise (Smith, 2016). Further complicating the event legacy narrative is the issue that what is perceived as a positive legacy by some may conversely be experienced negatively by others (Hiller, 2006).

A recent and high-profile example of events delivering questionable legacies comes from Rio de Janeiro. Following the announcement of the hosting of the 2014 FIFA World Cup and 2016 Summer Olympics, the city experienced a surge in real estate prices (Gaffney, 2016). While this was positive for property owners, developers and the government, low-income earners, many of whom were residents of *favelas* (shanty towns), were forced out of the city, thus limiting their access to public transportation and employment (Gaffney, 2016). Urban revitalisation projects may create economic benefits for the city, yet this can lead to marginalisation of some residents through displacement (Silk, 2014).

As major events are intended to attract international tourism and media attention, cities who stage them strive to present a positive image of themselves. While appearing spontaneous, a city's transformation is the result of meticulous and deliberate planning by city officials (Jamieson, 2004). Preferred narratives that serve dominant interests are highlighted while opposing elements are transformed or hidden from view (Silk, 2014). An example is the staging of late-night cultural events designed to attract diverse user groups and provide an alternative vision of the city at night, instead of one based upon alcohol-centred entertainment (Evans, 2012). Yet, in the construction of event spaces, social boundaries are implicitly drawn and those who do not fit within the dominant cultural framework of the city being marketed face exclusion (Jamieson, 2004).

This may be particularly problematic where eventfulness has been adopted, as entire cities become the stage for a rolling series of events (Richards & Palmer, 2010). Public streets, buildings and centres of civic activity are often appropriated, interrupting the usual dynamics of these spaces (Smith, 2016). This may be of benefit to marginalised communities when events are used to claim space for wider recognition and visibility of social issues (Ford & Markwell, 2017). However, events may also result in higher levels of security, commercialisation and privatisation, thereby narrowing access to, and use of, these 'public' spaces (Smith, 2016). Over time, this can lead to the privileging of certain identities while concomitantly excluding others, as usual activities and social life are displaced and even replaced (Kern, 2016). For this reason, events cannot simply be considered as assets in the service of legacy creation through economic development and destination enhancement. Instead, they function as sites where power is contested and practices of social inclusion and exclusion are performed (Kern, 2016).

Much of the research into event legacies has focussed on mega-events. However, this research has suggested that long-term benefits deriving from single, large-scale events may be compromised owing to their short duration (Smith & Fox, 2007). While ongoing planning has been identified for legacy creation, some event legacies may be unplanned and others may be negative (Preuss, 2014). Leveraging event portfolios has been suggested as a more sustainable alternative for the achievement of event legacies (Chalip, 2014), yet minimal empirical research has considered strategies that rely on multiple events. Reliance on eventful strategies for city development may result in unintended negative consequences and prior research suggests these may inordinately impact marginalised communities.

Method

A qualitative case study approach has been chosen to consider the intersection of homelessness and events within an eventful city. Case study research is valuable for the in-depth understandings of contemporary phenomena they generate within particular spatial and temporal boundaries (Creswell, 2013). This study focusses on the story of homelessness within Melbourne's CBD, beginning in June 2016 when results of a survey of the city's rough sleepers was released, through to February 2017 when two of the city's major events, the Australian Open and White Night, took place. The converging of homelessness and major events within this eventful city presented an opportunity to explore the ways that event strategies may marginalise vulnerable populations. This case study is thus an intrinsic one where the findings are representative of the case itself rather than being generalisable (Stake, 2013). Nevertheless, the insights that flow from the rich descriptions of this case study may provide the basis for future research (Creswell, 2013).

To develop detailed understandings, case studies rely on multiple sources of data collection from which thematic patterns emerge (Creswell, 2013). Three methods have been used in this research. First, active participant observation took place at White Night 2017 with photographs, video and research notes seeking to capture the way the theme of homelessness was portrayed within the event. Active participant observation was chosen to gain insider knowledge of White Night from the perspective of an attendee (Mackellar, 2013). The research was not directed at homeless individuals or groups and ethics approval was granted upon this basis. White Night takes places from 7pm to 7am and stretches across several kilometres of Melbourne's CBD. To ensure researcher safety, the data were collected with a companion, mobile phones were accessible and there was no deviation from the boundaries of the event. The second method was a semi-structured interview conducted with Visit Victoria, the state's destination marketing organisation and owner of White Night. Whilst this interview was concerned with developing broader understandings of Melbourne's events environment, the theme of homelessness and the city's events was explicitly explored. Finally, media reports and documentation from the

CoM have been textually analysed to understand the ways in which the story of homelessness is presented within the city. Patterns that emerged from the data have been coded and findings developed from the resulting themes (Creswell, 2013).

Melbourne's events strategy

Melbourne's events strategy was founded in the need for an alternative economic base following the demise of the manufacturing industry. The lifting of tariffs to support manufacturers in the 1960s led to business closures, increasing unemployment and the abandonment of buildings within the inner city (O'Hanlon, 2009). Government reports from the 1970s suggest that rapid deindustrialisation was threatening the city's financial and social stability (O'Hanlon, 2009). Meanwhile Sydney, Melbourne's traditional rival, was attracting high tourism numbers and significant business investment in the new financial, media and technology sectors (Sandercock & Dovey, 2002). In response, successive Victorian governments adopted an events-based strategy to rejuvenate the stagnating city and secure its future prosperity (O'Hanlon, 2009).

Beginning in the 1980s, a revitalisation programme saw the development of sporting, cultural and entertainment precincts, all within a few kilometres of the CBD (Sandercock & Dovey, 2002). The Victorian Major Events Company (now Visit Victoria) was established in 1990 to attract world-class sporting, cultural and business events to the state (Lowes, 2004). As well as pursuing ongoing tourism expenditure, these measures were undertaken to transform the city's image, rejuvenate its moribund atmosphere and encourage business investment (Sandercock & Dovey, 2002; O'Hanlon, 2009). Melbourne's events strategy has evolved to being one of eventfulness, where the city is the stage for an ongoing roster of events (Richards & Palmer, 2010). Central to its success is the suite of hallmark and major events, including the Australian Grand Prix, the Melbourne International Comedy Festival and the Australian Football League Grand Final, that have worked to position Melbourne as the events capital of Australia (Frost, 2012).

Rather than the decline that was predicted in the 1970s, Melbourne is now recognised as one of the most liveable cities in the world. However, accompanying its ascent is attendant gentrification within traditionally working-class inner-city suburbs (O'Hanlon, 2009). Increasing demand for more urban residential environments has diminished low-income housing stock. This situation has worsened in recent years with the escalation of real estate values across the metropolitan area, placing pressure on rental prices (Pawson et al., 2018). Research from the United Kingdom suggests that a reduction in housing affordability can rapidly affect levels of homelessness (Fitzpatrick et al., 2017). Within Melbourne, inequality has become more apparent, particularly with regard to the numbers of homeless people that can be observed on the city's streets (Pawson et al., 2018).

Homelessness in Melbourne

Since 2008, the CoM has performed a survey of Melbourne's rough sleepers, defined as those people who sleep in public places, including streets, parks, abandoned buildings and cars (CoM, 2016). 'StreetCount' takes place in the central city and along parts of its fringe during winter, when only those who cannot access suitable accommodation would be sleeping rough. The survey targets homeless people in areas they frequent; focusses questions on their experience of homelessness; and is performed by volunteers, many of whom have worked in the homeless sector (CoM, 2016). From 2014 to 2016, when the most recent survey took place, StreetCount showed the number of rough sleepers had increased by an extraordinary 74%.

Shortly after the 2016 StreetCount, its results were reported in Victoria's leading newspaper alongside detail of complaints made to CoM regarding homelessness. Reports of 'footpaths being overtaken by "squats"', 'drug use and the accumulation of rubbish and filth' and 'violent confrontations ... between some rough sleepers' have led to some calling on the council to 'simply "move on the homeless" out of sight' (Dow, 2016: paras. 2, 12, 17 & 29). Homelessness was framed as an undesirable problem for the city and a threat to Melbourne's identity. With the protection of city image vital in a competitive and global business and tourism environment, Melbourne's Lord Mayor was quick to argue that although 'we should be supportive of people that are vulnerable ... there are challenging, illegal behaviours that we shouldn't put up with, whether people are homeless or not' (Dow, 2016: para. 16).

The vulnerability of those who are homeless extends beyond lack of access to a safe, secure and comfortable place to sleep. Relationship breakdowns, poor mental health and traumatic experiences including domestic violence and childhood abuse are some of the common factors leading to homelessness (Chamberlain & Johnson, 2013). As such, it is an acute and challenging issue for those who endure it and for society as a whole. The development of policy targeting homelessness in Australia reflects this polarity, as concern for homeless people's welfare is precariously balanced against a desire to manage their behaviours (Regan, 2012). This tension is evident in the CoM's position on homelessness, whereby they seek to 'strike a balance between recognising the hardship that rough sleepers experience and the need to ensure public places are clean, safe and accessible for all members of the community' (CoM, 2018b: para. 3). As such, the CoM have an online portal that allows the public to report people who are sleeping rough or where public amenity or access may be affected by their possessions. Control may be exerted over homeless people via the *Activities Local Law of 2009*, where camping is restricted and acceptable public behaviour defined (CoM, 2018a).

While an essential function of local government is to ensure a clean, safe and accessible city exists for all, this vulnerable population may be easily targeted as they attempt to secure clean, safe and accessible places to sleep. In the days after the failed attempt to remove the Flinders Street Station homeless camp before the Australian Open, members of local and state government met with service providers to discuss the issue of homelessness in the city (CoM, 2017). Following this meeting, a request was made by Victoria Police to Melbourne City Council to review the *Activities Local Law of 2009* so they could provide a stronger response to homelessness in the future (CoM, 2017). On February 7, 2017, just over a week after the Open had concluded, the council voted in favour of amendments to the *Activities Local Law of 2009* to be followed by a community consultation period of 28 days. These proposed changes would have broadened the definition of camping, thereby preventing any form of sleeping in the city, and allowed for the confiscation of possessions with payment of a fee required before their return (CoM, 2017).

This was a controversial decision surrounded by high levels of public interest, media attention and objections from homeless groups. Those opposed to the changes claimed that homeless people would be effectively banned from the city and that higher rates of incarceration would result with fines unable to be paid (Hancock, 2017). The Lord Mayor argued that the intention was not to evict people from the city, while the Deputy Lord Mayor emphasised the need to protect ratepayers (Hancock, 2017). It was within this environment that the next major event of Melbourne's very busy event portfolio was presented, less than two weeks after the Council's decision and only three weeks after the Australian Open had ended.

Background to White Night Melbourne 2017

White Night Melbourne follows the lead of Paris' Nuit Blanche and is designed to expand the night-time economy, provide opportunities for destination promotion and encourage people to experience the city differently via novel and delightful artistic interventions (Evans, 2012). White Night first took place in 2013 when it drew crowds of 300,000 for 12 hours of spectacular light installations and projections, street theatre and musical performances. Since that time, it has been an unmitigated success for its state government owner, with crowd numbers increasing each year. In June 2016, shortly after the StreetCount results were published, the Major Events Minister announced that not only would White Night be extended to the regional Victorian city of Ballarat but that David Atkins had been appointed its new creative director.

Atkins has a reputation for creating spectacular, world-class event productions, having been creative producer for the 2000 Sydney Olympic Games and the 2010 Shanghai World Expo. Shortly after this announcement, calls for artists to participate in White Night 2017 were issued. Several months later in December 2016, at the release of the upcoming event's programme, it was revealed that homelessness would be a featured theme. An interview with the event's owner Visit Victoria revealed that Atkins is credited with the idea of incorporating this theme: 'that was David's idea and we supported it along the way' (Visit Victoria, 17 January 2018, pers. comm.). A newspaper report covering the announcement of the programme and its socially inclusive theme reports Atkins's stance: 'There is a moral obligation when you have the focus of half a million people, not only to engage and entertain them, but remind them about some issues' (Razak, 2016: para. 12). The popularity and exposure the event receives were to be leveraged to provide visibility to a difficult issue that affects an increasing number of people in the city.

Official and unofficial representations of homelessness

Close to 600,000 people donned jackets and scarves for an unusually cold February night to attend White Night 2017. Once again it was a record-breaking crowd that wandered the city's closed-off streets, marvelling at its brightly illuminated buildings. One of the participating buildings was St Paul's Cathedral, situated on the southern edge of the CBD. With its Victorian Gothic architecture, towering spires and prominent positioning opposite Flinders Street Station and Federation Square, it is one of Melbourne's most recognisable landmarks. As the church is a traditional place of shelter for those seeking refuge, the Cathedral is often used by members of the city's homeless community who gather along its perimeter. It was here that the theme of homelessness was represented within the White Night programme.

The video installation *Home Less* by local filmmaker Chase Burns was projected against an external wall (Burns, 2016). It featured an anonymous figure dressed in black, sitting cross-legged as if they were leaning against the wall of the Cathedral. Their head is dropped into their hands in a pose of silent resignation and their face obscured by the hood of an athletic sweater. Next to them is the familiar boxy shape and checked pattern of the cheap, zippered, woven-plastic bags associated with the uprooted: those who are in transition, whether stateless or homeless. Suddenly a harsh spotlight highlights the figure as if they are under the scrutiny of the audience and the city itself. The scene changes as a woman rendered in white floats out from within the dark body (Figures 9.1 and 9.2). With outstretched arms she rises high up, bringing the cathedral's spire into view and leaving the prone figure below. She then floats here for some time, her skirt billowing outward, while crashing waves make Rorschach-like patterns and bright colours pulsate across the scene to an electronic soundtrack (Figure 9.3). Several minutes

Figure 9.1 The protagonist in Burns's *Home Less* spotlighted against a wall of
St Paul's Cathedral.
Source: Amanda Ford.

later she descends, falling back towards the figure into which she disap-
pears. The homeless person is once again alone, depicted in their muted
colours against the hard walls of the city.

Home Less was the sole representation of homelessness within the official
programme. However, approximately 1 km north of St Paul's Cathedral, an
unofficial projection drew attention to homelessness at the State Library of
Victoria. Similar to the Cathedral, the Library sits opposite the entrance
of a major train station and is one of the city's most popular cultural landmarks. By day, it is crowded with people viewing its collections, using its
resources or seated on its sloped, grassy forecourt. During White Night,
video installations within the Library's iconic domed reading room are
an exceptionally popular attraction with attendees queuing for hours to

Figure 9.2 The ethereal woman begins her ascent from within the prone body.
Source: Amanda Ford.

gain entry. Projections also feature across its sandstone façade and it was here that protestors had hijacked this prominent landmark with their own guerrilla-style projection.

The Library's forecourt is a regular site for activist gatherings and, following the council's decision in the week before White Night to amend the *Activities Local Law of 2009*, the event presented an opportunity for homeless people and their allies to gain public support. Up to 100 participants with traditional placards, banners and chanting gathered in the southern corner of the forecourt to accompany the projection that was made possible via inexpensive and readily accessible technology (Harmon, 2017). The message "MELBOURNE IS FOR ALL. #NO HOMELESS BAN" was overlaid in bold, static white lettering across the Library's swirling,

Figure 9.3 The woman in white floats high up against the pulsating, coloured
        background.
Source: Amanda Ford.

coloured imagery at the peak of its roof line (Figure 9.4). This placement
and the contrast between the different styles of the Library's projection
and the protestors' message ensured that it was immediately noticeable to
onlookers. Additionally, the protest was included in the media's coverage
of White Night, with attention paid to their messages and proposed local
law changes.

Figure 9.4 The homeless protestors' message hijacked the State Library of Victoria's
         installation.
Source: Amanda Ford.

Discussion

White Night-style events seek to present a new identity for cities at night,
one that is accessible to a broad audience (Evans, 2012). This makes them
an effective asset to leverage within an event portfolio for the development
of a destination's image (Ziakas, 2013). Yet homelessness could be considered a narrative that is antithetical to destination identity (Silk, 2014). The
accusations made against CoM and Victoria Police following their action
towards the homeless camp prior to the 2017 Australian Open are grounded
in this opposition. However, Visit Victoria actively integrated the theme of
homelessness into White Night. Their reasoning for this decision is: 'this
is a night for Melbourne and this is a whole piece for Melbourne and the
homeless, that was a big issue at the time'. For Visit Victoria it was a way
to 'demonstrate that reality' (Visit Victoria, 17 January 2018, pers. comm.).
This symbolic representation of a marginalised group within the event was
an inclusive action by powerful actors. Rather than displacing homelessness

from the story of the city (Silk, 2014), White Night allocated it a space within the event itself.

Through *Home Less*, White Night became proactively engaged in a conversation that had occurred since the publication of the 2016 StreetCount figures. As an event that transforms the city at night, 'it's a message that would be talked about anyway, so let's acknowledge it and be upfront, and let's weave it into what we're saying' (Visit Victoria, 17 January 2018, pers. comm.). This suggests that *Home Less* may have been an act of transparency, designed to present a realistic depiction of Melbourne to the White Night audience. At the same time, with the intense media scrutiny that the story of homelessness had received, it also ensured any discussion of homelessness that surrounded the event included its organiser's voice. Prominent events such as the Olympic Games have received international media criticism for their displacing of vulnerable groups (Gaffney, 2016). This deliberate inclusion of the narrative of homelessness within the event ensured the city would be presented positively in media coverage received (Jamieson, 2004).

Whilst the event organiser's voice was represented within *Home Less*, it is unclear if homeless people themselves were being heard. Biographical information does not indicate whether Burns has experienced homelessness himself and homeless groups were not attributed in its production (Burns, 2016). As a creative event, White Night is valued by its owners for the 'capacity to be able to do that little bit more' through its messaging and to 'push the boundaries of what you're doing and where you're doing it' (Visit Victoria, 17 January 2018, pers. comm.). Major events such as White Night can be leveraged to provide visibility for marginalised communities and the issues they face (Ford & Markwell, 2017) and was a rationale for the homeless theme's inclusion by Atkins. Yet research suggests that if the visibility afforded by major events can serve to challenge existing conventions or 'push the boundaries', those who are part of the marginalised community must be involved in the messaging (Ford & Markwell, 2017).

Rather than offering an alternative interpretation of homelessness that encouraged new understandings within audience members, this artwork's messaging served to reinforce existing tropes (Silk, 2014). The form of homelessness conveyed by this artwork was one of bleak loneliness and isolation, with fantastical dreams the only escape. While a solitary existence may be one aspect of homelessness, the Flinders Street Station camp suggests community and group belonging can also be experienced. Dreams perhaps offer a temporary disconnection from a difficult reality for those who are homeless, yet it is access to affordable, long-term housing that is essential for tangible improvements to their lived experience (Regan, 2012). A more cynical reading of this dream imagery could interpret it as being drug induced, which is frequently, albeit erroneously, attributed as a leading cause of homelessness, rather than a strategy for dealing with its difficult realities (Chamberlain & Johnson, 2013). Although event space was allocated to this important social issue, the installation was within a religious setting readily associated with the provision of shelter for the needy. At the end of the video, audience members would ultimately walk away, leaving the homeless person caught in their endless loop of isolation and fantasy.

Other events across the world in the Nuit Blanche canon encourage charitable donations to important social causes (Evans, 2012), yet this opportunity was missed with *Home Less*. The only interpretive information was its title, its artist's name and the link to the accompanying soundtrack. There was an absence of material to educate audience members about homelessness or detail on ways assistance could be provided, nor was there information on support services for audience members who may be affected by homelessness. *Home Less* was not intended to be controversial by the event owners: 'it wasn't a political statement, it wasn't anything like that, it was just a really subtle way that we could bring that message in' (Visit Victoria, 17 January 2018, pers. comm.). While the event provided an opportunity for the issue to receive visibility, it was portrayed in a way that did not threaten its government investors. Instead, this was a non-controversial simulation of homelessness that for the time frame of the event served to displace the homeless people who would often occupy this space (Kern, 2016).

As well as this representation in the official programme, Visit Victoria had arranged a homeless refuge on the night to ensure that audience members weren't 'trampling all over their place to sleep' (Visit Victoria, 17 January 2018, pers. comm.). The refuge was reported as the Salvation Army Church, positioned in the CBD although outside of the White Night precinct, with food, coffee and sleeping provisions available and a free all-night concert featuring some of the event's musicians (Harmon, 2017). Visit Victoria asserts that, 'when you bring a major event to the city, we need to be cognisant of the people sleeping rough' (Visit Victoria, 17 January 2018, pers. comm.). It is debatable whether this awareness is directed towards safety concerns for homeless people or the image that high levels of homelessness suggests of the city. The handling of the homeless camps prior to the Australian Open and the efforts to amend the *Activities Local Law of 2009* suggest the latter is the focus. Supplying accommodation and facilities for homeless people whilst the city's streets were transformed by White Night is a positive step. Nevertheless, the sustainability of this action is questionable within an eventful city where major events are regularly scheduled and some run for weeks at a time. This temporary accommodation may also be interpreted as a device to discourage homeless people away from the event.

However, instead of avoiding the event, homeless people and their allies leveraged its popularity and exposure to draw attention to the adverse way changes to the *Activities Local Law of 2009* would have an impact on them. Rather than the passive and lone representation as suggested in *Home Less*, this was a vocal expression by the homeless community of their dissatisfaction. The stylistic devices of the event itself were employed in an act of artistic vandalism that interrupted, skewed and dominated the meaning of the Library's external projection with its bold, static text. Appropriating public spaces for events has been challenged in the literature as it can lead to their commercialisation, privatisation and being subject to greater amounts of security (Smith, 2016). Yet, in this instance, the Library was successfully co-opted for protest because it is a public building and frequent site for activism. Visibility of the protestors' messaging was ensured through the large crowds that attended the event and the media coverage that followed (Ford & Markwell, 2017). Yet, despite these official and unofficial representations of homelessness at White Night, the starkest reminder of the issue came from the few people who were observed sleeping at its margins, away from the bright lights and crowded streets.

Conclusion

The actions towards the Flinders Street homeless camp, proposed changes to CoM by-laws and unresolved crisis of homelessness within the city provided the catalyst for the protest at White Night. Yet the tight rotation of Melbourne's events calendar created an ongoing and prominent platform for the issue's exposure. The scale of White Night itself ensured that protestors' messages were widely reported in the media in the following days. This suggests that while governments may rely on eventful strategies such as portfolios to achieve policy objectives (Richards & Palmer, 2010), they may also be utilised for the promotion of social causes via strategic protest. Media and public reaction to the manner in which the CoM chose to approach homelessness in the city during this period was influenced by the backdrop of its major events. Their excessive cost, spectacle and use for city image creation were a sharp contrast to this acute social need.

Ultimately, proposed amendments to the *Activities Local Law of 2009* were unsuccessful following public criticism, while state government funding for homeless housing increased. This is not to suggest that the attention derived from Melbourne's major events directly led to these positive outcomes, nor that homeless people within Melbourne no longer experience marginalisation. However, pursuing a strategy of eventfulness means that Melbourne's regularly scheduled major events occur within the dynamic and unpredictable environment of the city. In this instance, the converging of government measures to control a marginalised group, activism and media coverage against a backdrop of major events enabled this serious social issue to achieve wider visibility. However, tangible social change is reliant on government commitment to achieving such outcomes and an engaged public to hold them accountable.

References

Burns, C. (2016) *Homeless. White Night.* Available from: www.chaseburns.com/project-8 [Accessed 16th May 2018].
Chalip, L. (2014) From legacy to leverage. In: Grix, J. (ed.) *Leveraging legacies from sports mega-events.* London, Palgrave Macmillan, pp. 2–12.

Chamberlain, C. & Johnson, G. (2013) Pathways into adult homelessness. *Journal of Sociology.* 49 (1), 60–77.

City of Melbourne (2016) *StreetCount 2016: final report.* Available from: www.melbourne.vic.gov.au/SiteCollectionDocuments/streetcount-2016-final-report.pdf [Accessed 16th May 2018].

City of Melbourne (2017) *Report to the Future Melbourne (finance and governance) committee: homelessness and public amenity.* Available from: www.melbourne.vic.gov.au/about-council/committees-meetings/meeting-archive/meetingagendaitemattachments/766/13734/feb16%20fmc1%20agenda%20item%206.2.pdf [Accessed 16th May 2018].

City of Melbourne (2018a) *Activities local law 2009.* Available from: www.melbourne.vic.gov.au/about-council/governance-transparency/acts-local-laws/Pages/activities-local-law-2009.aspx [Accessed 16th May 2018].

City of Melbourne. (2018b) *Homelessness.* Available from: www.melbourne.vic.gov.au/community/health-support-services/social-support/Pages/homelessness.aspx [Accessed 16th May 2018].

Creswell, J. (2013) *Qualitative enquiry and research design: choosing among five approaches* (3rd ed.). California, Sage Publications.

Deery, M. & Jago, L. (2010) Social impacts of events and the role of anti-social behaviour. *International Journal of Event and Festival Management.* 1 (1), 8–28.

Dow, A. (2016) The homeless crisis gripping Melbourne. *The Age,* 17 July. Available from: www.theage.com.au/national/victoria/the-homelessness-crisis-gripping-melbourne-20160715-gq6yog.html [Accessed 16th May 2018].

Dow, A. (2017) Council insists it is not clearing homeless camps because of Australian Open. *The Age,* 11 January. Available from: www.theage.com.au/national/victoria/council-insists-it-is-not-clearing-homeless-camps-because-of-australian-open-20170111-gtpc2n.htm [Accessed 16th May 2018].

Evans, G. (2012) Hold back the night: Nuit Blanche and all-night events in capital cities. *Current Issues in Tourism.* 15 (1–2), 35–49.

Fitzpatrick, S., Pawson, H., Bramley, G., Wilcox, S. & Watts, B. (2017) *The homelessness monitor: England 2017.* London, Crisis. Available from: www.yhne.org.uk/wp-content/uploads/Homelessness-Monitor-England-2017_FINAL.pdf [Accessed 16th May 2018].

Ford, A. & Markwell, K. (2017) Special events and social reform: the case of the Sydney Gay and Lesbian Mardi Gras Parade and the Australian Marriage Equality Movement. *Event Management.* 21 (6), 683–695.

Frost, W. (2012) Events and tourism. In: Page, S. & Connell, J. (eds.) *The Routledge handbook of events.* London, Routledge, pp. 75–86.

Gaffney, C. (2016) Gentrifications in pre-Olympic Rio de Janeiro. *Urban Geography.* 37 (8), 1132–1153.

Hancock, J. (2017) Melbourne homelessness: council votes to ban camping in the city. *ABC,* 7 February. Available from: www.abc.net.au/news/2017-02-07/homelessness-in-melbourne-city-council-bans-camping/8248506 [Accessed 16th May 2018].

Harmon, S. (2017) White Night Melbourne: spontaneous moments stand out on night of unsettling ironies. *The Guardian,* 20 February. Available from: www.theguardian.com/artanddesign/2017/feb/20/white-night-melbourne-shifting-hues-reveal-the-citys-many-faces [Accessed 16th May 2018].

Hiller, H. H. (2006) Post-event outcomes and the post-modern turn: the Olympics and urban transformations. *European Sport Management Quarterly.* 6 (4), 317–332.

Jamieson, K. (2004) Edinburgh: the festival gaze and its boundaries. *Space and Culture.* 7 (1), 64–75.

Kern, L. (2016) Rhythms of gentrification: eventfulness and slow violence in a happening neighbourhood. *Cultural Geographies.* 23 (3), 441–457.

Lowes, M. (2004) Neoliberal power politics and the controversial siting of the Australian Grand Prix motorsport event in an urban park. *Loisir et Société/Society and Leisure.* 27 (1), 69–88.

Mackellar, J. (2013) Participant observation at events: theory, practice and potential. *International Journal of Event and Festival Management.* 4 (1), 56–65.

O'Hanlon, S. (2009) The events city: sport, culture, and the transformation of inner Melbourne, 1977–2006. *Urban History Review.* 37 (2), 30–39.

Pawson, H., Parsell, C., Saunders, P., Hill, T. & Liu, E. (2018) *Australian homelessness monitor 2018.* Melbourne, Launch Housing. Available from: www.launchhousing.org.au/site/wp-content/uploads/2018/05/LaunchHousing_AHM2018_Report.pdf [Accessed 16th May 2018].

Preuss, H. (2014) 'Legacy' revisited. In: Grix, J. (ed.) *Leveraging legacies from sports mega-events.* London, Palgrave Macmillan, pp. 24–38.

Razak, I. (2016) White Night Melbourne to expand into Ballarat to 'share the wealth', organisers say. *ABC,* 18 December. Available from: www.abc.net.au/news/2016-12-12/white-night-melbourne-to-expand-into-ballarat/8113310 [Accessed 16th May 2018].

Regan, S. (2012) The Melbourne street to home experience: lessons for long-term homelessness. *Parity.* 25 (5), 27–28.

Richards, G. (2017) Emerging models of the eventful city. *Event Management.* 21 (5), 533–543.

Richards, G. & Palmer, R. (2010) *Eventful cities: cultural management and urban revitalisation.* Oxford, Butterworth-Heinemann.

Sandercock, L. & Dovey, K. (2002) Pleasure, politics, and the 'public interest': Melbourne's riverscape revitalization. *Journal of the American Planning Association.* 68 (2), 151–164.

Silk, M. (2014) Neoliberalism and sports mega-events. In: Grix, J. (ed.) *Leveraging legacies from sports mega-events.* London, Palgrave Macmillan, pp. 50–60.

Smith, A. (2016) *Events in the city: using public spaces as event venues.* London, Routledge.

Smith, A. & Fox, T. (2007) From 'event-led' to 'event-themed' regeneration: the 2002 Commonwealth Games legacy programme. *Urban Studies.* 44 (5–6), 1125–1143.

Stake, R. (2013) Qualitative case studies. In: Denzin, N. K. & Lincoln, Y. S. (eds.) *Strategies of qualitative inquiry* (4th ed.). California, Sage Publications, pp. 443–466.

Wahlquist, C. (2017) Melbourne city council denies homeless camps 'cleanup' linked to Australian Open. *The Guardian,* 11 January. Available from: www.theguardian.com/australia-news/2017/jan/11/melbourne-city-council-denies-homeless-camps-cleanup-linked-to-australian-open [Accessed 16th May 2018].

Wright, P. (2016) Melbourne ranked world's most liveable city for sixth consecutive year by EIU. *ABC,* 18 August. Available from: www.abc.net.au/news/2016-08-18/melbourne-ranked-worlds-most-liveable-city-for-sixth-year/7761642 [Accessed 16th May 2018].

Ziakas, V. (2013) *Event portfolio planning and management: a holistic approach.* London, Routledge.

Part III

Managing events at the margins of life, death and the universe

10 Understanding peripheral queer events

The case of Gay Ski Week, Queenstown, New Zealand

Willem JL Coetzee and Xiang Liu

Introduction

The Stonewall Riots in 1969 are widely considered to be a point of departure for a long but gradually improved process of liberation and acceptance of the Lesbian, Gay, Bisexual, Transsexual and Queer (LGBTQ) community (Hughes, 2006). And in the last half-century we witnessed tremendous developments in the societal tolerance and acceptance of homosexuality in many countries in the Western world (e.g. Western Europe, North America and Australia), but it is critical to acknowledge that a large number of African, Asian, Caribbean and Pacific countries do not recognise homosexuals and their right to freedom of expression (Vorobjovas-Pinta & Hardy, 2016). LGBTQ events and festivals are a significant milestone for the tourism industry. Gay pride parades alongside politics, celebrations, art and activism have opened gay spaces that have helped to sustain counter-hegemonic identities from New York to Sydney, Bangkok, Vancouver and Cape Town. In the past, the gay identity of tourist destinations relied on a recognisably bounded gay village via aesthetic qualities of gayness evidenced in the environment through rainbow flags, picturesque cafés, bars, clubs and saunas (Hughes, 2003). Destinations made use of this gay-friendly environment to promote their unique offering to attract gay people making a holiday destination decision. Due to societal tolerance and technological changes (for example, dating apps such as Grindr), borders between straight and gay villages have become blurred, and destinations are still exploring ideas to attract tourists from the LGBTQ community.

Destinations are well aware of the importance of their event portfolios in establishing a gay culture and space within a town or city, and they design LGBTQ events to create opportunities to earn 'pink' economic benefits for the destination. Hallmark events, such as the Sydney Mardi Gras, boast attendee numbers of over 7,000 and provide evidence of the importance of gay event tourism. According to Liberato et al. (2018), LGBT tourism is a growing phenomenon in the US tourism industry and represents a market that exceeds $54 billion a year or 10 percent of the industry. However, not all LGBTQ events are large-scale hallmark events – some are peripheral. One such peripheral event is the 'Gay Ski Week' (GSW) held in Queenstown, New Zealand. This event successfully attracts members of the LGBTQ community to participate in leisure snow sports and enjoy the wild-life and natural environment within a popular macho tourist destination. Our research suggests that GSW has a transformative effect for individuals from marginalised communities, such as members of the Chinese LGBTQ community who are marginalised within their own country. The Chinese attendees suggested to us that they leave the GSW with a feeling of hope and belonging and a sense of self-worth.

Literature review

In 1998, Pritchard et al. referred to the gay tourist market as an emerg-ing market, but since then the LGBTQ event tourism market has grown into a very competitive market. Earlier research on the LGBTQ traveller focussed on wealthier middle-class white gay men and their holiday moti-vations (Clift & Forrest, 1999), holidays and homosexual identity (Hughes, 1997), the growing lesbian and gay sport tourism industry (Pitts, 1999), 'pink' tourism (Hughes, 2006), identity and sex as aspects of gay tourism (Monterrubio, 2008), sexuality and holiday choices, and gay spaces (Visser, 2003). Recent studies (Berezan et al., 2015; Prayag et al., 2015) showed that the LGBTQ community is not as homogeneous as previously thought. For example, Wong and Tolkach (2017) explored the travel preferences of Asian gay men and identified several aspects that affect travel planning and travel preferences of Asian gay men. In response, this paper argues that the gay visitor from Asia is in search of much more than bars, clubs, saunas, drag shows, parades and rent boys. In fact, Asian LGBTQ travellers have be-come much more discerning in their search for meaningful experiences and self-actualisation.

According to the website of Tourism New Zealand (newzealand.com), Queenstown, New Zealand is known as the adventure capital of the world and a cosmopolitan town with a smorgasbord of outdoor activities. Queenstown has been described by Johnston (2006) as a testosterone-driven destination in a heteronormative New Zealand nature space that has been used in Tourism New Zealand-sponsored tourism advertising campaigns to attract a specific type of visitor. Frohlick and Johnston (2011: p. 51) de-scribed this campaign as 'dramatic nature spaces populated only by young, white, able-bodied, couples (male and female) tourists'. This approach is not unique to New Zealand: previous researchers (Phillips, 1995; Little, 2003) argued that natural spaces are often dominated by representations of conventional forms of heterosexuality – especially skiing and mountain sports, which are usually associated with the hegemonic construction of masculinity. Researchers have demonstrated how gendered embodiment, power and ski resorts are intimately linked. For example, Waitt (2005: p. 436) described sporting spaces as 'equipped more for the needs of white,

Anglo, male and heteronormative bodies', while Johnston (2006) described nature spaces as spaces with conservative, affluent, straight tourists. However, in New Zealand, the heteronormative lines are becoming softer and communities are more tolerant towards the LGBTQ community. It is therefore important that we should search for new clues to questions regarding niche markets within the LGBTQ community. In particular, we need to ask why would the gay Asian male attend GSW in Queenstown? What meaning does GSW have as a destination for gay Asian tourists? In this study, the research objectives were to identify Asian gay tourist motivations to attend a ski week event and to identify the potential impact of such an event on this marginalised community.

The LGBTQ tourist

Earlier research related to LGBTQ tourism focussed on homosexual identity while on holiday (Hughes, 1997; Ersoy, Ozer & Tuzunkan, 2012), the relationship between the tourism industry and the LGBTQ community (Pritchard et al., 1998), the dimensions that might influence the choice of destination for the gay tourist (Clift & Forrest, 1999) and sexual behaviour of members of the LGBTQ community while on holiday (Clift & Wilkins, 1995). According to Hughes (2002), feelings of social censure, a desire to be oneself, relationships with others and being anonymous push gay people to construct and validate their identity away from home. The holiday provides a temporal opportunity for LGBTQ people to interact with members of the LGBTQ communities (Hindle, 1994) and a chance to be a 'homosexual' (Hughes, 1997). It also provides an opportunity for validating their gay identity, by establishing a relationship with other gay community members (Hindle, 1994) by living and playing in gay spaces or gay-friendly places.

According to Johnston and Longhurst (2009) sexuality has a profound effect on the way people live in, and interact with, space and place. These authors focussed on the complex relationship that exists between bodies and places, materiality and discourse, and nature and culture. According to them, spaces exist inside sexual politics; therefore sex and space cannot be decoupled. Gay travel is seen as a quest for utopia – a place where one is 'free' from heterosexism (Waitt & Markwell, 2014).

Tourism has always been significant in promoting cultural understandings in that it offers an important way to engage with different cultures, even though most of these references refer to heterosexual cultures. Waitt and Markwell (2014) argue that the oppressive qualities of heteronormatively are a key factor driving the mobility characterising gay cultures of travel. There are many gay people who adopt a conventional masculine identity, but they continue to be affected and oppressed by heterosexualism. Social oppression motivates gay travellers to seek out specific places and events where they can discover their sexual identity and belonging through performing gender and sex roles.

Devall (1979) discussed the tradition of travel as an important method used by gay people in search of themselves. He viewed the emergence and subsequent growth of the gay travel industry as an extension of the gay culture – most importantly, in the way in which travel assisted in constituting gay subjectivities by assisting in the coming out process, by providing an opportunity to meet gay people in sexual or non-sexual settings and by ensuring a heightened awareness of collectivism and political action through participation in gay festivals and events (Devall, 1979). Both Hughes (1997) and Pritchard, Morgan and Sedgley (2000) have drawn upon a postmodern framework when investigating the relationship between sexuality and travel. Hughes et al. (2002) argued that holidays are an important means for gay people to discover their sexual identity. Travel is a significant way to escape the straitjacket of the everyday 'closet'. According to Waitt and Markwell (2014), gay tourism is like a pilgrimage or a quest for an individual and collective identity. The main influences on gay people's choice of a holiday destination is a gay-friendly space, safety and the feeling of being comfortable with like-minded people (Pritchard, Morgan & Sedgley, 2000). The intrinsic motivating factors that are common across social communities are the need for escape from the home-related environment, a sense of belonging and an opportunity to be oneself.

Many destinations (for example Ibiza, Cape Town, Vancouver and San Francisco) have realised the significance of gay tourism and are now branding themselves as premier LGBTQ destinations. Some cities, such as São Paulo, London, Madrid, Miami and Barcelona, even claim gay-capital status to lure the LGBTQ traveller and run marketing campaigns that focus exclusively on the LGBTQ community. These destinations often target tourism fairs and exhibitions specifically aimed at gay people that are often hosted by infamous gay tourist destinations (Clift & Forrest, 1999). This is due to the perception that gay people have significant disposable income and more time for travelling (Ersoy, Ozer & Tuzunkan, 2012). According to Stuber et al. (2002), gay tourism marketing provides value and generates 'pink dollars' and public attention. However, Coon (2012) argues against this; he states that the marketing strategies employed reveal the second-class citizen status still experienced by the LGBTQ tourist. Nevertheless, we believe it is important to take note of the various niche markets within the LGBTQ community, such as the gay Asian attendee.

Gay Asian travellers

Chinese nationals made 130 million trips overseas in 2017 and the new generation of Chinese tourist is searching for authentic experiences that fulfil individual needs. According to Sun, Zhang and Ryan (2015), Chinese people particularly desire a harmonious relationship between human beings and the natural environment during their holidays, and this is an important aspect when making a holiday destination decision. Research such as that by

Sun, Zhang and Ryan (2015) on heterosexual Chinese tourists and their behaviour and experiences at tourist destinations is well established, but there has been little research done on Chinese gay tourists in New Zealand. One study by Neville and Adams (2016) discussed HIV/STI and health promotion among gay and bisexual Chinese and South Asian men living in Auckland, New Zealand, which view the influence of different environments on their sexual behaviours.

Due to traditional conservative customs in China, the developing gay community is still experiencing negative social stigma and is still regarded as a marginalised community. A study on destination choice and risk avoidance conducted by Hughes (2002) has suggested that the perceived antagonism caused by either the law or by the disparate cultural norms has had an impact upon the travel geography of gay tourists. He further states that homosexuals are less likely to visit such countries and/or geographical areas such as China. Most LGBTQ people still prefer to live in traditional spaces for gender difference (Sullivan & Jackson, 2013). However, the non-gay-friendly environment and inequitable policies regarding LGBTQ people in most Asian countries drive them – especially young LGBTQ people – to travel to or live in another country that is more open to homosexuality. Engaging in the Asian gay community motivates them to identify their gender diversity and participate in the group of gay people along with a sense of belonging. The Asian gay community may be less likely to encounter racism and anti-immigrant sentiment, and they are more likely to experience silence about homosexuality rather than overt anti-gay discrimination.

Wilson and Yoshikawa (2004) reported on Asian gay people's experiences of racism in New York – in the gay community rather than amongst the general public – and they reported high levels of racism, specifically from white gay men towards gay Asian men. Asian gay communities provide Asian gay people with an umbrella of protection, as they may be a minority group in another country. However, Han, Proctor and Choi (2014) argued that Asian gay people have a passion for engaging in the local gay community, which may offer an opportunity for them to experience the relationships between Asian gay people and local white gay people.

Events

Many destinations are now exploring the new interest in destinations for gay people by hosting gay festivals and events. Festival and event spaces are positioned as integral to the ongoing process of establishing a gay community and gay culture. Waitt and Markwell (2014) argue that ritualised occasions of collective celebration are of considerable importance to gay people and are often in the public eye. Festivals and events provide an opportunity to gather people together in large numbers to participate in and create cultural expressions, but also to claim the gay space and to show pride in celebrating.

Gay events can provide a comfortable space that offers an opportunity to create a gay community or individual sexual identity.

Festival or event celebrations are important in all cultures as they provide an opportunity for the community to socialise and bond. They are also helpful in providing an opportunity for sharing different cultural beliefs. Furthermore, these events are gradually validated by both homosexuals and heterosexuals. Also, all the supporting services provided assist with further structural development in the tourism industry.

Specific festivals and events that attract gay and lesbian people provide clear evidence of the economic significance of gay tourism and cities are targeting the 'pink dollar'. Cities such as Amsterdam, Stockholm and Copenhagen actively promote LGBTQ rights, and this is illustrated by specific references to homosexual travellers within their tourism planning strategies. Furthermore, events such as the Gay Games, the Sydney Mardi Gras and the Eurovision Song Contest are well-known gay tourism events which are heavily promoted by the host cities (Vorobjovas-Pinta & Hardy, 2016). LGBTQ festivals and events act as a powerful driver for the international gay tourism industry and support the institutional apparatus of the tourism industry (Waitt & Markwell, 2014). LGBTQ festivals and events have the potential to transform both the attendee as well as the host community as they have social, economic and political transformative dimensions.

GSW in Queenstown, New Zealand

Queenstown's journey to becoming an internationally acclaimed four-season resort began with the support of New Zealanders who used it as a popular summer holiday destination. As better roads and facilities were developed the town became a picturesque overnight stop for coach tours and became a thriving winter ski resort when Coronet Peak opened in 1947. Today, with close to 2 million visitors per year, Queenstown is regarded as a tourist spot that strongly represents the beautiful landscape features of New Zealand, and the outdoor adventure and sport tourism in New Zealand. World-first innovations such as commercial jet boating and bungy jumping have forged Queenstown's enduring reputation as the 'Adventure Capital of the World' with a population of approximately 32,000 people.

The destination marketing organisation is working with the event organisers to host the annual GSW (with the new name Winter Pride Festival from August 2018). The festival encourages locals and visitors alike to come together and celebrate diversity. Most of the attendees are from Australia (45 percent) and New Zealand (45 percent). With 5,000+ Facebook followers and over 10,000 followers on Instagram the event organisers sell 4,500 tickets to the event annually with a number of attendees attending the free events during the week. GSW is an event in which gay people participate in leisure snow sports and experience wildlife and the natural environment.

The aim of the event is to celebrate love, community, diversity, visibility and inclusion. It is a festival that encourages 5,000 local residents and visitors alike to come together and celebrate their diversity.

Methods

The researcher conducted face-to-face interviews with 15 LGBTQ event attendees (Table 10.1) from Asia. Interviews were conducted in either Mandarin or in English, audio recorded with the interviewee's permission and manually transcribed by one of the authors before translation to English.

An inductive approach was used to analyse the transcriptions, which resulted in meta-thematic analysis and common themes being grouped together. The following upper-level categories were identified:

- Inclusive society
- Gay marriages
- Beautiful destination
- Inclusive community
- 'Family'
- Individuality
- Sexual identity
- Acceptance
- The event, and
- Sport

These are reported on in the following section.

Table 10.1 Research participants

Pseudonym	Age	Gender	Sexuality	Ethnicity	Current residence	Occupation
William	25–30	Male	Gay	Taiwanese	Australia	Designer
Yansen	30–35	Male	Gay	Malaysian	Australia	Graphic designer
Nix	25–30	Female	Bisexual	Chinese	New Zealand	Working holiday
Henry	25–30	Male	Gay	Chinese	New Zealand	Hospitality
Sam	30–35	Male	Gay	Asian	Australia	Manager
Tiger	30–35	Male	Gay	Chinese	Australia	IT manager
Iran	25–30	Male	Gay	Malaysian	New Zealand	Student
Tai	25–30	Male	Gay	Vientiane	Australia	Photographer
Jessy	25–30	Female	Lesbian	Chinese	New Zealand	Student
Prince	20–25	Male	Gay	Chinese	New Zealand	Graduating student
Eric	30–35	Male	Gay	Malaysian	New Zealand	Manager
Tama	20–25	Male	Gay	Thai	New Zealand	Waiter
Leo	25–30	Male	Gay	Chinese	New Zealand	Student
Skyr	25–30	Female	Lesbian	Taiwanese	New Zealand	Bartender
Tao	30–35	Male	Gay	Chinese	China	Businessman

Findings

According to our analysis, attendees felt a sense of transformation from being a marginalised individual to a well-rounded human being. From our analysis, it is clear that the inclusive New Zealand society (particularly Queenstown as host destination) and GSW played a transformative role.

Inclusive society

The 'gay space' permits gay people to feel comfortable and relax with others (Ersoy, Ozer & Tuzunkan, 2012). Gay people might go to a gay holiday destination that offers an intimate gay space and want to feel 'at home' when away from their hometown (Hughes, 1997). GSW could be seen as a safe space for the LGBTQ community to relax with like-minded people. Participants attended GSW because of their desire for a space to socialise with other gay people away from social constraints and intolerance, in a place with an open, gay-friendly, peaceful environment.

> It's a chance to out of the regular things, you know. You can have fun here, you can drink, and meet new people in that way.
> (Henry, 1 September 2016)

A similar view was provided by Tao:

> I'm here just looking around, see what it looks like, meet some new friends. This is very cool, people here is more open to the gay community, more friendly with it, compare with my home country ... I know a little about LGBTQ in New Zealand, but at least, now I know some, it's more gay-friendly, open, and people would love to go out to celebrate it.
> (Tao, 3 September 2016)

Gay marriage

One theme that was identified in the interviewees was legalisation of same-sex marriage in New Zealand. In May 2003, the Civil Union Bill was put before the New Zealand Government Cabinet and is legal since April 2005. The purpose of the bill was to provide for a civil union between same-sex couples. The government's primary objective was to provide a mechanism for same-sex couples to formalise their relationship and so provide legal recognition of a loving and committed relationship (Johnston & Longhurst, 2009).

A more open and friendly space for LGBTQ people provides an essential environment in which they can come out of the closet and be who they are, especially for visitors from countries in Asia and Africa, where LGBTQ members are still discriminated against. Additionally, the legalisation regarding same-sex marriage motivates LGBTQ people to confidently live with their sexual identity and build a family life with their partners as a family. For example:

> As far as I know about all of LGBTQ people around me, coming to New Zealand to be married is the most attractiveness to travel or look for a chance of living in New Zealand. The legalisation of same-sex marriage is a major factor of pulling LGBTQ people, in particular Asian LGBTQ people, to away from their home environment to travel or live in another country where provides a positive opportunity of living with their sexual identity.
>
> (Neo, 2 September 2016)

The importance of marriage was also mentioned by other participants:

> The GSW is one of a big thing, and doing better than before. People come here for gay marriage and seeing the view.
>
> (Henry, 1 September 2016)

> I actually don't know much about LGBTQ in New Zealand, but the only thing I knew is you can get married here. I think it's very good in New Zealand. Here is so welcome to gay people.
>
> (Tiger, 1 September 2016)

> I think LGBTQ in New Zealand is quite advanced. Maybe because of the legal same-sex marriage, so some people, like from Australia and Asian countries, they come to here celebrating their own pride. That's really good.
>
> (Iran, 1 September 2016)

The interviewees mentioned the legalisation of same-sex marriages in New Zealand as being an important element of their experience in the country. Private functions, such as LGBTQ weddings, might be an interesting market for Queenstown entrepreneurs to explore.

Beautiful destination

Previous research (Visser, 2003) suggested that urban space is important for LGBTQ communities; but according to Clift and Forrest (1999), as with heterosexual tourists, gay tourists place a high value on convenience, relaxation, sunshine and beautiful environment. Johnston (2006: p. 195) also states that 'queer tourism has prompted a flurry of critical attention and research that acknowledges and analyses gender and sexuality as key cultural constructs in the social construction of place, space and landscape'. Participants referred to the destination:

> Here is a beautiful place, so ... just beautiful - beautiful people, and nice activities.
>
> (Nix, 30 August 2016)

This is my first-time to travel in New Zealand. Here is so beautiful, and very nice. It's very relaxing to stay here.

(Tao, 3 September 2016)

Queenstown is fun, it's beautiful here. But, it's busy. However, if you drive likely an hour away from downtown, it's quiet, not many people around, it's peaceful.

(Yansen, 29 August 2016)

We found that, especially for LGBTQ tourists from China, where the harmonious relationship between members in society and the relationship between society and nature are increasingly important, respondents repeatedly referred to the natural beauty of the environment. Perhaps the natural environment has created a sense of enjoyment and relaxation that may lead to feelings of satisfaction with sexual identity, as is the case of tourism experiences outside the normal place of residence where the visitor will feel a sense of adventure and self-discovery.

Being part of an inclusive community

Both the social function and the symbolic meaning of a festival are closely related to a series of values that the community recognises as essential to its ideology and world view, its social identity, its historical continuity and its physical survival (Falassi, 1987). Queenstown is an inclusive community and has been a proud supporter of GSW since its inception in 2012. During 2018, Queenstown was nominated for a New Zealand LGBTQ award as a destination that promotes the LGBTQ community and where the LGBTQ members feel safe. LGBTQ festivals and events offer the opportunity to LGBTQ people to periodically come together at a destination to celebrate individual and collective identities of an imagined social community (Waitt & Markwell, 2014). Kelly et al. (2014) found that socialising with other LGBTQ people at events, such as a Pride event, was more likely to result in a memorable experience and a sense of being part of the LGBTQ community. One of the participants in our study mentioned that socialising with members of the gay community is especially relevant for gay Asian men:

Because of the conventional wisdom, the social judgement, and the non-friendly gay space, we prefer to hide within the regular life, instead of coming out to socialise with other gay people. Even more badly, some of us do not accept ourselves to be gay.

(Neo, 1 September, 2016)

In addition, 'meeting new people, talking to them, and make some new friends' was frequently mentioned by the interviewees. This reflects the view that, 'for Asian gay people, they hardly come out to participate in the gay community or LGBTQ events in their own countries'. However, with the growth of tourism out of Asia, the number of LGBTQ travellers will increase and they might return as friends. As one participant stated:

> The important thing for me is skiing and meeting some new friends. Because last year I was here alone, I was too shy to talk to other people at the beginning. But, this year I am back here with some of the friends I met from last year's GSW. It's very good. But, for myself, I think to engage in the gay festival makes me more like to talk, more keen to socialise with others.
>
> (Iran, 1 September 2016)

Leo and Eric shared similar views:

> It's a new experience for me, and also a chance to meet more gay people, or gay community members here.
>
> (Leo, 9 September 2016)

> This is a fun week, knowing people, meeting people, old friends and new friends. I wish I could have more time to spend with the people. However, I knew few good friends, so we can contact each other in the future. So that is good.
>
> (Eric, 9 September 2016)

'Family'

One of the iconic gay anthems is the 1979 Sister Sledge hit *'We are family' – all my Sisters and me*. Within the LGBTQ community members will often ask 'are you family?', meaning 'are you one of us' – a sense of family and community. Significantly, for Asian gay people, a sense of belonging is more necessary for them to feel part of the community because in their home country they are still disregarded. Many interviewees, particularly Chinese gay people, indicated that they were looking forward to more encouragement for the Asian gay community here:

> I think for Asian people, maybe do more social things here. But you know we have the language gaps; even if people can speak English, but for the further and deep conversations, they always have the language barriers. Maybe can have some language centre for supporting particular Asian gay people.
>
> (Nix, 30 August 2016)

> I think maybe they can encourage the Asian gay community to come here, to post and take the pictures of the Asian gay people already had been spent a really good time here, to attract more Asian gay people come.
>
> (Sam, 1 September 2016)

Because most of the Asian people always being shy. So, if Asian people found out about this event, they wouldn't go … maybe they would go, but they wouldn't have a lot of fun, honestly. So, I guess, if you really want to attract more Asian gay people, maybe do more like a party for Asian gay people particularly. You know there are seven days' events and have different themes every night; so probably would think about doing a particular one for Asian. Just make them enjoy the night, enjoy the whole event - they probably would think about to join other nights as well.

(Prince, 7 September 2016)

Individuality

The gay community can best be understood not as a unified subculture but rather as a category in which lesbians and gay men have developed collective identities, organised urban space and conceptualised their significant relationships (Weston, 2013). Often the LGBTQ tourist will be searching for these spaces and identities where they can feel interconnected through sexual identity and practices. As mentioned earlier there are still many countries, especially in Africa and Asia, which are not gay-friendly, where residents may even experience social constraints and intolerance.

During the interviews, participants suggested that it is not easy to be gay in Asia. The fear that family members will reject them leads many LGBTQ people to live a life of solitude and loneliness. Tourism can play a significant role in the well-being of such persons. It is now easier for travellers from Asia to travel to new destinations. They travel to unfamiliar places in search of a sexual identity that will make them happy. Most of the interviewees who have been living in overseas countries have blended into the local society and celebrate their identity with pride. Eric has lived in New Zealand for about eight years and was participating in GSW for the third or fourth time: first as a participant, then a volunteer. He is now trying to help more people come and enjoy the celebration, and takes pride in GSW:

I grew up in an Asian family, so I'm trying to open myself, trying to being who I am, to recognise and be happy being myself. So, I don't mind joining in the GSW, came out and celebrate the equality, the nature of humanity. And, as you can see, all of those people, gay people, lesbian people, they are very very respectful and understanding.

(Eric, 9 September 2016)

Sexual identity

Sexual identity itself may not be a biological problem, but more of a social construction located in particular historical contexts (Hughes, 1997). Eric's story reveals him living in a new place far from home and starting a new life being gay, which is a significant way to be oneself. Sexual experimentation in a variety of spatial contexts could be an important part of the process of coming out the closet for most interviewees.

Sexual identities are inherently bound up with the spaces. For most gay people who are denied space to be gay at home, looking for gay spaces to holiday at may provide a space to identify with other gay people in ways that may not be possible at home (Cox, 2002). As Nix said:

> I can see a lot of Chinese tourists here. For LGBTQ people, we get away from our own country - we don't have to hide anything anymore, free here and more open, you can just be who you are. I feel more comfortable and confident here, and I think I can get more confident to being myself after the gay events, even when I go back to China.
>
> (Nix, 30 August 2016)

As Nix's account reveals, it is the imagined distance between home and away that provides an opportunity to confidently feel able to take a 'risk' that is not easy to take at home. On the other hand, on returning home, they may feel the desire to make similar changes to their lifestyle at home. Away from home, the lower risk of being gay in a different country releases people from the restraints experienced at home.

Acceptance

The tensions of cultural, ideological and gender differences can be expressed through relatively mild joking relationships in public, while a shared language helps to develop mutual understanding at a more individual level (Pritchard, 2007). Some of the participants were overwhelmed by the acceptance they experienced, not only at GSW but also in New Zealand in general.

> From my view, comparing with all those aspects in China, New Zealand is more like a paradise for me. Without annoying judgements and social pressures, I can easily find out what I want to be. Also, after knowing some local gay friends, I realised people here do respect the differences, and the society is more compatible for new immigrations and I may plan my future development here.
>
> (Nix, 30 August 2016)

Most of the interviewees have been looking for acceptance through participation in LGBTQ festivals and events, and a connection with local LGBTQ communities. The different activities available during the holiday have a particular significance for gay people (Hughes, 2002). They enjoy their leisure time while on holiday by living, playing and interacting with other likeminded individuals, which provides an opportunity for Asian gay people to be gay and to validate their identity.

The event atmosphere

Being away from home at a holiday destination makes gay people feel relaxed and open to being who they are. Being in a party atmosphere and being exposed to a hedonistic life drive gay people to actively look for the pleasure and comfort of participating in the gay community (Clift & Forrest, 1999). Gay people desire to be as they are and to escape social censure, abuse or discrimination. A friendly gay space provides the opportunity for them to be gay; but the self-acceptance with which gay people openly interact with other gay people is more important and allows them to participate in the gay community with enjoyment.

> The self-enjoyment in the GSW activities is more important than others, particularly for us, Asian gay people … It's like people very curious about the gay group or LGBTQ group, and they are very friendly. That is very nice. And also, because I'm from China, it's not easy to be gay there, but in New Zealand here is more open - you can just be who you really are, being yourself, and you don't have to hide anything. Also, people here they treat you very friendly, makes you feel more confident and comfortable.
>
> (Nix, 30 August 2016)

Similar to Nix, most of the participants felt encouraged to participate in GSW activities and for them it was a way to celebrate their 'pride to be gay'. Some of them also acknowledged that the festival resulted in positive psychology and well-being, and a sense of transformation and self-acceptance. However, the festival has more to offer than just skiing. Local tour companies, restaurants, bars and clubs use their imagination during GSW to provide a gay-friendly atmosphere. Members of the LGBTQ community felt welcome and popular places of interest in the town were transformed with rainbow flags and posters. There was a general sense of a liberal attitude regarding homosexuality:

> I found out when I arrived in Queenstown, and one of my friends told me as well. And I knew there are something going to happen here, because I have seen a lot of guys hugging and kissing on the street. And, I thought OMG, why there are a lot of gay people here. And the rainbow flags in the town. So, I think, ok, yes, it is. This is cool. Before I came here, my friend told me about GSW, but we didn't decide to stay longer, but after I got here and saw these things about GSW, and I thought, ok, I am probably going to stay here a couple of nights.
>
> (Prince, 7 September 2016)

Sport

Traditionally, sport has been presented as an area of heteronormative masculinity (Waitt, 2003). But for LGBTQ people, sports activities like skiing and other mountain sports provide an opportunity to get close to the snow and mountains to enjoy outdoor activities:

> This winter season was the first time to try to ski. It was so exciting to experience a new sport that I have never done before. Moreover, I did not have a chance to do it when I was in my hometown in China, because where is located in a sub-tropical area. Skiing is not a very common sport for us. When I came to New Zealand, I was keeping looking forward to skiing.
>
> (Neo, 2016)

GSW provides a chance to not only associate with gay people in LGBTQ events but also be close to the snow and mountains for skiing. As with the second author's own experience, most of the interviewees first came to Queenstown to ski, and some even came from Australia. They were very excited to come to Queenstown for skiing. As two of the participants explained:

> Going to the skiing, enjoying the nature. It's not just about the party things. You get to do other things. Party for one or two nights, that's enough. I've been to Queenstown before, so I know what Queenstown looks like. With the event, I don't know, I've seen the advertisements before, like the Opening Party, the Pool Party. My expectation is always like the same, as a party is always a party. But, I think, the skiing is the most exciting thing, because I only skied once in Australia.
>
> (Yansen, 29 August 2016)

> Hmm, maybe the important thing is skiing, and meeting some new friends. And also enjoying being in a small town, taking a break and relaxing. Queenstown is a nice and beautiful place, and there are a lot of activities people can do here. And here it is very close to the mountains for skiing. So, it's a good place for GSW events, because one of main purposes of the GSW is skiing - so Queenstown is a good place. Also, there are many bars and night clubs: it's good for people having a party, drinking and have a lot of fun here. So, for skiing and parties, Queenstown is a good place.
>
> (Iran, 1 September 2016)

Conclusion

Previous research showcased Queenstown as an adventure destination for able white bodies. Our research suggest that things have changed in the last decade and that the inclusive society of Queenstown and New Zealand welcomes marginalised communities such as the LGBTQ community members from Asia. GSW is not as disruptive as suggested by previous researchers and our participants felt a sense of family, inclusivity within a beautiful environment. It is our view that GSW plays a pivotal role in the transformation of Queenstown as an inclusive destination.

Our research suggests that events such as GSW might have a transformative role to play in the lives of LGBTQ attendees from Asia. Participants referred to legal gay marriage and did not experience traces of social and sexual conservatism. The reason might be that as a discriminated group in other countries, these attendees from Asia might be feeling very relaxed and at home within the GSW community – a place where they can express their individuality and personality without the straitjacket of their home towns. An individual (in our case the Asian LGBTQ attendee) arrives at an event within a specific destination in a new society or country and departs as a transformed individual.

Mega sport events such as a World Cup or an Olympic Game can transform and unite a nation. The same might be true for small-scale events, such as GSW in Queenstown, where a small-scale sporting event can be a transformative tool. In this chapter we tried to showcase the transformative powers of a sporting event. The destination and the attendees were touched by the transformative power of an event and GSW is now a highlight on the events calendar of Queenstown, while the attendees feel less marginalised.

Diversity and managing diversity are critical dimensions for well-known tourist destinations to develop a market strategy to attract the LGBTQ community. Clearly, when tourism industries promote the gay imagining, it provides an opportunity for some gay people to come out of the closet and for others to celebrate their sexuality. Our research suggests that the Asian gay people who participated in GSW in Queenstown wanted more than the stereotypical 'bright lights and mirror balls'. They were seeking experiences and outstanding opportunities to be gay, to be associated with local LGBTQ communities and to enjoy themselves in the natural environment and the abundant outdoor activities.

References

Berezan, O., Raab, C., Krishen, A. S. & Love, C. (2015) Loyalty runs deeper than thread count: an exploratory study of gay guest preferences and hotelier perceptions. *Journal of Travel and Tourism Marketing.* 32 (8), 1034–1050.

Clift, S. & Forrest, S. (1999) Gay men and tourism: destinations and holiday motivations. *Tourism Management.* 20 (5), 615–625.

Clift, S. & Wilkins, J. (1995) Travel, sexual behaviour and gay men. In: Aggleton, P., Davies, P. & Hart, G. (eds.) *AIDS: safety, sexuality and risk.* London, Taylor and Francis, pp. 35–54.

Coon, D. R. (2012) Sun, sand, and citizenship: the marketing of gay tourism. *Journal of Homosexuality.* 59 (4), 511–534.

Cox, M. (2002) The long-haul out of the closet: the journey from smalltown to boystown. In: Clift, S., Luongo, M. & Callister, C. (eds.) *Gay tourism: culture, identity and sex.* London, Continuum, pp. 151–173.

Devall, W. (1979) Leisure and lifestyles among gay men: an exploratory essay. *International Review of Modern Sociology*. 9, 179–195.

Ersoy, G. K., Ozer, S. U. & Tuzunkan, D. (2012) Gay men and tourism: gay men's tourism perspectives and expectations. *Procedia-Social and Behavioural Science*. 41, 394–401.

Falassi, A. (1987) Festival: definition and morphology. In: Falassi, A. (ed.) *Time out of time: essays on the festival*. Albuquerque, University of New Mexico Press, pp. 1–10.

Frohlick, S. & Johnston, L. (2011) Naturalising bodies and places: tourism media campaigns and heterosexuality in Costa Rica and New Zealand. *Annals of Tourism Research*. 38 (3), 1090–1109.

Han, C. S., Proctor, K. & Choi, K. H. (2014) I know a lot of gay Asian men who are actually tops: managing and negotiating gay racial stigma. *Sexuality and Culture*. 18 (2), 219–234.

Hindle, P. (1994) Gay communities and gay space in the city. In: Whittle, S. (ed.) *The margins of the city: gay men's urban lives*. Arena, Aldershot, pp. 7–25.

Hughes, H. (1997) Holidays and homosexual identity. *Tourism Management*. 18 (1), 3–7.

Hughes, H. (2002) Gay men's holiday destination choice: a case of risk and avoidance. *International Journal of Tourism Research*. 4 (4), 299–312.

Hughes, H. L. (2003) Marketing gay tourism in Manchester: new market for urban tourism or destruction of 'gay space'? *Journal of Vacation Marketing*. 9 (2), 152–163.

Hughes, H. L. (2006) *Pink tourism: holidays of gay men and lesbians*. London, CABI.

Hughes, H. L., Clift, S., Luongo, M. & Callister, C. (2002) Gay men's holidays: identity and inhibitors. In: Clift, S., Luongo, M. & Callister, C. (eds.) *Gay tourism: culture, identity and sex*. London, Continuum, pp. 74–190.

Johnston, L. (2006) 'I do Down-Under': naturalizing landscapes and love through wedding tourism in New Zealand. *ACME: An International Journal for Critical Geographies*. 5 (2), 191–208.

Johnston, L. & Longhurst, R. (2009) *Space, place, and sex: geographies of sexualities*. Lanham, Rowman and Littlefield.

Kelly, B. C., Carpiano, R. M., Easterbrook, A. & Parsons, J. T. (2014) Exploring the gay community question: neighbourhood and network influences on the experience of community among urban gay men. *The Sociological Quarterly*. 55 (1), 23–48.

Liberato, P., Liberato, D., Abreu, A., Alén, E. & Rocha, Á. (2018) LGBT tourism: the competitiveness of the tourism destinations based on digital technology. In: Rocha, Á., Adeli, H., Reis, L. P. & Costanzo, S. (eds.) *Trends and advances in information systems and technologies*. Cham, Springer International Publishing, pp. 264–276.

Little, J. (2003) 'Riding the rural love train': heterosexuality and the rural community. *Sociologia Ruralis*. 43 (4), 401–417.

Monterrubio, J. C. (2008) Identity and sex: concurrent aspects of gay tourism. *Tourismos: An International Multidisciplinary Journal of Tourism*. 4 (2), 155–167.

Neville, S. & Adams, J. (2016) Views about HIV/STI and health promotion among gay and bisexual Chinese and South Asian men living in Auckland, New Zealand. *International Journal of Qualitative Studies on Health and Well-Being*. 11 (1), 30764. doi: 10.3402/qhw.v11.30764.

Phillips, R. S. (1995) Spaces of adventure and cultural politics of masculinity: RM Ballantyne and The Young Fur Traders. *Environment and Planning: Society and Space.* 13 (5), 591–608.

Pitts, B. G. (1999) Sports tourism and niche markets: identification and analysis of the growing lesbian and gay sports tourism industry. *Journal of Vacation Marketing.* 5 (1), 31–50.

Prayag, G., Disegna, M., Cohen, S. A. & Yan, H. (2015) Segmenting markets by bagged clustering: young Chinese travelers to Western Europe. *Journal of Travel Research.* 54 (2), 234–250.

Pritchard, A. (ed.) (2007) *Tourism and gender: embodiment, sensuality and experience.* London, CABI.

Pritchard, A., Morgan, N. J., Sedgley, D. & Jenkins, A. (1998) Reaching out to the gay tourist: opportunities and threats in an emerging market segment. *Tourism Management.* 19 (3), 273–282.

Pritchard, A., Morgan, N. J. & Sedgley, D. (2000) Exploring issues of space and sexuality in Manchester's gay village. In: Robinson, M. (ed.) *Expressions of culture, identity and meaning in tourism.* Newcastle, Centre for Travel and Tourism, University of Northumbria, pp. 225–238.

Stuber, M., Clift, S., Luongo, M. & Callister, C. (2002) Tourism marketing aimed at gay men and lesbians: a business perspective. In: Clift, S., Luongo, M. & Callister, C. (eds.) *Gay tourism: culture, identity and sex.* London, Continuum, pp. 88–124.

Sullivan, G. & Jackson, P. A. (2013) *Gay and lesbian Asia: culture, identity, community.* New York and London, Routledge.

Sun, M., Zhang, X. & Ryan, C. (2015) Perceiving tourist destination landscapes through Chinese eyes: the case of South Island, New Zealand. *Tourism Management.* 46, 582–595.

Visser, G. (2003) Gay men, tourism and urban space: reflections on Africa's 'gay capital'. *Tourism Geographies.* 5 (2), 168–189.

Vorobjovas-Pinta, O. & Hardy, A. (2016) The evolution of gay travel research. *International Journal of Tourism Research.* 18 (4), 409–416.

Waitt, G. (2003) Gay Games: performing 'community' out from the closet of the locker room. *Social and Cultural Geography.* 4 (2), 167–183.

Waitt, G. (2005) Sydney 2002 Gay Games and querying Australian national space. *Environment and Planning D: Society and Space.* 23 (3), 435–452.

Waitt, G. & Markwell, K. (2014) *Gay tourism: culture and context.* New York, Routledge.

Weston, K. (2013) *Families we choose: lesbians, gays, kinship.* New York, Columbia University Press.

Wilson, P. A. & Yoshikawa, H. (2004) Experiences of and responses to social discrimination among Asian and Pacific Islander gay men: Their relationship to HIV risk. *AIDS Education and Prevention.* 16 (1), 68–83.

Wong, C. C. L. & Tolkach, D. (2017) Travel preferences of Asian gay men. *Asia Pacific Journal of Tourism Research.* 22 (6), 579–591.

11 Barriers to access

Investigation of plus-size women consumer experiences at fashion events

Amanda Elliott and Rebecca Finkel

Introduction

There is a growing body of literature that suggests that plus-size consumers experience exclusion and stigmatisation from society (Carels et al., 2013; Nutter et al., 2016). The fashion industry in particular alienates plus-size women by offering them significantly fewer and less fashionable garments than thinner women, which reinforces society's assertion that 'the ideal consumer is a thin one' (Afful & Ricciardelli, 2015: p. 12). As fashion superstar Karl Lagerfeld of the Chanel design house famously stated, 'No one wants to see curvy women' (Gurrieri & Cherrier, 2013: p. 276). Along with the negative impacts that this prevalent sociocultural attitude has on plus-size consumers themselves, by underserving and marginalising the plus-size market, fashion retailers and event managers are potentially losing out financially as well (Tali, 2016). From a purely economic perspective, it would be beneficial to cater to bodies of all shapes and sizes; yet fashion and events both appear to have a strict limit in terms of sizes served. Fashion has been described by Williams, Laing and Frost (2014) as an ideal vehicle to investigate the relationships between events and society. Based on this relationship, it may be deduced that society's marginalisation of fat bodies has ramifications for fashion events.

The terms 'fat', 'fatness' and 'plus size' are used in this chapter because these terms are preferred by fat acceptance advocates and fat positive activists (Brown, 1989). This study uses the terms fat and plus size synonymously and interchangeably. A key argument against medicalised terms, such as 'obese', 'obesity' and 'overweight', is that they equate fatness with illness rather than treating fatness as a naturally occurring diversity (Dickins et al., 2011). These widely used terms are considered unsuitable as they contribute negatively to weight-based bias and further stigmatisation of fat people (Nutter et al., 2016).

A key problem with defining plus-size fashion is a lack of consistent terminology. Plus size as a term implies something larger than average. Smaller sizes that are not large enough to be called plus size are referred to as 'straight size'. This terminology stems from queer theory. Plus size represents the queer or aberrant, while straight size represents the normative (Gurrieri & Cherrier, 2013). This supports Saguy and Ward's (2011) assertion that straight sizes parallel with normative bodies and plus sizes parallel with so-called deviant bodies. In this context, deviant bodies are those that diverge from what society accepts as average, normal or ideal, and therefore this term is a synonym for fatness. In 2016, the American National Health and Nutritional Examination Survey determined that the average American woman wears a size 16–18, which is equivalent to a UK size 20–22. Thus, it is argued here that garments above the average size should be considered plus size, while garments below that average should be considered straight size. However, popular plus-size clothing brands cater to sizes much smaller than the average. What is perhaps unsurprising is the lack of consistency even among dedicated plus-size brands. For example, the smallest plus-size offered by ASOS Curve is an UK 18; Yours Clothing and Evans both are UK sizes 14+; while Simply Be consider strikingly small UK size 10 and upwards. The sizing is relatively more consistent among plus-size or curve model management agencies, although they are not without exception. Bridge Models state UK size 12+; BMA Models and MiLK Management all primarily represent curve models who wear UK sizes 12–18. The only two known exceptions to this size range are Olivia Campbell (represented by Bridge Models) and Tess Holliday (represented by MiLK Management), who wear UK sizes 22 and 26, respectively. For the purposes of this study, plus size is considered to be UK sizes 12–32+, which encompasses a broad range of this spectrum within the fashion industry (Christel, 2016).

This chapter focusses on those who identify as women because weight bias and stigmatisation disproportionately target women. Compared to other genders, women specifically are expected to adhere to rigid standards in terms of how they physically present themselves (Dickins et al., 2011). These gendered beauty standards are amplified by the fashion industry and, subsequently, by the plus-size fashion industry. Plus-size fashion in particular is a gendered issue because women are held to stricter body ideals of thinness than other genders, leading to disproportionate numbers of women investing tremendous amounts of energy to conform to those ideals (Fikkan & Rothblum, 2011). This, in effect, assigns hierarchical value to women's bodies, with thinness perceived as more attractive and morally superior.

Events are the primary mode for the dissemination of fashion and related body image messages. Fashion events, such as runway shows, fashion weeks, trade shows, fashion awards and ready-to-wear showcases, are the primary platforms for those in the fashion industry to set trends and establish prominence. For event venues, high-profile fashion events can bring glamorous reputation benefits as well as financial value. However, these event spaces are often exclusive and designed without considering the needs that various bodies may have (Imrie, 1998). Although most current event accessibility research focusses primarily on physical disability and wheelchair access (Van Der Wagen, 2007), there are additional physical barriers to be considered. It is also important to keep in mind that physical barriers are not the only elements blocking access for event attendees. Representation of only thin idealised bodies in event marketing materials or at the event itself also serves to prevent access and isolate potential plus-size event attendees (Afful & Ricciardelli, 2015). Lack of representation and similar, non-physical barriers are referred to as psychological barriers to access throughout this chapter.

Placed at the intersection of event accessibility research, fat studies and fashion event literature, this chapter explores the ways fashion events could become more accessible for plus-size women by investigating the existing physical and psychological barriers as well as evaluating plus-size consumer attitudes with regard to fashion events. A self-selecting sample of plus-size women who attended a fashion event in 2017 was surveyed via an online questionnaire. Participants were asked to document their experiences with access issues (both physical and psychological) and share their attitudes and feelings with regard to event experiences as a plus-sized consumer. This work is important for event managers to better understand and cater to the needs of plus-size women, who represent a growing portion of the population.

Stigma and fat identity

Previous studies across several fields of research have concluded that fat individuals are the targets of weight bias (also known as fat-hate, fatphobia[1] and fatmisia[2]) in many different areas, including the workplace (Fikkan & Rothblum, 2011), education (Rice, 2007), social and romantic relationships (Dickins et al., 2011), healthcare (Carels et al., 2013) and fashion (Wann, 2009). This stigmatisation manifests in many different forms. For example, within the medical industry, physicians are likely to provide unsolicited weight loss advice or to suggest weight loss by extreme measures such as bariatric surgery to fat women, even if their fatness is not limiting their health in any way (Carels et al., 2013). In the workplace, fat women are less likely to be hired as they are perceived by interviewers to be unreliable, undependable and unable to perform daily tasks (Fikkan & Rothblum, 2011). In education, elite universities and colleges are less likely to admit fat women based on similar assumptions that fat bodies are a result of personal lack of 'self control' and signify a 'weak' character (Rice, 2007).

Due to its patriarchal roots, anti-fat sentiment and stigma are aimed primarily at women (McHugh & Kasardo, 2011); fat women in particular do not fit within the patriarchal 'ideal' of what women should look like and present aesthetically. Thus, a hierarchy can be seen to exist based on weight. In modern Western societies like the United Kingdom and the United States, thin women benefit from privileges that make their lives far easier than those of their fat peers, such as being perceived as healthy, moral and high class based solely on their size (Fraser, 2009). In this context, thin women experience privilege through a vast array of social advantages (Donaghue & Clemitshaw, 2012). While fatness is equated with ugliness, thinness is equated with beauty (Gurrieri & Cherrier, 2013).

However, academics and activists assert that claiming fat as an identity can enable individuals to reclaim power and remove former shame and stigma (Nutter et al., 2016). Claiming the fat identity has been paralleled to coming out as a queer person. By coming out as fat, individuals repudiate society's thin beauty ideal (Gurrieri & Cherrier, 2013). Reclaiming terminology that has been used in hate speech is another parallel between fatness and queerness. Reclaiming the term 'fat' is considered empowering because it removes any previous sense of embarrassment, shame or guilt, and reframes the term as a neutral bodily descriptor, such as short or brunette (Dickins et al., 2011). Some individuals proceed one step further and use the term as a positive descriptor rather than as a neutral or negative one (Saguy & Ward, 2011). By claiming a fat identity and participating in fat spaces online, individuals can experience empowerment, increased social connectedness and improved mental and physical well-being (Dickins et al., 2011). This also is the case with fashion spaces, which traditionally ignore if not marginalise fat women; thus, there has been a surge of interest in plus-size fashion online. These fat-friendly online spaces highlight and celebrate fat women as stylish, beautiful and confident, which is not often how they are portrayed – if they are portrayed at all – in the mainstream world of fashion.

Thus, many diverse plus-size women have created their own spaces online in which they might participate in fashion. 'Fatshionistas' are those whose interest and participation in fashion or 'fatshion' (fat fashion) actively challenge the stereotype that fat people cannot be fashionable or attractive. Many fatshionistas run fatshion blogs where they share outfit photos and styling tips, and recommend places to shop for clothing (Gurrieri & Cherrier, 2013). Fatshion is recognised as a form of activism whose goal is to challenge the idealised feminine physique and to encourage those with marginalised bodies to participate in fashion as a means of liberation. For example, the Fatshion February initiative provides a space across social media platforms to emphasise that 'fat people are interested in fashion and need greater opportunities to find clothing that will fit them and designers that have their body sizes in mind' (Lupton, 2016: p. 5). The initiative was widespread around the world, and at the time of publishing, there are 6,065 public posts on Instagram utilising the #fatshionfebruary hashtag.

Fashion events

Since it first aired in 2009, the award-winning fashion competition television show *Project Runway* has been credited for increased public interest in and awareness of the fashion industry and subsequently fashion events (Marcketti, Lo & Gendle, 2009). Fashion-themed events may take many forms, such as fashion exhibitions in museums, runway events, product launches, fan events and fashion auctions (Williams, Laing & Frost, 2014). Fashion events play a vital role in fostering relationships between organisations and consumers. Because of this relationship, it is important for fashion event organisers to understand the needs of attendees. Fashion Week is a biannual fashion event that includes a vast programme of runway shows and is staged in New York, London, Paris and Milan. During each fashion week, the media turns their eyes to the respective host city to see the latest runway releases as well as street style trends. The host cities have been labelled the fashion capitals of the world due to their industrial ability to manufacture clothing and possession of the image and style required to promote fashion (Williams, Laing & Frost, 2014).

In her seminal book, Orbach (1978) highlights how the fashion industry both creates and enforces the fat-thin binary that positions thinness as aspirational. However, because modern trends in fashion are ephemeral, the industry must constantly transform to match what is currently on trend as well as what is socially conscious. This includes race, size, age and gender diversity. While great strides are being made towards diversity at Fashion Week, some host cities, designers and brands are fixed in their ways and seem reluctant to change. Milan has consistently hosted the least diverse Fashion Week and some brands, like Commes des Garçons, featured absolutely no models of colour (Tai, 2017). However, it is apparent that the fashion events industry is becoming less tolerant of those who are not diverse or inclusive. For example, James Scully, a prominent casting director in the fashion event industry, acted as a whistle-blower and named designers and brands that, like Commes des Garçons, preferred to only hire models who adhere to traditionally Eurocentric beauty standards (The Fashion Spot, 2017).

Fashion event accessibility

While some research has been carried out on physical event accessibility, much of the current literature concentrates on access solely in terms of physical disability (Van Der Wagen, 2007). From a legislative perspective, the European Union law states that fatness alone does not qualify as a disability and is therefore not protected under discrimination laws. However, fatness may be considered a disability if accompanied by physical limitations (Cathaoir, 2015). American legislation differs regarding fatness and disability; in 2008, the Americans with Disabilities Act (ADA) was broadened to include a greater scope of medical conditions. It is believed that under the revised ADA, fatness is considered a disability, which protects it from workplace discrimination (Shinall, 2016). However, even after the amendments to the ADA, it does not appear that fatness is considered a disability in America by default. Further contributing to inconclusiveness, a key study found that while there is correlation between fatness and disability, causation is not concrete. The study does not establish whether fatness causes disability, disability causes fatness or neither causes the other (Shinall, 2016).

One similarity between fatness and disability from a social perspective is that the deviant bodies involved are considered impaired and in need of repair (Rice, 2007). While both fat and disabled people experience harsh instances of discrimination, Fikkan and Rothblum (2011) found that discrimination is more prevalent for fat people. This mirrors Klaczynski, Daniel and Keller's (2009) findings that fat people are the most negatively stigmatised of any social group. Indeed, denying individuals physical access to the built environment further feeds stigma attached to deviant bodies (Imrie & Hall, 2001). Many public and private spaces have been designed and constructed without catering to bodily differences (Imrie, 1998). While this discussion of access is usually regarding physical disabilities, it can theoretically be applied to other bodily diversities such as physical size. As event management depends on the infrastructure of the host city, this is relevant to the events industry. Common infrastructural access issues include (but are not limited to) seating, stairs, lifts, ramps, transportation and toilets (Asmervik, 2002). These issues may be a potential risk for plus-size fashion event attendees with the addition of runways and staging if an event includes plus-size models, hosts or performers.

The experiences of living in a fat body in a world built for thin people not only have physical implications, but there are also psychological dimensions related to marginalisation. In their analysis on representation, Afful and Ricciardelli (2015) found that visibility and representation serve to normalise marginalised bodies, such as fat bodies. This normalisation has benefits for those who are marginalised as well as for those who are privileged. Repeated exposure to bodies that deviate from societal norms may have an impact on how those who read as having abnormal bodies are perceived, and it is argued that increased exposure to fat bodies in fashion media might result in a more positive perception of fat people (Oliver & Barnes, 1998). In a compelling study of varied body sizes in fashion media, Aagerup (2011) found that thin women identify with similarly thin models and dissociate from fat models. Perhaps unsurprisingly, he found that the converse is also true; fat women identify with similarly fat models and disconnect from thin models. Based on these findings, fashion brands create a psychological barrier when they use models in campaigns, runways and fashion media that do not reflect the brand's clientele. If consumers sense a disconnect between their looks or personality and that of the brand, then they will actively avoid the brand. Alternatively, if consumers sense a match, then they will develop a connection with and seek out that brand. This theory is referred to as self-image congruence, and it is applicable to the fashion industry (Aagerup, 2011). Additionally, both fat consumers and fashion brands can benefit from using larger models who represent their clientele. Seeing so-called deviant bodies similar to one's own may lead to self-acceptance, and therefore increased participation in self-expression via fashion (Gurrieri & Cherrier, 2013).

Research methods

This research utilised critical social theory to understand, analyse and criticise the structures and phenomena that oppress, dominate and exploit plus-size women within the context of fashion events. Quantitative approaches were adopted in the form of an online survey. Discussion of bodies can be an uncomfortable subject due to the stigma and shame often attached to them; therefore participants' comfort and well-being were considered paramount. As such, the research was approached from an ethics of care and acceptance (Bentz & Shapiro, 1998). When designing the survey questions, there was mindfulness of language used, such as of those terms referring to body size. This enabled the promotion of inclusiveness and avoidance of negative connotations, which also aided the elimination of the potential for bias (De Vaus, 2002).

Due to the nature of the research, potential respondents were required to meet three prerequisites for participation. To qualify, they must first identify as a woman, femme or nonbinary person who wears women's clothing. Second, they should wear plus-size clothing, which was defined as a UK women's size 12–32+ or international sizing equivalent. Finally, they must have attended at least one fashion event in 2017. All cases where these three criteria intersect make up the population for this study. The convenience form of non-probability sampling was used to compile data for this research. Respondents were primarily recruited online via the social networking site Twitter. The questionnaire comprised 15 questions of varying styles in order to achieve the highest quality and most thorough data possible. For questions regarding representation, motivation and consumer attitudes, a Likert-scale was used. These questions utilised a scale of five graded responses from strongly agree to strongly disagree, which has been shown to make questions more attractive to participants in order to improve response rates and reliability (Jupp, 2006). Open-ended questions provided an opportunity to expound about context and provide more qualitative insight into the research narrative. The online survey received a total of 47 responses via Google Forms, and 43 usable responses were admitted. Quantitative data were analysed using Google tools, and qualitative data were coded and meanings were derived by applying thematic analysis. This comprises a snapshot of plus-sized women's experiences at fashion events in order to provide insight into key themes and issues.

Findings and discussion

The results from this research focussed on physical and psychological barriers to access fashion events by plus-size women as well as their attitudes as consumers regarding both the fashion industry and fashion event managers. As Williams, Laing and Frost (2014) state, fashion events may take many forms; therefore participants were asked to document what types of fashion events they attended. The different events attended may identify or imply different motives for attendance, which is valuable knowledge for event managers. It was found that the most-attended type of event was consumer buying shows, which represented 38.6 percent of all events attended. Most events were named only once, but there were two events that were repeatedly identified: Simply Be's The Curve Catwalk during London Fashion Week, and The Curve Fashion Festival.

Event facilities are a crucial point of consideration for the majority of potential plus-size event goers, and 83.7 percent of respondents agreed or strongly agreed that they are more likely to attend a fashion event if they believe the event facilities will meet their needs as a plus-size consumer. In terms of plus-size consumer satisfaction with the event's facilities, 51.2 percent of respondents agreed or strongly agreed that event facilities met their needs as a plus-size consumer; however, it is still worth noting that respondents who selected neutral, disagree or strongly disagree represent 48.9 percent of all participants.

While the majority of respondents were satisfied with the facilities, there is still a considerable amount of room for improvement. For example, a recurrent theme in response to the question, 'In what ways can fashion events become more accessible for plus-size women?', was that seating is the greatest physical barrier to access for participants. While the majority commented that seating was an obstacle, several different issues were made regarding seating in general. A few respondents noted that seating was minimal throughout most event venues, which can be problematic when guests are standing for long periods of time. A couple of respondents recalled that the chairs provided were too poor quality to support fat bodies. One participant mentioned cheap plastic chairs and another mentioned low-quality folding chairs. Both of these participants expressed fear of the seats buckling under them and felt they had no choice but to avoid sitting entirely. Another recurrent issue was the size of chairs. A third of respondents described how the chairs were uncomfortably small and positioned too close together. They used words like 'cramped' and 'squished' to express their discomfort with event seating. These were not the only instances of discomfort noted regarding chairs. Many participants described how seats with arms are not acceptable for plus-size consumers. Some participants who mentioned chairs with arms described how uncomfortable and painful the chairs are, and how forcing their bodies into the chairs often led to soreness and bruising of their hips and thighs. Others described how they simply could not fit into armed chairs, so they were unable to be seated at all.

Seating was the most frequently occurring concern regarding physical access, but it was by no means the only one mentioned. Respondents also indicated that walkways, particularly those between rows of chairs, were very tight. A few respondents also described how toilets were 'very small' and 'uncomfortable'. This may be an example of a gendered access issue, as women's toilets exclusively utilise restrictive cubicles. The presence of menstrual waste receptacles further limits the amount of space within cubicles in women's toilets. Another respondent described a beach themed party that featured sand floors. This made walking difficult for those who were able and wheelchair access completely impossible.

In terms of psychological barriers, results found that 93 percent of events attended by research respondents featured models, yet only 63.4 percent of those events featured plus-size models. However, even when plus-size models were present, they still were found to adhere to traditionally conventional beauty standards. The plus-size models reported were still tall, toned and tended to have an hourglass shape. Participants discussed how plus-size models represent a 'perfect', 'ideal', 'curvy', 'sexy' standard that the average fat woman may not be able to live up to. Specific physical characteristics that were represented by the audience, but not the models, were recorded by survey participants. These characteristics included large bellies, double chins, stretch marks, shortness and small bums and breasts. This is perhaps unsurprising because plus-size modelling agencies primarily represent models on the lowest end of the plus-size spectrum, and to be hired as models these women need to conform to conventional beauty standards.

A key issue that was expressed was a lack of women of colour represented by the models. Furthermore, when models of different racial and ethnic backgrounds were present, they were mostly very light in skin tone. While it was not explicitly discussed in the literature, perhaps it should have been foreseen. If both fat people and non-white people are the targets of social inequity (Nutter et al., 2016), then it follows that people existing at the intersection of fatness and non-whiteness would be under-represented at these kinds of events. The paucity of scholarly studies and industry-focussed attention to these issues suggests there is opportunity for future research to provide more in-depth information about the diversity of lived experiences.

Consumer intentions to attend fashion events highlight that all but six research participants agree or strongly agree that they are more likely to attend a fashion event if they know that plus-size bodies will be represented by the models. Representation is clearly of paramount importance regarding most participants' intention to spend, and, therefore, it is argued that fashion event managers should cease using exclusively thin, aspirational models (Orbach, 1978) and begin using diverse models in all senses of the word. Perpetuating the psychological barriers to accessing fashion events for plus-size consumers only exacerbates the fat-thin binary which serves to isolate fat women (Wann, 2009). It is unlikely that fat women will want to attend events hosted by a brand that makes them feel unrepresented. As Leischnig, Schwertfeger and Geigenmueller (2011) concluded, fashion events have the potential to have a positive impact on the relationship between brand and consumer. However, the converse may also be true, and this psychological barrier to access could have a negative impact on that relationship.

A lack of plus-size representation in promotional materials is another psychological barrier to access for plus-size women at fashion events; for example, it is often the case that no plus-size women are visibly featured in fashion event marketing campaigns. If women sense a disconnect between their appearance or personality and that of the brand, then they are likely to distance themselves from that particular brand (Aagerup, 2011). Based on the findings from the current study, fashion event managers should be particularly intentional when designing the visual media for advertising campaigns. This was also found to be the case with regard to the fashion industry as a whole. An overwhelming majority (86.1 percent) of respondents stated that they do not see bodies like theirs represented within the fashion industry. These results support Orbach's (1978) assertion that plus-size women are not represented because the fashion industry does not consider their body type to be aspirational. By not representing more varying body types, designers, brands and media organisations within the fashion industry are isolating potential clients and customers. If these organisations diversified the portfolio of bodies they featured, a greater number of women may relate to them and become loyal to those brands.

Some survey respondents stated that they only feel represented at fashion events within the plus-size community. One respondent said that they 'only see images of those with a similar body type to [theirs] on Instagram and tumblr, not in the mainstream fashion industry'. Similarly, another participant said their body type is 'only represented by bloggers'. This suggests that fat women feel more valued and visible when co-creating their own fashion content in their own online spaces. By posting photos online, fatshion bloggers and fatshionistas create a sort of vigilante representation to make up for the lack of representation within the mainstream fashion industry (Gurrieri & Cherrier, 2013). Given the societal stigma, it is understandable that fat women would turn to a community of others with similar experiences. These safe spaces online allow them to create their own representation when it is lacking within the fashion industry.

With regard to fashion event managers specifically, only 27.9 percent of respondents agree or strongly agree that fashion event managers anticipate, understand and cater to the needs of plus-size consumers. The majority expressed that plus-size consumers are not seen to be a priority. One respondent said, 'the needs of plus-size consumers are totally ignored, and usually not even acknowledged in most cases'. Another participant said that fashion event managers 'only cater to their "usual" audience of thin folks'. This is, once again, likely caused by the fat-thin binary which isolates fat women in social settings, including fashion (Wann, 2009). Aligned with this, a comment from one participant mentioned how they had, 'never attended an event where plus-size women were a consideration'. Another participant noted that fashion event managers 'explicitly avoid us and discourage us from inclusion', where 'us' refers to plus-size consumers. For example, physical barriers illustrate that plus-size needs are not often considered by event management. One respondent explained that this may be the case because 'plus-size in the mainstream is a fairly new concept' and, therefore, most event managers are not in the habit of remembering that different bodies have different needs.

Conclusions and recommendations

This chapter has investigated the physical and psychological barriers to access for plus-size women at fashion events. Findings concurred with Asmervik (2002), who found that seating, toilets and wheelchair access were all threats to physical access, with seating being the most frequently occurring complaint. An overwhelming majority of participants (83.7 percent) agreed that they are more likely to attend a fashion event if they believe the event facilities will meet their needs as a plus-size consumer. This research also concurred with Griffiths (2017), who asserted that fashion events can often leave attendees feeling under-represented or unrepresented, which is a significant psychological barrier to participation. Larger or fatter bodies, non-hourglass-shaped bodies and large stomachs were the three most common characteristics which respondents stated were not represented in promotional materials or by models at events. A clear majority (86 percent) of respondents indicated that they are more likely to attend a fashion event if they know that plus-size bodies will be represented by the models. Similarly, the overwhelming majority (88.4 percent) of respondents are more likely to attend a fashion event if they have seen plus-size bodies represented in promotional materials. Additionally, research data indicated that few (9.3 percent) participants felt that their body is well represented within the fashion industry. Over half of the respondents (51.7 percent) felt that plus-size women are rarely represented within the fashion industry, and when they are represented, it is still an unrealistic representation. Several (13.8 percent) respondents noted that this may be because plus-size models are not representative of most plus-size consumers, and other respondents (13.8 percent) shared that only plus-size women with hourglass-shaped bodies are visible within the fashion industry.

Regarding consumer attitudes towards event managers, only 27.9 percent of respondents felt that fashion event managers anticipate, understand and cater to the needs of plus-size consumers. Almost half of participants (46.6 percent) disagreed and discussed several ways they feel let down by event managers. The most commonly reported issue (42.1 percent) is that plus-size consumers feel like they are not a priority for event managers. Given that consumer attitudes towards fashion event managers were mainly negative, it is evident that there is still much room for improvement. Therefore, in order to appeal to wider audiences in order to develop more inclusive and diverse event experiences, it is recommended that fashion event managers should be more mindful in featuring models of varying sizes and include more diversity in promotional materials and on runways. While event managers may have less control over diverse bodies at designer or brand product launches, they should make an effort to invite plus-size brands to fashion events rather than inviting brands that exclude plus sizes. Additionally, event managers should consider avoiding low-quality chairs and chairs with arms. If for any reason this is not possible, then alternative plus-size friendly seating options should be available as a contingency. Should an attendee request this seating accommodation, event staff should be thoroughly trained to be sensitive and compassionate in order to assist the guest effectively and without judgement.

This research has made a unique contribution to knowledge by synthesising event accessibility research, fat studies and fashion event literature. While these schools of thought are all established in their own right, more work needs to be carried out at their nexus. Indeed, there is a necessity for further research with larger sample sizes and more voices to share the breadth and depth of lived experiences. Both the literature and questionnaire data named several specific events which might also be analysed in the future for in-depth case studies, such as The Curve Fashion Festival. Although it was not mentioned in the literature, the issue of photo editing software such as Photoshop was mentioned on multiple occasions by survey participants. There is scope for further research on this topic, and future studies on psychological barriers to access at events may want to include this as a point of discussion. For example, if stretch marks, cellulite and double chins are not visible on plus-size models in advertising, then what role does Photoshop play in limiting psychological access? As more research is conducted in this area, it has the potential to improve understanding and inclusivity by providing more insight to combat stigma and promote greater accessibility in practice.

Notes

1 Fatphobia does not connote a fear of fat people; rather, it describes the acts of being harmful/hateful to fat people and treating them as deviant in society.
2 Fatmisia refers to biased behaviour targeting fat people.

References

Aagerup, U. (2011) The influence of real women in advertising on mass market fashion brand perception. *Journal of Fashion Marketing and Management*. 14 (4), 1361–2026.

Afful, A. A. & Ricciardelli, R. (2015) Shaping the online fat acceptance movement: talking about body image and beauty standards. *Journal of Gender Studies*. 24 (1), 1–12.

Asmervik, S. (2002) Cities, buildings and parks for everyone, a universal design compendium. In: Christophersen, J. (ed.) *Universal design*. Drammen, Husbanken, pp. 43–57.

Bentz, V. M. & Shapiro, J. J. (1998) *Mindful inquiry in social research*. London, Sage Publications.

Brown, L. S. (1989) Fat-oppressive attitudes and the feminist therapist. *Women and Therapy*. 8 (3), 19–30.

Carels, R. A., Burmeister, J., Oehlhof, M. W., Hinman, N., Leroy, M., Bannon, E., Koball, A. & Ashrafioun, L. (2013) Internalised weight bias: ratings of the self, normal weight, and obese individuals and psychological maladjustment. *Journal of Behavioural Medicine*. 36, 86–94.

Cathaoir, K. Ó. (2015) On obesity as a disability. *European Journal of Risk Regulation: EJRR*. 6 (1), 145–150.

Christel, D. A. (2016) Average American women's clothing size: comparing national health and nutritional examination surveys (1988–2010) to ASTM international misses & women's plus size clothing. *International Journal of Fashion Design, Technology and Education*. 10 (2), 129–136.

De Vaus, D. A. (2002) *Surveys in social research*. (5th ed.). London, UCL Press.

Dickins, M., Thomas, S. L., King, B., Lewis, S. & Holland, K. (2011) The role of the fatosphere in fat adults' responses to obesity stigma: a model of empowerment without a focus on weight loss. *Qualitative Health Research*. 21 (12), 1679–1691.

Donaghue, N. & Clemitshaw, A. (2012) 'I'm totally smart and a feminist... and yet I want to be a waif': exploring ambivalence towards the thin ideal within the fat acceptance movement. *Women's Studies International Forum*. 35, 415–425.

Fikkan, J. L. & Rothblum, E. D. (2011) Is fat a feminist issue? Exploring the gendered nature of weight bias. *Sex Roles*. 66 (9–10), 575–592.

Fraser, L. (2009) The inner corset: a brief history of fat in the United States. In: Rothblum, E. & Solovay, S. (eds.) *The fat studies reader*. New York, New York University Press, pp. 11–14.

Griffiths, S. (2017) *Where were we, simply be?* Available from: http://shemightbe.co.uk/where-were-we-simply-be/ [Accessed 14th July 2018].

Gurrieri, L. & Cherrier, H. (2013) Queering beauty: fashionistas in the fatosphere. *Qualitative Market Research International Journal*. 16 (3), 276–295.

Imrie, R. (1998) Oppression, disability and access in the built environment. In: Shakespeare, T. (ed.) *The disability reader*. London, Cassel, pp. 129–146.

Imrie, R. & Hall, P. (2001) *Inclusive design: designing and developing accessible environments*. London, Spon Press.

Jupp, V. (ed.) (2006) *The Sage dictionary of social research methods*. London, Sage Publications.

Klaczynski, P., Daniel, D. B. & Keller, P. S. (2009) Appearance idealisation, body esteem, casual attributions, and ethnic variations in the development of obesity stereotypes. *Journal of Applied Developmental Psychology*. 30, 537–551.

Leischnig, A., Schwertfeger, M. & Geigenmueller, A. (2011) Do shopping events promote retail brands? *International Journal of Retail and Distribution Management*. 39 (8), 619–634.

Lupton, D. (2016) Digital media and body weight, shape, and size: an introduction and review. *Fat Studies*. 6 (2), 1–16.

Marcketti, S. B., Lo, Y. & Gendle, N. S. (2009) Iowa State University fashion show: why do they attend? *Journal of Family and Consumer Sciences*. 101 (4), 49–50.

McHugh, M. C. & Kasardo, A. E. (2011) Anti-fat prejudice: the role of psychology in explication, education and eradication. *Sex Roles*. 66, 617–627.

Nutter, S., Russell-Mayhew, S., Alberga, A. S., Arthur, N., Kassan, A., Lund, D. E., Sesma-Vazquez, M. & Williams, E. (2016) Positioning of weight bias: moving towards social justice. *Journal of Obesity*. 2016, 1–10.

Oliver, M. & Barnes, C. (1998) *Disabled people and social policy: from exclusion to inclusion.* London, Longman.

Orbach, S. (1978) *Fat is a feminist issue.* London, Penguin.

Rice, C. (2007) Becoming 'the fat girl': acquisition of an unfit identity. *Women's Studies International Forum.* 30, 158–174.

Saguy, A. C. & Ward, A. (2011) Coming out as fat: rethinking fat stigma. *Social Psychology Quarterly.* 74 (1), 53–75.

Shinall, J. B. (2016) Distaste or disability? Evaluating the legal framework for protecting obese workers. *Berkeley Journal of Employment and Labor Law.* 37 (1), 101.

Tai, C. (2017) *Diversity report: landmark gains for nonwhite, transgender, and plus-size models on the Spring 2018 runways.* Available from: http://www.thefashion spot.com/runway-news/768143-runway-diversity-report-spring-2018/#05SpkU auDZTsmXrl.99 [Accessed 14th July 2018].

Tali, D. (2016) The 'average' woman is now size 16 or 18. Why do retailers keep failing her? Available from: https:// www.forbes.com/sites/didemtali/2016/09/30/ the-average-woman-size/#78453c3c2791. [Accessed 10th June 2018].

The Fashion Spot (2017) *Report: Fall 2017 was a banner season for runway diversity, especially in New York.* Available from: http://www.thefashionspot.com/runway-news/740117-runway-diversity-report- fall-2017/ [Accessed 18th July 2018].

Van Der Wagen, L. (2007) *Event management: for tourism, cultural, business and sporting events.* (3rd ed.). New South Wales, Pearson.

Wann, M. (2009) Foreword: fat studies: an invitation to revolution. In: Rothblum, E. & Solovay, S. (eds.) *The fat studies reader.* New York, New York University Press, pp. ix–xxv.

Williams, K. M., Laing, J. & Frost, W. (2014) Social conformity or radical chic? In: Williams, K. M., Laing, J. & Frost, W. (eds.). *Fashion, design and events.* Oxon, Routledge, pp. 1–23.

12 Creating safe space in a hostile place

Exploring the Marathon of Afghanistan through the lens of safe space

Madeleine Orr and Anna Baeth

Introduction

> This event allowed us to be in the public commons and be involved in changing the social standards for other women who will come after us.
>
> (Participant 2)

Afghanistan is a country afflicted by protracted political conflict, recurrent natural disasters and intractable economic inequality (Wily, 2004). Until 2001, the Taliban, a jihadist military group, controlled the country, imposing strict religious laws and restrictions on women and girls' participation in public life (Ahmed-Ghosh, 2003). Nearly 20 years after the fall of the Taliban, women have experienced some advancement in the way of access to politics, education and employment; however cultural restrictions and expectations continue to hinder full participation in public life and freedom of movement (Mehta, 2002; Alvi-Aziz, 2008; Billaud, 2015). For example, Bamyan Province was the first to have a female Governor, Dr Habiba Sarabi, appointed in 2005. Education has also advanced; elementary education is now free nationwide, and enrolment in high school is increasing. However, there continues to be more male students than female in schools, given the pressure for girls to participate in domestic tasks and child-rearing.

Afghanistan is frequently promoted in feminist literature as a prime testing ground for social interventions as it lies at the crossroads of Islamic fundamentalism and Westernisation (Mehta, 2002; Ahmed-Ghosh, 2003), which promises opportunities for women's empowerment and advancement. Notably, sport has been an unsuspecting force in the Afghan women's movement, being used as a vehicle for development and peace since the fall of the Taliban (Thorpe & Rinehart, 2012). One example includes the introduction of school volleyball teams for the improved confidence and self-esteem of young women (VanSickle, 2012). In the capital, Kabul, a non-governmental organisation (NGO) called Skateistan was founded in 2006 to introduce young people to the action sport of skateboarding as a means of social capital building and community development (Thorpe & Rinehart, 2012). Most recently, sport organisations and non-profits have partnered to use sport as a means for eliminating or reducing restrictions on the movement of women in public spaces (VanSickle, 2012).

In the following sections, we unpack the theories of sport for development (SFD) and safe space in sport. We present the case of the Marathon of Afghanistan (MOA), the country's first coed sporting event and illustrate how safe space was cultivated in and through this event. Next, we discuss the applicability of the merged safe space framework for different sport contexts. Finally, we conclude the chapter with the implications of this research within the disciplines of sport sociology, sport management, event management, tourism and anthropology.

Literature

Sport for development

Within the last decade, SFD has received significant attention from practitioners and sport scholars alike (Schulenkorf, Sherry & Rowe, 2016). However, SFD has been wholly under-theorised within the literature (Skinner, Zakus & Cowell, 2008; Darnell, 2012; Schulenkorf, Sherry & Rowe, 2016). In 2016, SFD research was synthesised and rigorously reviewed by Schulenkorf, Sherry and Rowe (2016). They found a majority of the literature on SFD to be focussed at the community level by sport management (Frisby & Millar, 2002; Kellett, Hede & Chalip, 2008; Schulenkorf & Edwards, 2012) and event management scholars (Mair & Whitford 2013), resulting in a strong contextual understanding of SFD but an ambiguous conceptual framework for SFD.

Hartmann and Kwauk (2011) argue that the 'multiplicity and ambiguity' around development make theorisation around SFD challenging: 'development can refer to something as philosophical as the progress of humankind or as practical as the social engineering of emerging nations' (p. 286). Because SFD is interpreted differently depending on the location, culture and peoples involved in the development project, no two cases will be the same, and thus SFD must be redefined within each new context.

For the purposes of this chapter, SFD will be defined as the 'use of sport to exert a positive influence on public health, the socialisation of children, youths and adults, the social inclusion of the disadvantaged, the economic development of regions and states, and on fostering intercultural exchange and conflict resolution' (Lyras & Welty Peachey, 2011: p. 311). Notably, virtually all scholars agree that positive outcomes from sport, and sport events, are not automatically bestowed (Spaaij & Schulenkorf, 2014). Rather, they must be planned for and managed (Coakley, 2011; Darnell, 2012; Schulenkorf, Sherry & Rowe, 2016).

Safe space theory

One emerging component of SFD is that of 'safe space' (Brady, 2005). The term safe space was first used consistently in the United States during the women's movement of the 1960s, where safety meant distance from patriarchal thought and was used to describe consciousness-raising groups (Kenney, 2001). Safe space, according to Kenney, 'in the women's movement, was a means rather than an end and not only a physical space but a space created by the coming together of women searching for community' (2001: p. 7). In 1976, French theorist Michel Foucault developed a multidisciplinary understanding of power and safe spaces as components of everyday relationships: 'Power is not something that is acquired, seized, or shared, something that one holds on to or allows to slip away... power is exercised from innumerable points, in the interplay of...mobile relations' (Foucault, 1976: p. 94). Power and, in turn, safety, Foucault argued, were predicated on relationships. This conceptualisation of power had

> profound practical implications: [as people are now] responsible for the ways in which [they] reproduce existing power relations at their most micro levels. A space isn't "safe" just because everyone is committed to the same movement. The dominant power relations still find their way into the room.
>
> (Harris, 2015: p. 3)

Of late, individuals, organisations and institutions have adopted safe space as a way to dissipate dominant power relations and embody the social changes they want to see in the world (Harris, 2015).

Much like SFD, safe space is 'still contested and underdeveloped', making it applicable (and researchable) only within specific contexts (Spaaij & Schulenkorf, 2014: p. 3). In the case of the MOA, Spaaij and Schulenkorf's (2014) definition of safe space as a multidimensional, figurative space constructed through social relationships will be used. They envisaged five primary dimensions of safe space, each interconnected with the others, defined and contextualised within Afghani culture in the following section.

Political safe space

The political dimension of safe space is: 'sharing a sense of community, where people feel less inhibited and more supported to share their experiences or views and to express their sporting and other identities' (Spaaij & Schulenkorf, 2014: p. 6). A politically safe sporting space is perceived to be neutral from political and social conflict and may include the support of varying political, military and religious figures, as well as coaches, teachers and community leaders (Stidder & Haasner, 2007). To date, Bamyan has often been considered one of the – if not the – safest provinces in Afghanistan, given its remote location; its historically Buddhist ties; and the political opposition of the dominant local tribe, the Hazara, to the Taliban (Donati, 2012). In 2011, Bamyan was the first province in Afghanistan to have NATO security removed and instead, put in the hands of regional police officers, all of whom were locally recruited (Graham-Harrison, 2013).

Sociocultural safe space

A goal of 'familiarity: such that the people, practices and relations that exist within a safe space are comfortable and familiar' (Hunter, 2008: p. 8) is what Spaaij and Schulenkorf (2014) call the sociocultural dimension of safe space (p. 6). This dimension encompasses a 'notion of cultural safety, which promotes environments "where there is no assault, challenge or denial of [a person's] identity, of who they are and what they need" (Williams, 1999: p. 213)' (p. 6). Particular to Afghanistan, an analogous liberation of women coincided with the defeat of the Taliban (Rostami-Povey, 2007). Despite extremely repressive conditions under Taliban rule, women were able to exercise certain methods of autonomy and agency, practices that have carried over into current Afghani culture. Unlike Western cultures, women in Afghanistan view gender as (somewhat) fluid and tied intimately to faith. In several communities in Afghanistan, women were able to 'negotiate gender in different forms and... sometimes find themselves in positions of domination, able to exercise power within the family and community as well as subordination' (Rostami-Povey, 2007: p. 6). One exemplar of this domination was when women would employ men to play the role of mahram (the practice of women being accompanied by men in public) for them. In employing men, they were then able to behave in a non-submissive way. This cooperation between certain men and women in mahram allowed those against the Taliban to survive by publicly displaying the submission of a woman to men in front of the pro-Taliban community members. Even in the most unsafe of times under Taliban rule, women created their own sociocultural safety by using traditional Afghani culture to their advantage.

Physical safe space

The physical dimension of safe space includes a place that is accessible, accommodating and physically safe. Physical safety in Afghanistan is perhaps the most difficult dimension to attain as Afghanistan currently ranks the second least peaceful country in the world according to the Global Peace Index. In 2016, 69.8 percent of Afghanis reported that they sometimes, often or always felt fear for their personal safety, the highest level in over a decade (The Institute for Economics and Peace, 2017). Ground conflicts (primarily with the Taliban) count for the highest percentage of injuries and deaths in Afghanistan (UNAMA, 2017). Further, in 2017 there was a 23 percent increase in casualties of women and a 9 percent increase in the deaths of children in Afghanistan (UNAMA, 2017). High-profile attacks by suicide bombers are particularly prevalent in Kabul and are often planned in advance by the Taliban (US Department of State, 2017).

Psychological safe space

The psychological dimension refers to protection from psychological or emotional harm and is typically concerned with the establishment of trust, a sense of engagement and a common identity. Identities in Afghanistan are contentious. While more young people feel connected to their country than ever before, many find themselves drawn to the same regional traditions and ethnic politics that defined the lives of their parents (Dupree, 2002).

> In the heady days after the 2001 international intervention... nearly everyone was connected by mobile phones, and Afghan media— virtually non-existent during the years of Taliban rule—came into its own. Women entered the workforce in numbers not seen since the days of communist rule... private schools and universities opened, and government-funded schools also expanded, with more girls attending.
>
> (Gossman, 2017: p. 5)

Despite these social changes, trust and common identity among Afghan people have been difficult to establish and maintain in recent years.

Experimental safe space

The fifth dimension of safe space proffered by Spaaij and Schulenkorf (2014) is experimental safe space, which is most closely aligned with the aforementioned definition of SFD. One understanding of safe space as a site of innovation comes from Hunter (2008), who 'argues that the experimentation encouraged... within a safe space is "a product of the dynamic tension between known (safe) processes and unknown (risky) outcomes"' (Spaaij & Schulenkorf, 2014: p. 7). The shared belief, according to Edmondson (1999), by members of a group that the group is safe, allows for interpersonal risk-taking. It is this tension between group safety and interpersonal risk that allows for transformation social change. Experimental safe space, however, is not possible without strong relationships between group members and, more importantly, strong communication. As several peace and conflict scholars note, transformative social change requires collective communication and action amongst a group (Lederach, 2005).

Case and context

A case study of the MOA in the Bamyan Province was conducted to understand how sport managers create safe space during the event management process.

A brief introduction to Bamyan, Afghanistan

Bamyan Province is located in the heart of the country along the Hindu Kush range between 2,000 and 3,000 meters above sea level. Bamyan, which translates to 'the place of shining light' in Persian (Central Statistics Organization, 2013), is comprised of seven administrative districts, 500,000 people and around 2,000 villages (Wily, 2004). The precise demographics of the region are unclear as the population has been in flux over the past several decades and agencies use different boundaries to delineate villages.

The province is ethnically diverse, with the largest ethnic group being the Hazara people, followed by Sadats and Sayeeds which are two significant majorities. The Hazara people are Imami Shi'a,[1] a strong distinction from the non-Hazaras in the province (who adhere to Sunni[2]), the source of much conflict. Many different languages are spoken in the region, and the number has increased in the last decade as families and social groups return from their exile during the Taliban rule (Wily, 2004). Economically, the vast majority of Bamyan residents earn their keep as farmers. Supplementary economic activities include spinning and weaving and the trade of qurut (dried milk curds) and leather (Mousavi, 1998). Despite the implementation of the Education Law of 2008 that mandates nine years of primary education, the literacy rates remain low at 38 percent (Central Statistics Organization, 2013). There are significant disparities between male and female literacy rates: for men above ten years of age, the literacy rate is 50.1 percent; for women above ten years of age, it is not even half that (Central Statistics Organization, 2013). The low literacy rate in Bamyan is not unusual for a rural area due to long distances between schools and to the diversity of languages spoken which makes centralised education difficult.

In 2013, a group of local and international volunteers began the planning process for what would become the MOA, held in the Bamyan Province. The inaugural event was held in October 2015, on a weekend morning. The date was not announced ahead of time to ensure the safety of the event and to allow organisers the flexibility to change the date should they feel it necessary. The event was coed; however there are some cultural barriers for women to run in public including low awareness and practice of running among Bamyan people, lack of proper shoes and clothing, and a limited sense of safety on public roads. To address these barriers, the MOA organisers partnered with Free to Run, a woman-run non-profit that uses running and sport to empower girls and women in conflict zones (Free to Run, 2018).

Methods

Semi-structured interviews with organisers (Organisers 1, 2 and 3), local and international participants (Participants 1, 2, 3 and 4), a partner organisation (Partner 1) and sponsoring organisations (Sponsors 1 and 2) were conducted ($n=10$). The respondents were mostly men (7 of 10) and internationals from the United Kingdom, Canada and the United States (6 of 10). Each interview was conducted over Skype in the Spring of 2017 and lasted 30–45 minutes. Purposeful sampling was achieved using the MOA website and local media coverage of the event. In line with suggestions by Cohen and Arieli (2011) on field research in conflicted environments, snowball sampling was used to access, involve and gain the subjects' trust in the data collection processes. Purposive, snowball sampling is particularly useful in capturing a range of views, opinions and knowledge from the respondents (Cohen & Arieli, 2011; Richie et al., 2013). Specific to the MOA, snowball sampling was used to identify additional participants who may contribute new insight or knowledge about the production and planning of the event. Data collection stopped once all referred English-speaking respondents had been interviewed and no new referrals or data were available (Creswell & Creswell, 2017). Interviews were transcribed and deductively coded by the first author for themes derived from the safe space framework: notably political, physical, social, psychological safe spaces (Spaaij & Schulenkorf, 2014).

To supplement the interview data, a content media analysis of newspaper articles was conducted (Creswell & Creswell, 2017). Articles were collected using keyword search of the event title ('Marathon of Afghanistan') on Google News; 17 were retained (Creswell & Creswell, 2017). The first author manually coded the articles using the same deductive themes as the interview analysis (Fereday & Muir-Cochrane, 2006). The second author then coded a subsample of interviews ($n=3$) and articles ($n=5$) as a means of establishing intercoder reliability of the coding results (Campbell et al., 2013).

Research was limited by language barriers, as very few race participants spoke English, and low availability of news articles due to restrictions around event publicity for security reasons. Additionally, steps were taken in this chapter to restrict the release of information that may compromise the safety of the event. Considering the focus of this book on marginalised events and people, a certain level of abstraction was maintained in the quotes and evidence offered to protect those involved, consistent with recommendations for working with research subjects in vulnerable or hostile environments (Goodhand, 2000).

Findings

Three key findings emerged in this study. First, the interviewees and news articles uniformly stressed the importance of safety in the event. Second, thematic analysis suggested safe space was found for all five dimensions. Third, each type of safety was made possible by a carefully curated network of relationships and partnerships that normalised running, provided security and served other essential roles at the event. Given the potentially dangerous circumstances of the event, safety was conscientiously planned for by organisers, partners and participants. The dimensions of safe space in the MOA, and the relationships that produced them, are discussed in the following.

Political dimension

The first type of safety planned for this event was political safety. Organisers secured the support of local authorities in the earliest stages of planning, knowing the event would be impossibly unsafe without their agreement and involvement in protecting the race. Traditional methods of securing political support for events, such as getting rights to occupy a space, are non-existent in Bamyan:

> There's no paperwork, there's nothing… even in advance, you won't get an official agreement to do [the event]. In Afghanistan there's no system in place or permit system to organise events in because no one's ever done any before.
>
> (Organiser 1)

Thus, political support was fostered through informal meetings and conversations:

> we did sound out the Governor and the Chief of Police and they seemed happy to do it. And then the week before, [one organiser] had to go see the Governor again and shake hands, drink tea, and get the agreement for it, and then go see the Chief of Police, various ministers, some other people. Everybody has to be consulted and included.
>
> (Organiser 3)

The organisers approached these meetings with the strategy of highlighting the benefits for each person they met. For example, with the Governor, the potential for the event to improve the reputation of Bamyan as a safe province was made clear: 'for the Governor it shows that he's doing a good job, that his province is safe enough to put on an event like this' (Sponsor 1). The process of building political safety was long, beginning in the early stages of planning and extending to race day and beyond. Indeed, on race day, many political figures were present for the award ceremony to publicly show their support and lend credence to the event: 'All were male officials, speaking in their native language. The speeches happened after the race. People seemed to really appreciate seeing them there, even the spectators and the locals' (Participant 3). This show of public support reinforced a second type of security: sociocultural safety. For participants in the race and resident onlookers, the involvement of local authorities indicated the acceptance of running as an activity and the appropriateness of women participating.

Sociocultural dimension

Until the MOA began in 2015, there was no culture of running in Bamyan: 'culturally, it is not part of what we do – there are other priorities (family, food, work, etcetera) which come before such 'leisure' activities' (Participant 2). To provide for the sociocultural safety of participants in the race, organisers had to partner with a range of organisations and individuals to normalise the activity and communicate the safety of the event with locals: 'We worked with the local communities, families, teachers, elders, by providing lots of information and education on how the event is managed and the steps we're taking to keep their girls safe' (Partner 1). One organisation that was instrumental in advancing this dimension of sociocultural safety was Free to Run, an NGO that provides running training to women and girls in conflict areas.

The greatest barrier to participation, according to local running coaches and marathon participants, is fear of security issues and low awareness of the sport. Free to Run and the MOA have overcome this barrier by having coaches and community leaders speak in schools and meet with parents, with great results: 'because we've been doing this for a couple years, it's much much easier now for us to speak with parents and convince them to allow their daughters to participate now' (Partner 1). In this sense, the organisations have built and capitalised on relationships with teachers and community leaders as a means of providing sociocultural safety.

Physical dimension

The most commonly mentioned type of safe space in this data set was physical safety. This was also the dimension that was referred to most explicitly. The course of the marathon was designed as a point-to-point race, beginning in one town and ending in another, crossing a section of the Hindu Kush mountains along a main highway. The highway is one of few that cross provincial lines in the country and thus can be a target for attacks. Furthermore, the entire race is over 3,000 meters above sea level, and for many participants, the MOA was their first-ever experience running for sport; therefore the injury risk was high. Given these circumstances, strategies for assuring physical safety at the event included not only security but also health precautions.

Organisers explained that the key to physical safety was partnerships with external parties such as the military and the local police. These parties considered terrorist chatter and incidents in the region and provided guidance to the event organisers regarding an appropriate date and time for the race. Further, they offered viable methods for patrolling and securing the course on race day. Indeed, there was a military and police presence at the event to protect racers: 'a military convoy that went up and down the course to make sure that the first and last racers were safe' (Organiser 1). This presence was felt by racers throughout the race, especially the women. Given there was no culture of women participating in sport in this region, and the fears that local residents may misunderstand the event, the security personnel on the course were instructed to pay close attention to the women. One female racer recalled:

> I noticed it particularly when I was separate from the other runners, and always about 500m ahead of me or behind me, there was a white truck. I asked [the organiser] afterwards and he said that it was the National Defense Service.
>
> (Participant 3)

As with any event, the health of the athletes and prevention of injury are paramount to successful delivery: 'it's a very dry, sunny climate – essentially mountainous desert. But in reality, that's no obstacle as long as the organisers have worked out the logistics of providing drinks and first aid support at the appropriate places on the route' (Participant 4). The strategy to provide for the well-being of athletes along the course was to partner with external organisations, a continuation of the strategy used to reduce traffic and protect the athletes from security threats. In this case, one partner was a sponsor who offered athletes snack bars. Additionally, Free to Run provided some training for women runners to prepare them for the event, which reduced the risk of injury for some participants. The programming by Free to Run also helped normalise the activity of running, lending to the psychological safety of the event, discussed in the following.

Psychological dimension

Psychological safety at the event was best represented by this quote: 'There's far more confidence among runners. We're starting to feel safer in public' (Participant 2). As discussed, the efforts by Free to Run and the MOA organisers to normalise the event resulted in psychological safety by allowing the community to feel more familiar with the activity and the runners to feel more comfortable and confident participating, which translated to psychological safety.

Psychological safety was not reserved for runners; rather it extended to spectators, local residents and community members: 'the good part was it gave us a good feeling that we [the host community] can help and support the event, and create a safe place for running' (Sponsor 2). The event fostered feelings of pride and unity for local residents who welcomed runners from other areas of Afghanistan and international tourists for the event, many of whom were housed in homestays. The event organisers partnered with local residents to offer affordable accommodation, which produced a stronger sense of involvement among local residents who hosted tourists and a greater degree of community pride.

Experimental dimension

In this case, the experimental dimension of safe space, which includes creative risks that must be taken by organisers and participants, given the particularities of the circumstance, is numerous. The most obvious was the choice not to announce the date publicly. Given the unpredictable nature of the region's security, organisers chose to keep the date and location of the race a secret until a couple days before the event, allowing them the flexibility to change it should risks be too great on the chosen day. One organiser explained: 'Part of the challenge for us is that we can't market the event in advance, for security reasons, so we have to just turn up and sweep people up and convince them to take part in this race' (Organiser 1). This no-date method of managing the race meant participants had little advance notice, demanding flexibility by participants and confidence in the organisers. The event relies on strong word-of-mouth networks, phone messaging and secret Facebook pages to communicate with racers. This marketing method would be untenable without built relationships that allow the personal communication to take place.

Discussion and conclusion

This study explored the production of safe space in the MOA through interviews and news articles, and found that all dimensions of safe space were produced through intentional relationship building and planning. For example, the political dimension was made possible through relationships with local authorities, and the physical dimension was provided in part by partner organisations, such as the police. Further, relationship building allowed all five dimensions of safe space to culminate. While relationships with local authorities created a political safe space, they simultaneously cultivated the physical, psychological and experimental dimensions of safe space. Relationship building thus allowed for each dimension of safe space to be developed in tandem and to build upon one another. Without the relationships with politicians, police and military groups, local running clubs and NGOs, the tourism sector, sponsors, schools and community members, the MOA would not have been possible, or at the very least it would not have been as safe.

There appears to be a chronological order in which the dimensions of safe space, and specifically, the relationships on which they rely, were built. In this case, political relationships were developed with local authorities first, which, in turn, made police and military organisations more approachable. Without the support of the politicians (particularly in Bamyan), the police may not have been so generous with their support. The political and physical dimensions would later serve as the backbones of sociocultural safety: when Free to Run staff and MOA employees marketed the event to local residents, the support of politicians and the police served as a key selling point to assuage fears over event security. While this chronology of safe space production may not be consistent across events, it certainly provides a useful illustration of how the dimensions of safe space build upon each other and support each other.

The MOA is particularly useful for illustrating the uniqueness of each dimension of safe space and the variability of each sporting context.

204 Madeleine Orr and Anna Baeth

Considering this study explored the beginning of the MOA and its first two years of races, the relationship building process is particularly easy to identify compared to more established events and organisations.

The multiple methods of data collection used in this study may serve as a model for future research on sport events in conflicted regions or where participant safety is at risk. Further, considering this study focussed on a unique case, this research could be replicated in different events with a larger or differently diverse sample size of respondents. Future research might use quantitative methods to determine the relative importance of each dimensions of safe space to the success of the event and weigh the mediating role of relationship building in each dimension of safe space.

Interdisciplinary considerations

The unique contributions of this study include: first, the use of safe space development through a rare look at a sporting event in a country afflicted by political conflict; second, relationship building as a means of building safety; and third, the culmination of safety in all five dimensions of safe space theory. The dimensions of this study can – and arguably should – be leveraged within other disciplines to likewise collect data on similar events or, alternatively, to build similarly safe, sporting events. Thus, to close this chapter, some interdisciplinary considerations are presented as further contributions of this study to the literature. This list is not exhaustive; rather, the intent is to highlight the interdisciplinarity of this work, the potential of the safe space framework outlined here and how relationship building could be used in other domains.

Within sport management and event management literature, this research is helpful for highlighting the applications of safe space in a new context and, specifically, in conflict zones. From a practical perspective, the management of events in conflict zones, and in any region with social inequities, can (and we argue should) include a careful consideration of the elements of safe space. In addition, because many events attract tourists, including the MOA, the potential to promote the safety of the event and the region may incentivise future travel. This framework and example might be a helpful starting point for tourism and event managers to begin building relationships that will create safe space, such as the MOA's partnership with Free to Run. This is especially relevant in regions that are politically, economically or socially unstable.

Within the discipline of sport sociology, this work offers considerations for managing a coed event in spaces that are generally oppressive towards women. Because running is often practiced in public spaces, the MOA can be indicative of, and potentially influential to, the cultural norms of the host community. Further, this case offers a unique insight into the ways contentious and closely held religious and political beliefs about womanhood can be managed through sport and public activity. This chapter may offer an avenue for exploring the theoretical and practical intersections of gender, sport and safe space within gender and women's studies.

Notes

1 Shi'ites believe that Imams are rightful successors of Muhammad and possess divine knowledge and authority (Nasr, 2007). They also provide guidance and authority on the Quran (Ibrahim, 2008).
2 Sunnis believe that Muhammad did not designate a successor and thus follow the practices of Muhammad's companions (Esposito, 2003). Sunnis make up an estimated 85+ percent of the 1.62 billion Muslims around the world (Pew Research Center, 2009).

References

Ahmed-Ghosh, H. (2003) A history of women in Afghanistan: lessons learnt for the future or yesterdays and tomorrow: women in Afghanistan. *International Journal of Women's Studies.* 4 (3), 1–14.

Alvi-Aziz, H. (2008) A progress report on women's education in post-Taliban Afghanistan. *International Journal of Lifelong Education.* 2, 169–178.

Billaud, J. (2015) *Kabul carnival: gender politics in postwar Afghanistan.* Philadelphia, University of Pennsylvania Press.

Brady, M. (2005) Creating safe spaces and building social assets for young women in the developing world: a new role for sports. *Women's Studies Quarterly.* 33 (1), 35–49.

Campbell, J., Quincy, C., Osserman, J. & Pedersen, O. (2013) Coding in-depth semi-structured interviews: problems of unitization and intercoder reliability and agreement. *Sociological Methods and Research.* 42 (3), 294–320.

Central Statistics Organization (2013) *Statistical Yearbook 2012–2013.* Available from: http://cso.gov.af/en/page/1500/4722/2012-2-13 [Accessed 18th April 2018].

Coakley, J. (2011) Youth sports: what counts as 'positive development'? *Journal of Sport and Social Issues.* 35, 306–324.

Cohen, N. & Arieli, T. (2011) Field research in conflict environments: methodological challenges and snowball sampling. *Journal of Peace Research.* 48 (4), 423–435.

Creswell, J. & Creswell, J. (2017) *Research design: qualitative, quantitative, and mixed methods approaches.* Thousand Oaks, Sage Publications.

Darnell, S. (2012) Global citizenship and the ethical challenges of 'sport for development' and peace. *Journal of Global Citizenship and Equity Education.* 2, 1–17.

Donati, J. (2012) Afghanistan's safest province falling prey to Taliban. *Reuters.* Available from: www.reuters.com/article/us-afghanistan-bamiyan/afghanistans-safest-province-falling-prey-to-taliban-idUSBRE89F1MG20121016 [Accessed 19th May 2018].

Dupree, N. (2002) Cultural heritage and national identity in Afghanistan. *Third World Quarterly.* 23 (5), 977–989.

Edmondson, A. (1999) Psychological safety and learning behavior in work teams. *Administrative Science Quarterly.* 44 (2), 350–383.

Esposito, J. (2003) *The Oxford dictionary of Islam.* Oxford, Oxford University Press.

Fereday, J. & Muir-Cochrane, E. (2006) Demonstrating rigor using thematic analysis: a hybrid approach of inductive and deductive coding and theme development. *International Journal of Qualitative Methods.* 5 (1), 1–11.

Foucault, M. (1976) *The history of sexuality, volume 1: an introduction.* Translated by R. Hurley. London, Penguin Press.

Free to Run (2018) Our work. Available from: www.freetorun.org/our-work/ [Accessed 18th April 2018].

Frisby, W. & Millar, S. (2002) The actualities of doing community development to promote the inclusion of low income populations in local sport and recreation. *European Sport Management Quarterly*. 2 (3), 209–233.

Goodhand, J. (2000) Research in conflict zones: ethics and accountability. *Forced Migration Review*. 8 (4), 12–14.

Gossman, P. (2017) Afghanistan's deadly identity politics: how corruption and ethnic division undermine governance. *Human Rights Watch*. Available from: www. hrw.org/news/2017/07/24/afghanistans-deadly-identity-politics [Accessed 19th May 2018].

Graham-Harrison, E. (2013) Bamiyan was a safe haven in Afghanistan – but what now? *The Guardian*, 14 May. Available from: www.theguardian.com/commentisfree/2013/ may/14/bamiyan-Afghanistan-safe-foreign-troops [Accessed 19th May 2018].

Harris, M. (2015) What's a 'safe space'? A look at the phrase's 50-year history. *Splinter*. Available from: https://splinternews.com/what-s-a-safe-space-a-look-at-the-phrases-50-year [Accessed 20th May 2018].

Hartmann, D. & Kwauk, C. (2011) Sport and development: an overview, critique, and reconstruction. *Journal of Sport and Social Issues*. 35 (3), 284–305.

Hunter, M. (2008) Cultivating the art of safe space. *Research in Drama Education: The Journal of Applied Theatre and Performance*. 13 (1), 5–12.

Ibrahim, M. (2008) *Sociology of religions: perspectives of Ali Shariati*. New Delhi, Prentice-Hall of India.

Kellett, P., Hede, A. & Chalip, L. (2008) Social policy for sport events: leveraging (relationships with) teams from other nations for community benefit. *European Sport Management Quarterly*. 8 (2), 101–121.

Kenney, M. (2001) *Mapping gay LA: the intersection of place and politics*. Philadelphia, Temple University Press.

Lederach, J. (2005) *The moral imagination: the art and soul of building peace*. London, Oxford University Press.

Lyras, A. & Welty Peachey, J. (2011) Integrating sport-for-development theory and praxis. *Sport Management Review*. 14, 311–326.

Mair, J. & Whitford, M. (2013) An exploration of events research: event topics, themes and emerging trends. *International Journal of Event and Festival Management*. 4 (1), 6–30.

Mehta, S. (2002) *Women for Afghan women: shattering myths and claiming the future*. New York, Palgrave Macmillan.

Mousavi, S. (1998) *The hazaras of Afghanistan: a historical, cultural, economic and political study*. Surrey, Curzon Press.

Nasr, V. (2007) *The Shia revival: how conflicts within Islam will shape the future*. New York, W.W. Norton.

Pew Research Center (2009) Mapping the global Muslim population. Available from: http://www.pewforum.org/2009/10/07/mapping-the-global-muslim-population [Accessed 19th May 2018]

Richie, J., Lewis, J., Nicholls, C. & Ormston, R. (2013) *Qualitative research practice: a guide for social scientists* (2nd ed.). London, Sage Publications.

Rostami-Povey, E. (2007) *Afghan women: identity and invasion*. London, Zed Books.

Schulenkorf, N. & Edwards, D. (2012) Maximizing positive social impacts: strategies for sustaining and leveraging the benefits of intercommunity sport events in divided societies. *Journal of Sport Management*. 26 (5), 379–390.

Schulenkorf, N., Sherry, E. & Rowe, K. (2016) Sport for development: an integrated literature review. *Journal of Sport Management*. 30 (1), 22–39.

Skinner, J., Zakus, D. & Cowell, J. (2008) Development through sport: building social capital in disadvantaged communities. *Sport Management Review*. 11 (3), 253–275.

Spaaij, R. & Schulenkorf, N. (2014) Cultivating safe space: lessons for sport-for-development projects and events. *Journal of Sport Management*. 28 (6), 633–645.

Stidder, G. & Haasner, A. (2007) Developing outdoor and adventurous activities for co-existence and reconciliation in Israel: an Anglo-German approach. *Journal of Adventure Education and Outdoor Learning*. 7 (2), 131–140.

The Institute for Economics and Peace (2017) *Global peace index 2017*. Available from: http://visionofhumanity.org/app/uploads/2017/06/GPI17-Report.pdf [Accessed 3rd July 2017]

Thorpe, H. & Rinehart, R. (2012) Action sport NGOs in a neo-liberal context: the cases of Skateistan and Surf Aid International. *Journal of Sport and Social Issues*. 37 (2), 115–141.

United Nations Assistance Mission in Afghanistan (UNAMA) (2017) *Afghanistan annual report on protection of civilians in armed conflict: 2016*. Available from: https://unama.unmissions.org/sites/default/files/protection_of_civilians_in_armed_conflict_annual_report_2016_final280317.pdf [Accessed 6th July 2017]

US Department of State (2017) *Country report on human rights practices for 2016*. Available from: www.state.gov/j/drl/rls/hrrpt/humanrightsreport/index.htm?year=2016 [Accessed 12th July 2017]

VanSickle, J. (2012) The impact of physical activity and sport in the lives of women. *Journal of Physical Education, Recreation and Dance*. 83 (3), 3–5.

Williams, R. (1999) Cultural safety: what does it mean for our work practice? *Australian and New Zealand Journal of Public Health*. 23 (2), 213–214.

Wily, L. (2004) Land relations in Bamyan province: findings from a 15 village case study. *Case Study 14644, Afghanistan Research and Evaluation Unit*, pp. 1–80.

13 'It allowed me to deliver the biggest show of their national tour'

An examination of contemporary live music festivals in peripheral and geographically isolated locales

Christina Ballico

Introduction

Despite their popularity as a way through which to stage and engage with contemporary live music activity, challenges exist in being able to stage music festivals in locales that are geographically isolated and operationally peripheral from centralised music markets. As discussed in this chapter, these challenges relate to a range of logistical and financial factors. Considering this dynamic, this chapter examines the experiences of a select number of music festival promoters who, between 1999 and 2009, were responsible for a number of contemporary music festivals staged in Western Australia, in both its capital city of Perth and in regional areas of the state. The festivals included here are the Big Day Out, Blackjack, Rollercoaster, Southbound, St Jerome's Laneway Festival, Wave Rock Weekender and West Coast Blues n Roots. These festivals are recognised within the local sector as playing a vital role in the development and sustention of the indie pop/rock music industry and scene of Perth as well as in the careers of the promoters who have developed and staged them – and, in turn, in the viability of the festival market in Western Australia. Perth, located towards the state's south-west coast, is a city geographically isolated from other major centres and capital cities around Australia, as well as in its own state. As such, it has been historically positioned as being on the periphery of national and international music activity and, due to its geographical isolation, requires dedicated investments of a financial, resource and temporal nature in order to stage live music events programmed with national, and particularly international, musicians (Brabazon, 2005; Ballico & Bennett, 2010; Bennett, 2010b; Stratton & Trainer, 2016).

It was during the late 1990s through to the late 2000s period (the focus of this discussion) that Perth's contemporary indie pop/rock music scene came to national prominence, with its associated local music industry growing in relation to both the scale and recognition of its activities and associated events. This can be attributed to three key factors. First, an increase in interest in Perth's contemporary music scene by national and international music industry and media players. Second, the introduction of a range of arts – and specifically music – focussed, peer-assessed grant programmes developed and administered by the West Australian State Government. Third, an increase in disposal incomes attributed to a resources boom, which made an increase in festival activity – and more broadly live music touring within and to the state – financially viable (Ballico, 2018; Ballico & Carter, 2018). An increase in festival activity within national and international markets further spurred this increase in activity in Western Australia.

Drawing on in-depth qualitative semi-structured interviews undertaken between 2010 and 2012 as a part of a broader research project that examined the growth and development of Perth's indie pop/rock music industry and scene (cf. Ballico, 2013), this chapter comments upon the social and cultural contributions that these select contemporary music festivals have made to the state. In doing so, it examines the ways in which the promoters offset their financial investments associated with staging such events and brings to the fore the challenges for music festivals occurring in peripheral locales. Building on Ballico (2018), this chapter is contextualised within three key discussions. First, the importance of, and contribution made by, arts and culture activities in geographically isolated and peripheral locales, and the challenges and benefits associated with working within and from such places (Ballico & Bennett 2010; Bennett 2010a, 2010b; Felton, Collis & Graham, 2010; Gibson, Luckman & Willoughby-Smith, 2010; Warren & Evitt, 2010). Second, the use of the music festival format as a way through which to engage live music in peripheral and isolated markets (Gibson & Connell, 2016). Third, the impact of the saturation point of the contemporary festival music sector in Australia (Johnston, 2013; Lewis, 2013; Baroni, 2014; Northover, 2015; Purtill, 2015; Ballico, 2018).

In presenting this discussion, this chapter recognises that a broad spectrum of work has been published on the music festival format and its role in the staging of live music activity. Such work encompasses a wide range of issues and perspectives such as: the motivations for, and attendance of, audiences (Lee, Lee & Wicks, 2004; Tyrrell & Ismail, 2005; Gelder & Robinson, 2009); the varying ways in which festivals can be staged and managed (Paleo & Wijnberg, 2006; Getz, 2008; Pegg & Patterson, 2010; Oakes & Warnaby, 2011); and festivals as a driver for tourism (Gibson & Connell, 2003). In addition, other work, such as that undertaken by Cashman (2013); Cummings (2005); Gibson (2007); and Dowd, Liddle and Nelson (2004), has linked the structure and staging of music festivals to aspects of place and space, and how such forms of musical engagement can individually exemplify a unique music scene. Illustrative of societal concerns about the culture of festival attendance, research has also engaged with ancillary facets of attendance including ways in which to manage and respond to drug use and injury at these types of events (Osler, Shapiro & Shapiro, 1975; Archer et al., 2012; Hutton et al., 2015). While much of this literature sits beyond the discussion presented here, its breadth demonstrates the multifaceted nature of the music festival format, the challenges associated with their staging – regardless of their specific format and associated location – and the pressures facing the market in domestic and international contexts.

The eight festivals included in this discussion range in size, scale and duration, with the discussion presented focussing specifically on the logistics associated with bringing the events to the state. As discussed, each of these festivals has experienced challenges associated with their staging in a market which not only has been historically viewed as peripheral to the national live music circuit but also must contend with higher investments of time and money in order to overcome its geographical isolation. As explored, despite such challenges, the social and cultural contributions music festivals make in isolated locales, and to the culture of music consumption, are strongly recognised by the promoters who staged them. It was these contributions which often influenced the development of these festivals and ensured they remained in the market despite the financial pressures associated with doing so. As discussed, promoters have overcome this through the diversification of their business model; by staging live music events and tours throughout the year; and by undertaking an array of different activities, such as event ticketing, live music booking, music booking and/or management, and venue booking and/or management. Table 13.1 lists the interviewees; their festivals, which are the focus of this discussion; and the broader diversification of their businesses.

This chapter will first present a discussion regarding arts and culture in peripheral and geographically isolated locales within the context of music festivals as a useful way through which to stage large-scale live music activity. This is followed by an overview of Perth's contemporary music industry and scene, with a particular focus on the ways in which live music – and especially music festival – activity is staged in the state. The specific motivations for establishing the festivals in Western Australia are then discussed.

Table 13.1 Interviewee and music festivals staged and business diversification

Interviewee	Festivals	Business diversity
David Chitty	Southbound St Jerome's Laneway Festival West Coast Blues n Roots	Live music touring Venue booking Venue management
Jeff Halley	Rollercoaster	Live music touring Music management Venue booking Venue management
Ken Knight	Big Day Out	Live music touring
Paul Sloan	Blackjack Rock-It Wave Rock Weekender	Event ticketing Live music touring Music booking Music management

The chapter concludes with an examination of the challenges associated with staging such events and the ways in which the promoters have overcome them.

Arts and culture in peripheral and geographically isolated locales and the music festival format

The complexities of undertaking arts and culture activities in peripheral and geographically isolated locales are well established in creative industries literature (cf. Ballico & Bennett, 2010; Bennett, 2010a; Felton, Collis & Graham, 2010; Gibson, Luckman & Willoughby-Smith, 2010; Warren & Evitt, 2010). Reflecting and expanding on this literature, the research reported here reveals that operating in a geographically isolated and peripheral market has heightened the focus placed on festivals as a way to stage large-scale live music events while also presenting a range of logistical challenges relating to their staging and long-term viability. Further impacting this was the festival sector's saturation point – resulting from an influx of new events to the state, as well as around Australia. This led to an increase in competition for high-profile musicians to perform at the festivals, a significant shift in the format, structure and scale of particular festivals, as well as an increase in competition for audiences (Ballico, 2018).

Festivals are recognised as a useful way in which to engage arts and culture activities – such as music – within peripheral and geographical isolated locales (Gibson, 2007). The festival format is able to engage a range of performers; develop and utilise large-scale facilities; and, in turn, engage large audiences. The staging of festivals can counteract the high investments of time, money and staging resources required to overcome connecting with audiences in isolated locales. Reflecting on music festivals as a way through which to consume music, Shuker (2005: p. 105) explains:

> Festivals play a central role in popular music mythology. They keep traditions alive, maintaining and expanding their audience base, legitimising particular forms of that tradition, and giving its performers and their fans a sense of shared, communal identity.

Most of the festivals included here took place over an afternoon/evening; however two (Southbound and Wave Rock Weekender) were staged over several days. All festivals took place in large, public spaces – generally parks and outdoor sports stadiums – with music hosted across numerous stages, and a range of food and beverage options were also made available to patrons. In addition, for these multi-day events, camping facilities were offered to attendees at a cost. Music performances were staged from the hours of late morning through until midnight, with the festivals staged in the Perth metropolitan area as well as in the south of the state. Audience capacity ranged from several thousand to upwards of 30,000 people. Reflective of the ways in which the market has changed, of the eight festivals discussed here, only three remain in the market today – Southbound, St Jerome's Laneway Festival and Wave Rock Weekender.

Overview of Perth's contemporary music scene and associated festival sector

Located towards the south west coast of Australia, Perth the capital city of Western Australia is both geographically isolated from the rest of the country and within its own state. This is due to a populous concentrated on the metropolitan area, as well as the state being predominantly covered by arid desert which also results in sparsely populated regional centres, particularly in the state's north. Western Australia is the fourth-most populated state in Australia (with 2.6 million residents or 10.49 percent of the country's population residing in the state), with its capital of Perth being the fifth-most populated capital city in the country. However, it ranks seventh (of eight) with regards to population density, with 1.02 people for every square kilometre (ABS, 2017; Ballico & Carter, 2018). Reflecting this, Western Australia's live music touring circuit is largely focussed on the inner city and surrounding suburbs as well as in Fremantle (25 km south of the Perth central business district) and the state's south, with the festival activity discussed here similarly focussed in these areas. Recognising the challenges associated with working in such a market, the local industry has strong links with the national music industry based in the eastern states cities of Sydney (New South Wales) and Melbourne (Victoria). These connections exist with larger record companies, national music media outlets and larger national live music touring and festival promoters who are based in these cities. All promoters included in this discussion have accessed such networks when staging their events and, more broadly, in the operating of their overarching businesses.

The theme of geographical isolation and the ways in which it permeates local music activity – from a creative and business perspective – greatly informed the project from which this chapter draws. This isolation was also implicated in the unexpected nature of the interest in Perth music during the study's broader time frame of 1998–2009.[1] This study comprised semi-structured interviews with 48 participants. Of these, 25 of the participants were musicians and 23 were key music industry members. Interviews were conducted over a two-year period (2010–2012), with many being undertaken in face-to-face settings. A small number were conducted by phone or via email, with most lasting on average 45 minutes and some taking as long as two hours. All face-to-face and phone interviews were audio recorded and then transcribed verbatim by the researcher, before being lightly edited to remove redundant and awkward phrasing. Narrative reality (Gubrium & Holstein, 2009) was adopted as a methodology for this project, which resulted in a strong focus not only on the lived experiences of the interviewees but also on the ways in which they constructed their stories. These perspectives similarly shape the discussion presented here in relation to the activities of the four live music festival promoters and the eight festivals they staged at one time or another between 1999 and 2009. As touched upon earlier, these festivals were staged within the Perth metropolitan area, as well as in the south of the state. The physical placement of these festivals has reflected the population spread, flows of tourism and ease of access for audiences in the state, as well as a desire to engage and support specific regional communities. Broadly, festivals have been established due to the recognition of their ability to facilitate large-scale live music activity in the state and due to their ability to provide a unique live music experience.

Motivations for establishing music festivals

Music festivals are a particularly lucrative model through which to facilitate large-scale live music activity in Western Australia. The four promoters included here valued the format as a way to simultaneously engage a number of well-established national and international musicians at the same time and, in turn, maximise the capital investments of time, money and staging resources required to facilitate such events. In turn, this format has allowed musicians to capitalise on being able to perform to large audiences – which has been particularly useful for Perth musicians (cf. Ballico, 2018) – and with a calibre of acts with which they otherwise may not get the opportunity to. As a result, the music festival sector in Western Australia grew considerably between 1999 and 2009, with a particular increase in activity from 2006 (Table 13.2).

Decisions regarding the specific locales in which festivals were to be staged – which also influenced their establishment – encompassed place activation, community engagement and tourism considerations. These considerations were made as a result of festivals providing a unique social event, the ways in which they were able to engage and support specific regional communities and how they could leverage existing flows of tourism in order to maximise experiences and audience numbers. For example, Southbound is held in Busselton, 220 km south of Perth, because, as promoter David Chitty explains:

> I always enjoyed going down to [... the] region [and] loved down south, and over the years - post high school - I just noticed that there's just a mass exit from Perth for the youth to go to that region around the Christmas New Year period. There's never really been anything that's captured and reflected that youth culture on holidays near the beach. And we thought if we did Southbound it would give, the youth a music focal point at that time of the year.
>
> (D. Chitty, 10 June 2010, pers. comm.)

Table 13.2 Music festivals staged between 1999 and 2009

Year	Festival 1	Festival 2	Festival 3	Festival 4	Festival 5	Festival 6	Festival 7	Festival 8
1999	Big Day Out	Rock-It						
2000	Big Day Out	Rock-It						
2001	Big Day Out	Rock-It						
2002	Big Day Out	Rock-It						
2003	Big Day Out	Rock-It						
2004	Big Day Out	Rock-It	West Coast Blues n Roots					
2005	Big Day Out	Rock-It	West Coast Blues n Roots	Southbound	Rollercoaster			
2006	Big Day Out	Rock-It	West Coast Blues n Roots	Southbound	Rollercoaster	Wave Rock Weekender		
2007	Big Day Out		West Coast Blues n Roots	Southbound	Rollercoaster	Wave Rock Weekender	Blackjack	
2008	Big Day Out		West Coast Blues n Roots	Southbound	Rollercoaster	Wave Rock Weekender		
2009	Big Day Out	Rock-It	West Coast Blues n Roots	Southbound		Wave Rock Weekender		St Jerome's Laneway Festival

Similarly, Sloan's Wave Rock Weekender is held in Hyden, 330 km south-east of Perth, due to a desire to

> address the breakdown in community and the sort of commercialisation of music, to put something that's much more real together and boutique [...] I mean it's meaningful and it's very personal to me, that event, because it's sort of more of an expression of how important I think music is in getting people together.
>
> (P. Sloan, 1 August 2011, pers. comm.)

The perspectives of Chitty and Sloan illustrate the contribution of festivals in the cultural economy of specific – and especially regional – places and further reinforce the ways in which place activation can be achieved with music festivals (cf. Gibson & Connell, 2003; Dowd, Liddle & Nelson, 2004; Cummings, 2005; Gibson, 2007; Cashman, 2013). Southbound and Wave Rock Weekender are both staged in regional areas and, as such, are required to consider additional logistics, such as the provisions of accommodation for attendees and the impact of additional traffic on main arterial highways in and out of their locations, and within the Perth metropolitan area. Both festivals have offered – for a fee – camping options for attendees, as well as a range of group transport options such as buses and shuttles in and out of the festivals and key regional areas (Southbound) or in and out of the Perth metropolitan area (Wave Rock Weekender). Demonstrative of how much of an impact road travel to and from these events can have on arterial highways, the 2016 edition of Southbound was cancelled as a result of bushfires that occurred in Waroona, a town roughly half way between Perth and Busselton. Waroona is located on a major thoroughfare between Perth and Busselton, with the bushfires requiring major road detours to be put in place, causing delays and concerns for public safety (Campbell & Leitch, 2016). While the remaining six festivals have been staged in the Perth metropolitan area, challenges still exist as a result of the geographical isolation of the city in relation to the rest of the country. These metropolitan-staged festivals similarly experience challenges in relation to providing transport options for audiences and the need to supply accommodation for musicians and travelling stage crew. The interviews with their promoters also reveal the ways in which they work to overcome these challenges and the ways in which broader shifts in the marketplace have impacted upon their event's viability.

Challenges of staging festivals in the west

While the festival format is recognised as a way through which to overcome Western Australia's geographical isolation and peripherality, it is this very isolation and peripherality which caused a raft of challenges to the events being able to be staged. These challenges relate to a range of logistical, equipment and financial considerations. In addition, as the festival format continued to grow in popularity, the number of events taking place in Australia's national festival circuit grew, with competition between events increasing. This increase in competition resulted in festivals not only needing to diversify what they offered to audiences, but also saw musicians attempting to capitalise on the increased activity and request higher than previous performance fees.

At the most basic level, Perth's geographical isolation, coupled with the state's widespread population, influenced the promoters' need to engage with east coast counterparts in order to host Western Australian-based legs of national festivals (such as the Big Day Out) or in order to engage international artists at Western Australian-only festivals alongside east coast national headline shows. Taking such an approach can reduce the pressure on promoters in attracting musicians (particularly international ones) to the state. In turn, such an approach can be of a benefit to international musicians as they have additional performance opportunities. For example, as Chitty, who has partnered with the promoters of the east coast-based Falls Festival and Sunset Sounds in order to stage Southbound, explains 'it wouldn't have been [easy] had we tried to bring in acts on our own' (D. Chitty, 10 June 2010, pers. comm.). Similarly, as Sloan explains, while the live music market has grown exponentially in order to become viable for international touring artists and music festivals to be staged regularly in the west, engagement alongside eastern states activity is required as 'making [artists] come to WA's not difficult, making them come here exclusively is almost impossible' (P. Sloan, 1 August 2011, pers. comm.). Sloan has leveraged the music festival format to such a degree that on numerous occasions he has staged festivals in order to facilitate engagement of musicians who are undertaking headline stadium and club shows on the east coast.

For example, Blackjack was a festival he staged in 2007 in order to facilitate a headline show for the US rock band The Pixies. As Sloan explains, doing so proved useful when circumventing the regulatory hurdles associated with large-scale live music activities:

> The reason I called it Blackjack is only because the year before, in order to get approval through [local] council to do a Motley Crüe show for someone else, I called it Blackjack so they didn't see what bands were playing [...] I didn't want to freak people out that it was Motley Crüe and Motorhead [...] So when I put the application to [the local] council it was for a 'Blackjack' concert and I didn't name acts and it just made it sound softer than it was. So, I got approval through [... and] if the event's happened before [... it] helps you get the approval through.
>
> (P. Sloan, 1 August 2011, pers. comm.)

In addition, he staged the Rock-It festival in 2009 – for the first time in four years – as it afforded the United States rock band Kings of Leon the opportunity to perform in the west. As he reflects, 'it allowed me to deliver the biggest show of their national tour'. To this end, the music festival format has facilitated additional performance opportunities for musicians, and additional live music experiences for audiences, that otherwise would not have been able to occur. The challenges of attracting live music touring to the west are further compounded by attitudes held by promoters working outside the state, who do not always recognise the viability of the Western Australian music market.

The associated higher financial expenditure needed in order to bring events west resulted in some festivals hosting a reduced line up. For example, the Big Day Out was unable to offer Perth audiences the full range of musical offerings. As its promoter, Ken Knight explained, 'it costs you more money to bring the Big Day Out to Perth than it does to go Brisbane, Sydney, Melbourne [and] Adelaide [combined]' (K. Knight, 7 September 2011, pers. comm.). Knight says that the additional financial costs associated with bringing the event to Perth were incurred as a result of additional accommodation requirements for performers and touring event staff – as a result of the festival being largely programmed with musicians and who reside outside of Perth – as well as the need to bring in additional staging infrastructure into the state. Knight explains, in length, about this process:

> 27 semi-trailer loads of gear [have] to come all the way to Perth and go all the way back [...] We chase the trucks across the desert with empty trucks, just in case a truck breaks down [... and] then once it's got to Perth it needs to go back. And there's also the other tyranny of distance - even the majority of Australian bands, for example, either come from Melbourne or Sydney [... So] when you buy airfare tickets [for all those people] your Perth return tickets is going to cost as much as it costs to do the whole rest of the country. Your production, your PAs [Public Address systems], you've already got a lot of it over [on the east coast]. Someone big may have dumped it up in Brisbane on the way out and then they actually take it back to Melbourne where it came from [...] So, then you have to freight – airfreight – all their backline and stuff like that. And that costs an incredible amount of money.
>
> (K. Knight, 7 September 2011, pers. comm.)

The costs associated with staging the event in the west, coupled with a change ownership of the overarching company that staged the national event, would see this event cease in 2012. The overarching company Altered State would be declared insolvent in 2014, following the failure to pay a $1 million profit to another promoter for which they had been contracted to operate a bar at another national touring festival in Western Australia (Baroni, 2014). Additional pressures were also experienced around the event continually needing to change where it was hosted within the metropolitan area, as well as additional costs associated with site management (of around

$1 million) and in order to subsidise (at around $60,000) audience members making their way to and from the event via public transport (Ballico, 2018).

The continued increase in staging costs as well as an increase in competition within the market led to a diversification of what promoters would offer at events, such as skate parks, art exhibitions and luxury camping facilities. While this increase in competition was credited by some promoters in pushing for a better quality festival experience to be provided, it also resulted in fatigue amongst audiences due to the sheer number of festivals being staged. In addition, looking to capitalise on their newfound bargaining power as a result of an increase in competition, performance fees for musicians increased – as recalled by Knight – with high-profile international artists saying, 'we're coming down, we want to play the Big Day Out, otherwise we'll put our shows on at the same time as your Big Day Out' (K. Knight, 7 September 2011, pers. comm.). Ultimately these factors led to an increase in ticket prices for audiences and, in turn, pushed out some smaller operations and impacted upon the viability of the festival model more generally. As Halley – who staged the Rollercoaster festival between 2005 and 2008 – explained, the market 'was just too saturated' (J. Halley, 8 June 2011, pers. comm.) for the event to remain viable after its fourth iteration.

This highly volatile nature of the festival market, coupled with the concentration of events taking place in the months of September and May, has resulted in a diversification of the businesses of all promoters. All staged stand-alone headline shows throughout the year in order to remain active and financially viable, and in order to generate profits that can help offset the high financial investments and potentially low (or no) returns associated with the staging of music festivals. In some instances, their businesses have diversified to include event ticketing, live music booking, music management, venue booking and/ or management. Reflecting the challenges of being able to remain active within the live music sector, two of the promoters included here no longer stage festivals. Halley's business now focusses solely on artist management, artist booking and venue management, while Knight's ceased operations altogether in 2014.

Conclusion

In conclusion, this chapter has explored the multifaceted role music festivals play within the live music market of Western Australia. This has been in relation to the ways in which the format has provided a means through which to overcome the geographical isolation and cultural peripherality of the state, as well as how such influences impacted upon the ways in which such events were staged. As discussed, the festival format has provided a mechanism through which the state's geographical isolation can be overcome by providing a model through which the large-scale live music activity of high-profile national and international music artists can be facilitated. In addition, the considerations made of where festivals are to be staged – particularly in relation to regional centres – can support, and be leveraged by, the desire to support specific regional communities and towns, as well as flows of tourism. Despite changes to the structure of the festival market and the specifics of what individual festivals offer the market, the format continues to be valued as a way to overcome the isolation and peripheral nature of Western Australia's music sector. At the same time, however, the experiences of Chitty, Halley, Knight and Sloan illustrate that while the geographical isolation and cultural peripherality have heightened the role of festivals, they can only go so far in overcoming such influences due to broader market forces and resulting competition. It is this saturation that continues to place pressure on the market, leading to a decrease in the festivals being staged and a diversification of what they offer, and ultimately limiting the ways in which the geographical isolation can be overcome as a result.

Note

1 1998 is not included in the time frame considered in this discussion as none of these festivals were staged that year.

References

Archer, J. R., Beaumont, P. O., May, D., Dargan, P. I. & Wood, D. M. (2012) Clinical survey assessing the appropriate management of individuals with acute recreational drug toxicity at a large outdoor festival event. *Journal of Substance Use.* 17 (4), 356–362.

Australian Bureau of Statistics (ABS) (2017) *3101.0 - Australian demographic statistics, Sep 2017.* Available from: www.abs.gov.au/ausstats/abs@.nsf/mf/3101.0 [Accessed 6th June 2018].

Ballico, C. (2013) *Bury me deep in isolation: a cultural examination of a peripheral music industry and scene.* Unpublished PhD dissertation. Perth, Edith Cowan University.

Ballico, C. (2018) Everyone wants a festival: the growth and development of Western Australia's contemporary live music festival sector. *Event Management.* 22 (2), 111–121.

Ballico, C. & Bennett, D. (2010) The tyranny of distance: viability and relevance in regional live music performance. *The UNESCO E-journal of Interdisciplinary Research in the Arts.* 1 (5), 1–11.

Ballico, C. & Carter, D. (2018) A state of constant prodding: live music, precarity and regulation. *Cultural Trends.* 27 (3), 203–217.

Baroni, N. (2014) Soundwave WA promoter declared insolvent. *Music Feeds,* 6 June. Available from: http://musicfeeds.com.au/news/soundwave-wa-promoter-declared-insolvent-over-1m-bar-tab/ [Accessed 11th May 2018].

Bennett, D. (2010a) Creative migration: a Western Australian case study of creative artists. *Australian Geographer.* 41 (1), 117–128.

Bennett, D. (2010b) State of play: live original music venues in Western Australia. *Perfect Beat: The Pacific Journal for Research into Contemporary Music and Popular Culture.* 11 (1), 49–66.

Brabazon, T. (ed.) (2005) *Liverpool of the South Seas: Perth and its popular music.* Perth, University of Western Australia Press.

Campbell, K. & Leitch, C. (2016) Southbound music festival cancelled over bushfires. *Perth Now,* 8 January. Available from: www.perthnow.com.au/news/wa/southbound-music-festival-cancelled-over-bushfires-ng-bbb736c98c05857d3a634bb b77af4700 [Accessed 7th June 2018].

Cashman, D. W. (2013) Fabricating space: postmodern popular music performance venues on cruise ships. *Popular Entertainment Studies.* 4 (2), 92–110.

Cummings, J. (2005) Australian indie music festivals as scenes. In: Julian, R., Rottier, R. & White, R. (eds.) *TASA Conference 2005: community, place, change.* University of Tasmania, The Australian Sociological Association, pp. 1–9.

Dowd, T. J., Liddle, K. & Nelson, J. (2004) Music festivals as scenes: examples from serious music, womyn's music, and skatepunk. In: Bennett, A. & Peterson, R. A. (eds.) *Music scenes: local, translocal, and virtual.* Nashville, Vanderbilt University Press, pp. 149–67.

Felton, E., Collis, C. & Graham, P. (2010) Making connections: creative industries networks in outer-suburban locations. *Australian Geographer.* 41 (1), 57–70.

Gelder, G. & Robinson, P. (2009) A critical comparative study of visitor motivations for attending music festivals: a case study of Glastonbury and V Festival. *Event Management.* 13 (3), 81–196.

Getz, D. (2008) Event tourism: definition, evolution, and research. *Tourism Management.* 29 (3), 403–428.

Gibson, C. (2007) Music festivals: transformations in non-metropolitan places, and in creative work. *Media International Australia incorporating Culture and Policy.* 123 (1), 65–81.

Gibson, C. & Connell, J. (2003) 'Bongo Fury': tourism, music and cultural economy at Byron Bay, Australia. *Tijdschrift voor economische en sociale geografie.* 94 (2), 164–187.

Gibson, C. & Connell, J. (2016) *Music festivals and regional development in Australia.* London, Routledge.

Gibson, C., Luckman, S. & Willoughby-Smith, J. (2010) Creativity without borders? Rethinking remoteness and proximity. *Australian Geographer.* 41 (1), 25–38.

Gubrium, J. F. & Holstein, J. A. (2009) *Analyzing narrative reality.* Thousand Oaks, Sage.

Hutton, A., Savage, C., Ranse, J., Finnell, D. & Kub, J. (2015) The use of Haddon's matrix to plan for injury and illness prevention at outdoor music festivals. *Prehospital and Disaster Medicine.* 30 (2), 175–183.

Johnston, C. (2013) The crisis rocking Australia's music festivals. *Sydney Morning Herald,* 19 October. Available from: www.smh.com.au/entertainment/music/the-crisis-rocking-australias-music-festivals-20131019-2vtbx.html [Accessed 23rd December 2015].

Lee, C. K., Lee, Y. K. & Wicks, B. E. (2004) Segmentation of festival motivation by nationality and satisfaction. *Tourism Management.* 25 (1), 61–70.

Lewis, M. (2013) Future looks bleak for Australian music festivals after Homebake cancelled hot on the heels of Harvest and Pyramid festivals. *Daily Telegraph,* 24 October. Available from: www.dailytelegraph.com.au/entertainment/sydney-confidential/future-looks-bleak-for-australian-music-festivals-after-homebake-cancelled-hot-on-the-heels-of-harvest-and-pyramid-festivals/story-fni0cvc9-122 6745117247 [Accessed 23rd December 2015].

Northover, K. (2015) Soulfest 2015: Poor tickets sales cause shock festival cancellation. *Sydney Morning Herald*, 14 October. Available from: www.smh.com.au/entertainment/music/soulfest-2015-poor-tickets-sales-cause-shock-festival-cancellation-20151014-gk8jqn.html#ixzz3v7Hzokgk [Accessed 23rd December 2015].

Oakes, S. & Warnaby, G. (2011) Conceptualizing the management and consumption of live music in urban space. *Marketing Theory*. 11 (4), 405–418.

Osler, D. C., Shapiro, F. & Shapiro, S. (1975) Medical services at outdoor music festivals: risks and recommendations. *Clinical Pediatrics*. 14 (4), 390–395.

Paleo, I. O. & Wijnberg, N. M. (2006) Classification of popular music festivals: a typology of festivals and an inquiry into their role in the construction of music genres. *International Journal of Arts Management*. 8 (2), 50–61.

Pegg, S. & Patterson, I. (2010) Rethinking music festivals as a staged event: gaining insights from understanding visitor motivations and the experiences they seek. *Journal of Convention & Event Tourism*. 11 (2), 85–99.

Purtill, J. (2015) Why Soundwave collapsed and what it means for future festivals. *ABC*. Available from: www.abc.net.au/triplej/programs/hack/why-soundwave-collapsed-and-what-it-means-for-future-festivals/7042852 [Accessed 23rd December 2015].

Shuker, R. (2005) *Popular music: the key concepts* (2nd edn.). London and New York, Routledge.

Stratton, J. & Trainer, A. (2016) Nothing happens here: songs about Perth. *Thesis Eleven*. 135 (1), 34–50.

Tyrrell, B. J. & Ismail, J. A. (2005) A methodology for estimating the attendance and economic impact of an open-gate festival. *Event Management*. 9 (3), 111–118.

Warren, A. & Evitt, R. (2010) Indigenous hip-hop: overcoming marginality, encountering constraints. *Australian Geographer*. 41 (1), 141–158.

14 Events management for the end of life

Mortality, mourning and marginalisation

Chantal Laws and Katie Deverell

Introduction

Celebrations and rites of passage play an important function within human society (Richards, Marques & Mein, 2014; Laing & Frost, 2015) and have done for millennia (Falassi, 1987; Ayot, 2015). For celebrations marking the passage of an individual life, the emphasis placed on certain thresholds for example the transition from childhood to adulthood (Van Gennep, Vizedom & Caffee, 1960) are 'much more than mere reflections of social order' (Thomassen, 2012: p. 23). These thresholds offer an opportunity for transformation through a liminal state, within which participants are literally and symbolically marginalised before being re-incorporated into society in a new way (Turner, 1969/2017). Andrews & Leopold (2013: p. 36) recognise that funeral rites in particular reflect one of the greatest symbolic and literal shifts, from 'person to ancestor, from present world to beyond' and therefore constitute a rich area of study. Life stage celebrations can be characterised as a form of private planned event (Getz & Page, 2016). As the events body of knowledge has matured, it has been acknowledged that such occasions present a distinct area of both study and professional practice (Daniels & Loveless, 2013), and are expressions of a certain world view (Spracklen & Lamond, 2016), yet they remain an under-investigated aspect of professional events work.

Currently within the Anglophone world there is a marked tendency to focus research on events with a positive celebratory character (such as birthdays, weddings and anniversaries) and on the formative rites of passage leading into adulthood (Pleck, 2000; Andrews & Leopold, 2013). However, Goldblatt (1997) predicted that changing demographics would lead to new opportunities for marking the milestones of later life, suggesting that future events managers would need 'to design a total life cycle event environment providing services including accommodation for these important events in a resort or leisure setting' (p. 9). The growth of retirement communities, particularly in the North American context, and the prediction that in the United Kingdom 25 percent of those born in the late twentieth century will live to 100 years suggest that later life is a time for activity and engagement, not disengagement from society (Clifont, 2009; Jepson, Stadler & Wood, 2018). By extension, we can extrapolate that attitudes towards end of life and demand for information and services will also change. Indeed, the Office for National Statistics (ONS, 2017) identified a recent sharp spike in the UK national death rate, leading to greater need for services at the end of life. Indicators are that planning for end of life is an increasing concern with the UK National Association of Funeral Directors (NAFD) estimating their industry was worth £1.5bn in 2016 (Beame, 2016).

In this way, later life stage and end of life events now constitute a growing area of the modern events and hospitality industries, where wider shifts in contemporary society are well reflected. These shifts include the effects of secularisation (Andrews & Leopold, 2013), cross-cultural awareness fostering heterotopic attitudes towards death (Laing & Frost, 2015), the contestation of accepted traditions of mourning (Walter, 2005), the de-sequestration of death (Stone, 2012) and alternative modes of consumption (Otnes & Lowrey, 2004; Beame, 2016). All of these speak to the central concept of contestation within the critical event studies approach (Lamond & Platt, 2016).

Reappraising the role of events management for end of life within a critical event studies framework presents an opportunity for a more nuanced understanding of the private sphere of events, beyond the dominance of standard event typological models (Lamond & Platt, 2016). Moreover, an approach which challenges prevailing negative attitudes towards ageing and end of life (Tornstram, 2005), and addresses the impact of marginalisation in how mortality is acknowledged, expressed and made meaningful through the planned event experience (Getz, 2012) is much needed.

In this chapter we unpack these twin topics of marginalisation and mortality, exploring the conceptual and practical ways in which our understanding can be further enriched. We draw on the professional event design experience of the second author to consider how current mourning practice foregrounds issues of personalisation, meaning making and place, using an illustrative vignette to explore implications for roles and relationships. We conclude by pointing the way for further research developments in this area.

Setting the scene

Before considering particular issues around the management of end of life events, it is helpful to frame this discussion in the context of marginalisation, reflecting how both personal and professional perspectives are shaped by the cultural history of mourning.

Defining marginalisation and the end of life

With regard to life stage events focussed on later and end of life, the concept of marginalisation is not only present through treatment within the events management literature but also in more general attitudes towards ageing, dying and the grieving process. In many respects, whilst late modernity and postmodernity have been marked by the rise of individualism and the cult of the self (Miller & Brewer, 2003; Bruce & Yearley, 2006), in reflecting on the end of life Machin (1998) and others identify that the personal dimension of grief and mourning has been suppressed within a system of rational bureaucracy of health and social care.

Both the centrality of the self and the intercession of administrative systems in the organisation of daily life are symptomatic of something that Giddens (1991) termed the 'sequestration of experience'. Here the rhythmical structuring of life cycles through ritual, tradition and intergenerational experience is made separate from individual lifespan. Giddens further argued that death was subject to processes of concealment which helped to foster a sense of ontological security in high modernity. And yet 'Death remains the great extrinsic factor of human existence; it cannot as such be brought within the internally referential systems of modernity' (p. 162). This ultimate otherness of death is problematic in Giddens's argument; yet Elias (1985, 1994) posits that there is an interplay between the other and the known through *the figuration* or network of social relationships by which 'the unknown and ineffable are tamed' (Stanley & Wise, 2011: p. 953). Adopting Elias's viewpoint, the sequestration of death can therefore be perceived as part of a continuum of practices where the de-sequestering of death is also favoured among alternative methods to achieve ontological security (Stone, 2012).

Lastly, the issue of who has died, and how, may involve value judgements that privilege some forms of death and mourning over more mundane kinds of passing (Coombs, 2014; Green, 2016). Death-phobia at both the individual and the societal level is also a contributing factor in the creation of taboo topics, which groups such as The Order of the Good Death (www.orderofthegooddeath.com/) and the Death at Winchester Facebook Group (www.facebook.com/groups/104742819300/) actively seek to address through death positivity. Caitlin Doughty, a mortuary graduate and founder of The Order, states:

> The Order is about making death a part of your life. That means committing to staring down your death fears - whether it be your own death, the death of those you love, the pain of dying, the afterlife (or lack thereof), grief, corpses, bodily decomposition, or all of the above. Accepting that death itself is natural, but the death anxiety and terror of modern culture are not.
>
> (Doughty, 2011: para. 4, lines 1–5)

Death and funerals are now not only a key area for academic study but also an increasing focus of public discussion. For example, at 'Death Cafe' events people (often strangers) gather to eat cake, drink tea and discuss death. Their objective is 'to increase awareness of death with a view to helping people make the most of their (finite) lives' (Deathcafe.com, 2018: para. 2, lines 1–2). Since 2011 over 6,608 Death Cafe events have been held in 56 countries.

Changing attitudes towards end of life in late modernity

As identified in the introduction, mourning is configured in particular ways within the Anglophone world, and established practices are heavily influenced by historic attitudes. However, over the course of the twentieth century social conventions have been challenged by disrupting influences such as conflict and economic upheaval (Bedikian, 2008). As Crabtree (2010) notes, the funeral industry is always responsive to prevailing sociocultural attitudes, and this is particularly pertinent for those born from the 1940s onwards, often identified as the Baby Boomer generation (Wuthnow, 2010), as they have experienced both profound social change and increased longevity.

Clark (2018) observes that death and dying are now 'having a moment' (para. 2, line 2) with growing media coverage of funerals and end of life issues. These topics are also current concerns for public policy, debate and planning. The ageing population in Western societies is forcing issues of end of life to be discussed more widely, particularly as the Baby Boomer generation are used to making more personalised choices, more likely to challenge received wisdom and more technologically engaged than their parents' generation (Storch, 2017).

As Holloway et al. (2013: p. 30) state both academic and popular writing on funerals reflect 'a growing trend towards secularisation and personalisation'. Although the funeral remains a significant ceremonial event with psycho-social-spiritual character and purpose, its content and format are evolving. As such, the bereaved and funeral professionals are actively engaged in co-creating the meaning of these end of life events. As well as facilitating and guiding existing choices, professionals are often involved in interpreting exactly what is required. Rather than following a set of prescribed traditions, or the formalities and scripture of a religious ritual, there is a focus on drawing out meanings and beliefs and incorporating different needs by attending to the nuances in each situation.

The death care industry

As part of the professionalisation of end of life services, a discrete set of related business has been identified which is termed either the funeral or death care industry. The latter phrase originates in the United States, with the Department of Commerce (Lawton, 2016: p. 1) defining it as 'divided into three segments: the ceremony and tribute (funeral or memorial service); the disposition of remains through cremation or burial (interment); and memorialization in the form of monuments, marker inscriptions or memorial art'.

The US industry is identified as highly fragmented, with a prevalence of SMEs and family-owned business across a range of funeral services, which overall generated $14.2 billion for the US economy in 2016. The supply structure is quite similar to other life stage events, such as weddings, where the person responsible for organising the event acts as a coordinating hub in their client-facing role (Daniels & Loveless, 2013). Lawton further identifies that innovation across the supply chain is a growing trend. This is reflected in UK consumer data collected by Mintel (Mitskavets, 2014), highlighting increased demand for innovative product design and personalisation, and better advertising of available products and services to give consumers clear and free choice in deciding their end of life wishes.

One of the ways in which consumers access the latest market developments is by attending exhibitions and shows. Lawton (2016) identifies a number of international expos catering to the funeral industry from large established shows to smaller fairs, such as Uitvaartbeurs Amsterdam (2018) which recently hosted its third edition and addressed more controversial topics such as assisted dying. The United Kingdom's biannual National Funeral Exhibition attracts over 4,000 funeral industry professionals (National Funeral Exhibition, 2018) and is wholly owned and organised by the National Association of Funeral Directors (NAFD, 2018). This professional association, established in 1905, lobbies government at all levels on issues related to death and bereavement as well as providing education and qualifications for those wishing to enter the death care professions. Internationally, the National Funeral Directors Association (NFDA, 2018) fulfils a similar mission and there are many other professional associations representing the sub-sectors that make up the wider death care industry. The business-to-business (B2B) and business-to-consumer (B2C) events hosted by the funeral industry in themselves represent a segment of the wider events industry (Bladen et al., 2018) – another under-explored aspect in the events literature.

Having set the scene, we now consider how the issues outlined earlier are evinced and challenged in practice, focussing on how events can open up new spaces, places and approaches to marking the end of life.

Spaces, places and practices for end of life events

According to Kong (in Maddrell & Sidaway, 2016: p. xv) 'Death foregrounds the most important social and cultural values that we live our lives by, including those values that we acknowledge and express, but also those that are neither ordinarily recognised nor explicit'. These values are intimately connected with the spaces, places and practices for mourning events.

The somewhat sporadic treatment of end of life events across a range of subject literatures (Green, 2016), and almost complete absence from the events management literature, is partly attributable to a reluctance to discuss death but also due to the fact that organising these events has long been the province of families – particularly women – and seen to belong to the private domestic sphere (Stanley & Wise, 2011; Hochschild, 2012). Until the 1950s most people died at home and dead bodies were often cared for in the home until the funeral. Now over half of all deaths occur in hospital, and the removal and care of the deceased are more likely to be handled by a professional funeral director, who also takes responsibility for arranging the funeral (Goulding & Miller, 2017). This sequestration of death (Giddens, 1991) is often reinforced through institutional settings and a limited supply chain for professional services; yet de-sequestration is also evident in the changing discourse of dying, death and bereavement (Stone, 2012; Maddrell & Sidaway, 2016; Andersson, 2017).

Mundane or everyday kinds of death in particular are being opened up for public consumption (Coombs, 2014), often through direct personal interactions by the dying using blogs, live streaming and social media platforms (Andersson, 2017) or through the Ritual Fields 'Before I die I want to _____' global art project (Chang & Reeves, 2018). This project, initiated in 2011 as a participatory installation to open up conversations and spaces around death and grieving (Figure 14.1), is also used in workshop settings to consider alternative approaches to dying and living.

In common with wedding planning, the proliferation of choices opens up not only new possibilities but also new roles and market opportunities as people seek paid expertise to help organise these most personal aspects of their lives. As Hochschild (2012) identifies, services related to end of life care, death and funerals are increasingly being outsourced, no longer carried out by the family but paid for and undertaken by professionals. Families

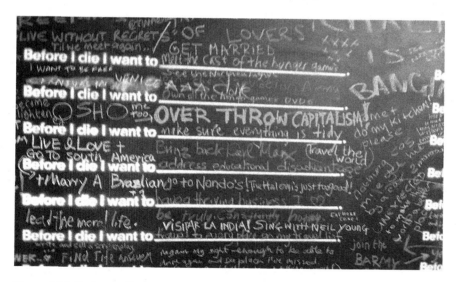

Figure 14.1 Before I die I want to_____ board, interactive exhibit at 'Death: The Southbank Centre's Festival for the Living 2012'.
Source: Katie Deverell.

still express their feelings for the deceased, and grief at their loss, but they are doing so in a context far more oriented to consumerism. This requires more attention to the design aspects of an event to achieve a personalised result.

Event design perspectives

Event design is a recognised area of the events management literature (Berridge, 2012) and an important function for the events professional (Silvers, 2012; Sharples et al., 2014). Such design is far more than a practical proposition as events act as 'catalysts, symbols, conduits, and lenses that enable people to function within and reflect upon their own role in society' (Richards, Marques & Mein, 2014: p. 4). Drawing on the work of Falassi, Laing and Frost (2015) recognise the continued significance of ritual practice in modern events, identifying life stage events as an area where the contrast between traditional and contemporary approaches can be clearly contrasted. Furthermore, by considering the total experience environment or experienscape of an end of life event, we can map the interplay of meanings and associations found in or at places of death and for the dying. Maddrell and Sidaway (2016) acknowledge that the deathscape engages with art and design to demarcate and privilege these spaces and places.

We identified earlier how changing attitudes lead to changing expectations and demand for services at the end of life. The Order of the Good Death recognise this shift and showcases designers working at the forefront of this change. There are photographers and videographers choosing to specialise in this area, with one UK photographer coining the term 'Funeography' for her work (BBC News, 2010). Floristry is another area where providers are adjusting their services to incorporate alternative approaches, with sustainable and natural flowers increasingly in demand. Instagram and Pinterest are key sites for sharing design inspiration, and as identified by Gibbs et al. (2015) these platforms are ideal for creating affective and influential content.

Increasing secularisation and personalisation is leading to a shift in the meaning and experience of funerals. As noted by Holloway et al. (2013) the purpose is less about committing a person into God's care and more about creating a space to remember a life and make sense of loss. This approach places greater emphasis on how a person lived their life, their beliefs, personality traits and the memories of mourners.

Holloway et al.'s (2013) study of 46 funerals in the North of England found two common features that define their essential character and purpose. First, that participants are actively engaged in the staging of a dramatic narrative of the deceased's life and that second: 'Rather than accepted wisdom that today's funerals are about celebrating the life rather than focusing on the death, we found that making sense of the relationship between life and death was an important pre-and-post-requisite to the life-centred funeral' (p. 35).

This sense-making is a key aspect of contemporary funeral design, impacting both religious and secular funerals. Historically most ceremonies took place in church, and with religious rites and practices already laid down there was little scope for event professionals to influence their content or design. Generally, funeral directors (those often responsible for the logistical organisation) have been concerned with the dignified care and disposal of bodies rather than the ceremonial content. The key aspects of the funeral ceremony have usually been left to a religious leader or celebrant to organise with friends and family.

In a similar way to weddings, funerals are now evolving beyond recognised traditions and prescribed rituals to more curated, personalised experiences. This may involve the use of different types of music and words, family decorated coffins or even a fully themed event. Indeed, research carried out for The Co-Operative Funeral Care (2015: p. 7) suggests that the funeral director role is developing to be more like that of an event planner, with 'two fifths (43 percent) of UK adults seeing similarities between the roles'. These changes have also been observed by the Church of England, whose services are adapting to include more personal touches and popular music in addition to hymns and bible readings. Reverend Ian Meredith (2015) notes the rise in popularity of civil celebrants, observing that the number of Christian funerals is dropping dramatically, and suggests some possible remedies, including changing services, so they are more about the life of lost loved ones than God.

The Office for National Statistics reported that in 2001, 15 percent of people in England and Wales considered themselves to be non-religious (ONS, 2004), and by 2011, this percentage had grown to 25 percent (ONS, 2011). Increasing secularisation and a move away from organised religion to a more individualised spirituality have led to fundamental shifts in the nature and purpose of funerals where even those identifying as religious may not seek purely religious ceremonies. Research from Sun Life's (2017) annual Cost of Dying report shows that more than 50 percent of funeral directors have seen a decrease in religious services, and 80 percent have seen an increase in 'celebration of life' type services. Furthermore, an increasingly multicultural society creates a need to blend different practices and beliefs. In practice, demand is not always for purely secular services; rather it is the opening up of ceremonial content to enable more nuanced references to spirituality or the incorporation of different (or no) faiths into one service.

More widely, the design emphasis on delivering experiences is influencing the way private events are organised (Daniels & Loveless, 2013; Brown, 2014). As people look to create something more individual and unique, practices that were once seen as marginal are becoming mainstream. For example, many crematoria no longer employ an organist to play hymns but use a computerised system to broadcast all types of music. The content of ceremonies may include the use of Facebook posts, diary entries, letters, song lyrics, family written poetry or keepsake orders of service (Kuyvenhoven, 2017a).

The drive towards personalisation may incorporate elements such as the handing out of mementoes to remember the deceased, e.g. a Kit Kat, lily bulbs or a packet of seeds.

End of life events are also taking advantage of new technology, incorporating slideshows, video footage or favourite TV theme tunes. Several crematoria and funeral venues have installed webcast facilities to help connect friends and family overseas. With a culture increasingly drawn to visual displays there is growing interest in decorating ceremony spaces to reflect hobbies and interests. These can include things the deceased made, collected or enjoyed – a bottle of beer, a football scarf, a painting, embroidery or even cardboard cut-outs of film characters. All these changes place new demands on venue managers and events professionals, often requiring a shift in role and perspective as well as new equipment, use of time and skills.

Amid all these new consumables, it is important to remember there is a growing issue of funeral poverty. In 2017, the Royal London National Funeral Cost Index report found that average funeral costs had risen 3 percent to £3,784, with one in five people now struggling to afford to pay. This in itself has led to the development of new services, with direct cremation or no-frills funerals aimed at reducing costs to the bereaved. With more choices to navigate, there are increasing dilemmas for consumers in deciding how to spend and who to trust. In the United Kingdom several new funeral directors have emerged advertising a modern approach and emphasising their commitment to transparency, honesty and freedom of choice. They market themselves as empowering and enabling, seeking to work in partnership with the bereaved rather than promising to take care of everything on their behalf.

Place and possibilities

The space and place in which events take place offer both possibilities and constraints. Traditionally in the United Kingdom most funerals have taken place in either a church or a crematorium, neither of which have generally been designed around the need for more personal and participatory events. Mourners wanting to come up to touch or place something on the coffin may have to negotiate awkward, slippery or narrow steps and there can be restrictions on lighting candles or little space to accommodate live music or displays. It is hard to remove religious iconography where a more secular ceremony is preferred as many older crematoria have large fixed crucifixes. The limits to the flexibility of these traditional settings means there is a small but growing trend to using alternative spaces for funerals (Storch, 2017) and a move to redesigning funeral spaces to better meet the needs of the bereaved (Kuyvenhoven, 2017a).

With changes in services one of the greatest practical issues remains the time allocated for each event. The fact that crematoria often hold back-to-back ceremonies significantly reduces the possibility to adapt the layout, seating or even do much to dress the space, as everyone has to be in and out of the room within 30–40 minutes. This time constraint is one of the most common complaints made by families and ceremony leaders (Storch, 2017). For example,

> The funeral was for a great uncle and it was held in Manor Park Crematorium. I remember the music starting (which I'm sure came from a CD player) and then a man said a few words and then a coffin disappeared... I remember thinking how sad it was... This just felt as though it was too quick and didn't really say a lot about my uncle's life... I wouldn't have called it a 'good' funeral it was probably one of the worst I have been to as it was so short.
>
> (Bailey, 2012: p. 275)

It is therefore not surprising that new spaces are emerging to facilitate end-of-life events. Since 1993 the number of green burial sites in the United Kingdom has grown (West, 2015), and several incorporate ceremony buildings which market themselves as offering greater service time, flexible seating, audiovisual equipment and the ability to hold the wake. Of course, natural burial grounds have their own constraints, with several of the smaller, more rustic ones having no toilet or catering facilities or any shelter from the elements. Some funeral directors have expressed concerns about taking their cars and shoes into dusty or muddy areas, particularly when they have to move straight to another service. A recent Farmer's Weekly article (2016) encouraging farmers to think about diversifying, reports that 15 years ago there was one green cemetery in the United Kingdom, and now there are over 270. The article further outlines how a burial ground can be created on as little as half an acre and redundant farm buildings can be converted to accommodate funeral ceremonies.

As people become more aware of possibilities and choices there is a small yet growing interest in ceremonies being held in the deceased's home or garden, a favourite pub, sports ground, hotel or village hall, bringing new entrants into the field of end of life events. In the same way that hotels, historic homes and local landmarks have long marketed themselves as unique venues for weddings (Leask & Hood, 2001; Whitfield, 2009; Weidenfeld & Leask, 2013), some are now hiring their premises for funerals. Event venue managers who have begun to offer wakes and funeral teas may soon find themselves hosting the whole funeral, leading to a more complex set of roles and relationships to manage.

Roles and relationships

As new demands emerge, so too have the variety of event planning roles and services available, including those designed to help navigate this growing stream of choices. As well as modern funeral directors and celebrants, there are now funeral singers, media and music libraries and digital death managers. Companies offer woollen, cardboard or bespoke printed coffins, specialised stationery and funeral favours. Following cremation there are companies to turn ashes into jewellery, paperweights or fireworks, as well as urns and receptacles for scattering or storage.

In common with other industries, internet and social media technologies are transforming the planning of end of life care and events. Consumers are able to find information for themselves, compare prices and select different options. Not only are charities such as Dying Matters and the Natural Death Centre raising public awareness, but a plethora of websites have sprung up offering advice or providing listings of funeral directors and celebrants (West, 2015). Rather than an expert arranging and taking care of everything, a contemporary funeral is becoming more of an actively co-created event where people design and choose what they want. As Kuyvenhoven (2017b: para. 33, lines 4–7, 9–10) notes:

> The business model is changing: in the nearby future, the demand for full funeral packages will decrease. Clients will only buy particular services from the funeral director … Funeral directors who would like to survive in this rapidly changing world better stay ahead of the game through constant innovation and agility towards new developments.

Much can be learnt from wider event professionals about creating and managing personalised and meaningful experiences within these changed roles. The move away from a prescribed ritual or set of activities requires the ability to handle complex negotiations, drawing out nuances, unexpressed needs and respecting different beliefs. Celebrants and funeral directors may often find themselves in the role of mediators, particularly where there are differences of opinion as to the content of a ceremony or the desired choices. This means it is essential for event professionals not just to attend to an event's efficient execution but to understand its ritual and therapeutic purpose. The growing demand for a sincere and authentic portrayal of the life of the deceased also alerts us to ask questions as to whose voices are being heard and who has the power to speak and organise (Bailey, 2012). This raises the important issue of skills and training. Expertise in developing and building relationships, and the adoption of a creative and flexible approach, is becoming increasingly important to deliver meaningful and memorable end of life events. As Litten (1991) says of funerals 'they are highly important and emotional social events forming the final ritual in the calendar of life' (p. 4). Often the design process itself is considered a valuable part of the event experience, with feedback from families stating that time spent talking through ideas not only created a better ceremony but also helped with the grieving process (Holloway et al., 2013).

These are special events with huge emotional significance and so subtle nuances and attention to detail matter. As O'Rourke, Spitzberg and Hannawa

(2011: p. 734) note, 'because funerals are group experiences, they represent a social context in which relationships can be established, renewed and otherwise managed...they provide an opportunity for socialisation' where the bereaved try to make sense of their loss.

As ceremonies become more actively experienced events there is greater interest in making them interactive. Rather than delivering the whole funeral, the ceremony leader may become more of an MC, introducing tributes given by friends and family, orchestrating the playing of live music or assisting with candle lighting. Adding elements of participation may require time for placing items on the coffin, assistance handing out drinks to raise a toast or facilitating open space for spontaneous tributes and reflections. This emphasis on co-creating a more involving and meaningful experience means that in addition to bearing the coffin, mourners may take responsibility for lowering it at a burial or pressing the button to close the crematorium curtains. In this way different demands are being placed on the event professionals involved. As modern funeral director Louise Winter (@poetic_endings) recently tweeted: 'If you're thinking about planning your funeral with a professional, find someone who understands the value of funerals and why we have them. Stay away from professionals who reduce funerals to three pieces of music and a pre-paid plan' (2018).

The preceding discussion has outlined an increasingly complex set of roles and requirements and highlighted the need for empathetic management of the process by those involved in coordinating end of life events. We now turn to a short vignette to illustrate how one celebrant (the second author) approaches these responsibilities.

Illustrative vignette

Vignettes are employed in both quantitative and qualitative approaches to the study of lived situations. They are 'short stories or concrete scenarios and examples of situations, people or individuals and their behaviours that are written about or pictorially depicted in specified circumstances' (Azman & Mahadir, 2017: p. 28). They are commonly deployed in professional or vocational environments (Wilks, 2004) and to elicit responses to certain scenarios (Braun & Clarke, 2013). Here, we are using the vignette technique to illustrate the key thematic strands of design, place, roles and responsibilities in planning an end of life event.

"FAMILY, FRIENDS, FLYING AND FUN"

The funeral planning began with a family meeting. Memories and photographs were shared with the celebrant who made suggestions, helping to draw out different views and feelings. The deceased preferred

things understated, nothing too 'over the top' or sentimental. His philosophy 'to look on the bright side' guided the choices the celebrant
and family made, designing a ceremony to suit.

With a woodland burial agreed on, the widow, children and grandchildren visited the site to choose the exact spot where 'grandad' would
be buried. Personal stories, connections and characteristics all influenced their selection. A preference was expressed for a quiet and light
aspect with mature trees, and it was agreed that it would be nice if
there was a clear view above, so he 'could still see planes fly over'. The
tree chosen was an established oak which was felt to represent the deceased's strength of character. Being near to fields it offered a similar
view to that he'd enjoyed at home. Involving the whole family in the decision enabled a certain emotional investment in the process and made
the setting feel more familiar and less daunting. Viewing the ceremony
room, the family could begin to imagine what the funeral would be like
and were able to discuss seating, layout and the availability of audiovisual equipment. With the venue holding two events a day there was
scope for a longer ceremony and possibilities to personalise the space.

The funeral began in the ceremony hall, a large, light room with views
over the wood and its wildlife. Some personal items were placed near
the front, creating a focal point and reflecting key interests: a model aer-
oplane, a teddy in flying goggles and a photo of the deceased with his
pilot's licence. The wooden coffin, chosen to suit his personality, was
topped with flowers selected for seasonality, colour and meaning. Family
members carried the coffin, enabling those who didn't feel able to speak
to make a meaningful contribution and show respect and appreciation.

The ceremony was designed around four key elements that it was felt
summed up the deceased: "Family, most important, friends, flying and
fun". Tributes from an old friend, work colleague and son-in-law enabled different aspects of his personality to be drawn out, along with important achievements. A slideshow of photographs with music was put
together by another friend using images to portray the seven decades
of the deceased's life, highlighting significant moments and relationships. Words from the celebrant, and selected poems, emphasised his
character, values and interests. Although the deceased had no religious
beliefs, a period of reflection was incorporated for those with faith to
say a private prayer. Within the ceremony the celebrant acknowledged
the difficulties the family had been through in recent months and the
sadness and grief the death had brought, whilst voicing many funny
stories and anecdotes. These recollections emphasised core aspects of
the deceased's personality as well as less well-known incidents and attributes. Within the ceremony there were sad, poignant and funny moments: eliciting both laughter and tears from the mourners.

As the main part of the ceremony drew to a close, everyone was invited to walk through the wood to the burial spot (Figure 14.2). This procession created a moving and ritualised moment, drawing the mourners together and focussing them in the present. Once at the tree the celebrant invited everyone to gather around, saying a few words to mark the symbolic moment of goodbye. As the coffin was lowered people were invited to lay flowers or sprinkle some earth. The grandchildren each gave a sunflower, with a personal message, as for several years the deceased had given them sunflowers grown from seed. The celebrant closed the ceremony with some words of hope, reflecting the natural surroundings and acknowledging the seasons and cycles of life. Mourners were invited to stay as long as they wished before joining the family at a local hotel. The deceased had enjoyed entertaining and it was suggested he'd be delighted to be treating everyone one last time.

The hotel is a well-established wedding venue and was pleased to host the wake, providing ideas of possible layouts, table arrangements and menus. The family were able to decorate the space using personal items, including a large map of all the places the deceased had visited, for which the venue supplied an easel. Having large grounds with mature trees the venue created a sense of connection to the ceremony as well as privacy.

The gathering was well attended, with further sharing of memories and stories. This collective experience helped mourners connect with each other and express their thoughts and feelings. It was felt that the ceremony had 'hit exactly the right note. It was really uplifting and exactly what we wanted. I felt we gave him a really good send-off... it was exactly true to him'.

Figure 14.2 Epping Forest, Natural Burial Ground, location of vignette story.
Source: Katie Deverell. For further details on the location see: www.greenacrescelebrate.co.uk/park/epping/

This vignette serves to illustrate our key themes, demonstrating how contemporary shifts play out in practice to impact on design, place, roles and responsibilities. The celebrant acts as a co-creator, facilitating choices, mediating different needs and supporting the family to design a meaningful ceremony which reflects the values, beliefs and personality of the deceased. The support of the staff and funeral director enables involvement from the mourners, e.g. advising how to bear the coffin and providing technology and facilities. The resulting event allows those involved to give shape and meaning to their experience whilst also enacting a formal rite of passage.

Conclusion

We began by stating that the existing literature on end of life events was somewhat fragmented; yet what has emerged is a wealth of material that those studying, researching and working in events can draw on if they look beyond the immediate boundaries of their subject area. Here, we have brought together some of the key issues within a critical event studies framework to illustrate how well placed many event providers are to respond to the future challenges for end of life provision. Driven by demographic change, an unprecedented number of people dying in future decades will put new strains on families, communities, services and governments. It also has implications for representations of death and dying within society and for the overall orientation of health and social care. Events can offer rich and accessible experiences to help navigate these societal complexities, but only if delivered with sensitivity and awareness. As such, they demand a complex skill set yet can offer managers a rewarding and memorable professional environment with an obvious return on experience through the collective and inspirational eventscape that they help to create. Festivals research (Jackson, 2014; Jepson & Clarke, 2014; Wilks & Quinn, 2016) has begun to map such complex social interactions and these approaches would also find fertile ground here.

As end of life events move further into the mainstream they must be regarded as more than just another source of revenue and work for the events industry (Hochschild, 2012), rather an area to which events professionals can bring useful expertise to improve the overall experience (Bladen & Kennell, 2014; Jackson, Morgan & Laws, 2018). After all, the current focus on issues involving design/place/roles affords new opportunities for researching how these events can be enhanced across the individual and collective experience.

As Holloway et al. (2013) have outlined, the content and format of end of life events is changing, requiring more creative design skills as well as an understanding of ritual and its purpose. Many of the issues shaping end of life events: secularisation and the emergence of new forms of ritualised expression (Ayot, 2015), the emphasis on personalisation, the impact of technology and web-based media and new forms of families and relationships are also impacting on wider event design. There are both practical and theoretical implications to be explored as roles shift towards co-creation, creative design and meaning making rather than administering and managing (Richards, 2014).

Private events are amongst the most valued and significant occasions in our lives, marking key points in our individual and collective experience. They are planned for, spent on and shaped by wider consumer culture. As such memorable and impactful occasions, they deserve to be treated more seriously. We will all one day encounter our mortality and mourn for those who have gone before. The unique and universal resonance of end of life events must surely place them at the heart of our explorations rather than at the margins.

References

Andersson, Y. (2017) Blogs and the art of dying: blogging with, and about, severe cancer in late modern Swedish society. *OMEGA – Journal of Death and Dying*, 1–20. doi: 10.1177/0030222817719806.

Andrews, H. & Leopold, T. (2013) *Events and the social sciences*. London, Routledge.

Ayot, W. (2015) *Re-enchanting the forest: meaningful ritual in a secular world*. Bristol, Vala Publishing Co-operative.

Azman, H. & Mahadir, M. (2017) Application of the vignette technique in a qualitative paradigm. *Gema Online Journal of Language Studies*. 17 (4), 27–44.

Bailey, T. (2012) *Going to funerals in contemporary Britain: the individual, the family and the meeting with death*. Doctor of Philosophy thesis, University of Bath.

BBC News. (2010) *Audio slideshow: the funeral photographer*. Available from: www. bbc.co.uk/news/uk-11678482 [Accessed 15th January 2018].

Beame, S. (2016) A grave business: the rise of alternative funerals. *BBC News*, 7 January. Available from: www.bbc.co.uk/news/business-35235590 [Accessed 13th October 2017].

Bedikian, S. A. (2008) The death of mourning: from Victorian crepe to the little black dress. *OMEGA – Journal of Death and Dying*. 57 (1), 35–52.

Berridge, G. (2012) Designing event experiences. In: Page, S. & Connell, J. (eds.) *The Routledge handbook of events*. London, Routledge, pp. 273–288.

Bladen, C. & Kennell, J. (2014) Educating the 21st century event management graduate: pedagogy, practice, professionalism, and professionalization. *Event Management*, 18 (1), 5–14.

Bladen, C., Kennell, J., Abson, E. & Wilde, N. (2018) *Events management: an introduction* (2nd ed.). London, Routledge.

Braun, V. & Clarke, V. (2013) *Successful qualitative research: a practical guide for beginners*. London, Sage.

Brown, S. (2014) Emerging professionalism in the event industry: a practitioner's perspective. *Event Management*. 18 (1), 15–24.

Bruce, S. & Yearley, S. (2006) *The Sage dictionary of sociology*. London, Sage.

Chang, C. & Reeves, J. A. (2018) *Ritual Fields: before I die project*. Available from: http://ritualfields.com/project/before-i-die/ [Accessed 10 July 2018].

Clark, D. (2018) *Focus: a moment for dying and death?* 6 February 2018. Available from: https://discoversociety.org/2018/02/06/focus-a-moment-for-dying-and-death/ [Accessed 10th July 2018].

Clifont, J. (2009) Ageing and well-being in an international context. *Institute of Public Policy Research*. Available from: www.ippr.org/files/images/media/files/

publication/2011/05/ageing_international_context_1732.pdf [Accessed 20th June 2018].

Coombs, S. (2014) Death wears a T-shirt – listening to young people talk about death. *Mortality*. 19 (3), 284–302.

Crabtree, L. S. (2010) *The changing discourse of death: a study of the evolution of the contemporary funeral industry*. Master's thesis, University of Kentucky.

Daniels, M. & Loveless, C. (2013) *Wedding planning and management: consultancy for diverse clients* (2nd ed.). London, Routledge.

Deathcafe.com (2018) *What is death cafe?* Available from: http://deathcafe.com/what/ [Accessed: 19th July 2018].

Doughty, C. (2011) *The order of the good death: about.* Available from: www.orderof-thegooddeath.com/about [Accessed 23rd March 2018].

Elias, N. (1985) *The loneliness of the dying*. London, Continuum.

Elias, N. (1994) *The civilizing process*. Oxford, Blackwell.

Falassi, A. (1987) *Time out of time: essays on the festival*. Albuquerque, University of New Mexico Press.

Farmer's Weekly (2016) *So you want to… open a green burial ground.* Available from: www.fwi.co.uk/business/so-you-want-to-open-a-green-burial-ground [Accessed 10th July 2018].

Getz, D. (2012) *Event studies: theory, research and policy for planned events* (2nd ed.). London, Routledge.

Getz, D. & Page, S. J. (2016) *Event studies: theory, research and policy for planned events* (3rd ed.). London, Routledge.

Gibbs, M., Meese, J., Arnold, M., Nansen, B. & Carter, M. (2015) #Funeral and instagram: death, social media, and platform vernacular. *Information, Communication & Society*. 18 (3), 255–268.

Giddens, A. (1991) *Modernity and self-identity: self and society in the late modern age*. Cambridge, Polity Press.

Goldblatt, J. (1997) *Special events: best practices in modern event management*. Hoboken, Wiley and Sons.

Goulding, T. & Miller, H. (2017) Funeral poverty: the crisis for Britain's poorest that begins the day your loved one dies. Mass graves, debt cycles and how 'Big Death' undertakers make money from the grief of British families. *The Independent*, 15 April. Available from: www.independent.co.uk/news/uk/home-news/funeral-poverty-crisis-mass-graves-debt-cycles-big-death-loved-one-dies-undertakers-video-a7682151.html [Accessed 10th July 2018].

Green, L. (2016) *Understanding the life course: sociological and psychological perspectives* (2nd ed.). Cambridge, Polity Press.

Hochschild, A. R. (2012) *The outsourced self: intimate life in market times*. New York, Metropolitan Books.

Holloway, M., Adamson, S., Argryou, V., Draper, P. & Mariau, D. (2013) 'Funerals aren't nice but it couldn't have been nicer'. The makings of a good funeral. *Mortality*. 18 (1), 30–53.

Jackson, C. (2014) *The lived experience of the popular music festival-goer*. Doctoral dissertation, Bournemouth University.

Jackson, C., Morgan, J. & Laws, C. (2018) Creativity in events: the untold story. *International Journal of Event and Festival Management*. 9 (1), 2–19.

Jepson, A. & Clarke, A. (eds.) (2014) *Exploring community festivals and events*. London, Routledge.

Jepson, A, Stadler, R. & Wood, E. (2018) Exploring older event communities: a co-creative approach to exploring the wellbeing effects of participatory arts events for the over 70s. *AEME 2018: Events Education and Research: Coming of Age*, Leeds Beckett University, 4–5 July 2018.

Kuyvenhoven, R. (2017a) Why we need to rethink funeral spaces. *Rituals Today*. Available from: www.ritualstoday.co.uk/why-we-need-to-rethink-funeral-spaces/ [Accessed 10th July 2018].

Kuyvenhoven, R. (2017b) The future of funerals: what the UK funeral industry can learn from the Dutch. *Rituals Today*. Available from www.ritualstoday.co.uk/the-future-of-funerals-what-the-uk-funeral-industry-can-learn-from-the-dutch/ [Accessed 18th July 2018].

Laing, J. & Frost, W. (eds.) (2015) *Rituals and traditional events in the modern world*. London, Routledge.

Lamond, I. R. & Platt, L. (eds.) (2016) *Critical event studies: approaches to research*. London, Palgrave Macmillan.

Lawton, W. (2016) Industry focus: death care. Available from: https://build.export.gov/build/groups/public/@eg_main/@byind/@healthtech/documents/webcontent/eg_main_113189.pdf [Accessed 10th July 2018].

Leask, A. & Hood, G. L. (2001) Unusual venues as conference facilities: current and future management issues. *Journal of Convention & Exhibition Management*. 2 (4), 37–63.

Litten, J. (1991) *The English way of death: the common funeral since 1450*. London, Robert Hale Ltd.

Machin, L. (1998) Making sense of experience: death and old age, *Journal of Social Work Practice*. 12 (2), 217–226.

Maddrell, A. & Sidaway, J. D. (2016) *Deathscapes: spaces for death, dying, mourning and remembrance*. London, Routledge.

Meredith, I. (2015) How to regain funerals from civil celebrants. *Church Times*, 19 June. Available from: www.churchtimes.co.uk/articles/2015/19-june/comment/opinion/how-to-regain-funerals-from-civil-celebrants [Accessed 26th March 2018].

Miller, R. L. & Brewer, J. D. (2003) *The AZ of social research: a dictionary of key social science research concepts*. London, Sage.

Mitskavets, I. (2014) *Funerals and funeral planning - UK - August 2014*. Available from: http.academic.mintel.com [Accessed 19th June 2018].

NAFD (2018) *About us*. Available from: http://nafd.org.uk/about-us/ [Accessed 20th June 2018].

National Funeral Exhibition (2018) *About us*. Available from: www.nationalfuneral-exhibition.co.uk/ [Accessed 26th June 2018].

NFDA (2018) *About NFDA*. Available from: www.nfda.org/about-nfda [Accessed 20th June 2018].

O'Rourke, T., Spitzberg, B. H. & Hannawa, A. F. (2011) The good funeral: toward an understanding of funeral participation and satisfaction. *Death Studies*. 35 (8), 729–750.

Office for National Statistics (ONS) (2004) *2001 Census: Religion in the UK, 2004 Edition*. Available from: http://webarchive.nationalarchives.gov.uk/20160128144717/http://www.ons.gov.uk/ons/rel/ethnicity/focus-on-religion/2004-edition/index.html [Accessed 20th July 2018].

Office for National Statistics (ONS) (2011) *Full story: what does the census tell us about religion in 2011?* Available from: www.ons.gov.uk/peoplepopulationandcommunity/

culturalidentity/religion/articles/fullstorywhatdoesthecensustellusaboutreligionin2011/2013-05-16 [Accessed 20th July 2018].

Office for National Statistics (ONS) (2017) Deaths. Available from: www.ons.gov. uk/peoplepopulationandcommunity/birthsdeathsandmarriages/deaths [Accessed 13th October 2017].

Otnes, C. C. & Lowrey, T. M. (2004) *Contemporary consumption rituals: a research anthology*. London, Taylor & Francis.

Pleck, E. H. (2000) *Celebrating the family: ethnicity, consumer culture, and family rituals*. Boston, Harvard University Press.

Richards, G. (2014) Imagineering events as interaction ritual chains. In: Richards, G., Marques, L. & Mein, K. (eds.) *Event design: social perspectives and practices*. London, Routledge, pp. 14–24.

Richards, G., Marques, L. & Mein, K. (2014) *Event design: social perspectives and practices*. London, Routledge.

Royal London (2017) A FALSE DAWN Funeral costs rise again after a one year respite. Available from: www.royallondon.com/Documents/PDFs/2017/Royal-London-National-Funeral-Cost-Index-2017.pdf [Accessed 28th March 2018].

Sharples, L., Crowther, P., May, D. & Orefice, C. (eds.) (2014) *Strategic event creation*. Oxford, Goodfellow Publishers.

Silvers, J. R. (2012) *Professional event coordination*. Hoboken, John Wiley & Sons.

Spracklen, K. & Lamond, I. R. (2016) *Critical event studies*. London, Routledge.

Stanley, L. & Wise, S. (2011) The domestication of death: the sequestration thesis and domestic figuration. *Sociology*. 45 (6), 947–962.

Stone, P. R. (2012) Dark tourism and significant other death: towards a model of mortality mediation. *Annals of Tourism Research*. 39 (3), 1565–1587.

Storch, E. L. (2017) *Funerals: life's final event. How alternative venues influence the experience and design of a funeral*. Master's thesis, University of Westminster.

Sun Life (2017) *Cost of Dying Report 2017: a complete view of funeral costs over time* (11th ed.). Available from: www.sunlife.co.uk/siteassets/documents/cost-of-dying/cost-of-dying-2017.pdf/ [Accessed 28th March 2018].

The Co-Operative Funeral Care (2015) Funeral trends 2015: the ways we say goodbye. *Media Report*. Available from: www.co-operativefuneralcare.co.uk/globalassets/media-report-funeral-trends-2015-pdf.pdf [Accessed 31st October 2017].

Thomassen, B. (2012) Revisiting liminality: the danger of empty spaces. In: Andrews, H. and Roberts, L. (eds.). *Liminal landscapes*. London, Routledge, pp. 37–51.

Tornstram, L. (2005) *Gerotranscendence: a developmental theory of positive aging*. New York, Springer Publishing Company.

Turner, V. (2017) *The ritual process: structure and anti-structure*. London, Routledge.

Uitvaartbeurs Amsterdam (2018) Home. Available from: www.uitvaartbeurs. amsterdam/ [Accessed 14th April 2018].

Van Gennep, A., Vizedom, M. B. & Caffee, G. L. (1960) *The rites of passage*. Chicago, University of Chicago Press.

Walter, T. (2005) Three ways to arrange a funeral: mortuary variation in the modern West. *Mortality*. 10 (3), 173–192.

Weidenfeld, A. & Leask, A. (2013) Exploring the relationship between visitor attractions and events: definitions and management factors. *Current Issues in Tourism*. 16 (6), 552–569.

West, K. (2015) Celebrants in the UK. *Final Fling*, 22 December. Available from: http://blog.finalfling.com/celebrants-in-the-uk/ [Accessed 10th July 2018].

Whitfield, J. E. (2009) Why and how UK visitor attractions diversify their product to offer conference and event facilities. *Journal of Convention & Event Tourism.* 10 (1), 72–88.

Wilks, L. & Quinn, B. (2016) Linking social capital, cultural capital and heterotopia at the folk festival. *Journal of Comparative Research in Anthropology and Sociology.* 7 (1), 23–39.

Wilks, T. (2004) The use of vignettes in qualitative research into social work values. *Qualitative Social Work.* 3 (1), 78–87.

Winter, L. / @poetic_endings (2018) If you're thinking about planning your funeral with a professional, find someone who understands the value of funerals and why we have them. Stay away from professionals who reduce funerals to three pieces of music and a pre-paid plan. [Twitter] 26th April 2018. Available from: https://twitter.com/poetic_endings/status/989617412877307904 [Accessed 20th July 2018].

Wuthnow, R. (2010) *After the baby boomers: how twenty-and thirty-somethings are shaping the future of American religion.* Princeton, Princeton University Press.

15 Concluding upon marginalisation and events

Allan Stewart Jepson and Trudie Walters

Introduction

We begin the final chapter of our book with an admission to you, the reader, that no one can ever really conclude upon phenomena such as the margins and marginalisation; these concepts are iterative, evolving, expanding and blurring traditional postmodernist societal and political boundaries, which is why as scholars we must bring attention to them. The one certainty in research on the margins and marginalisation is that as scholars we must push against the traditional boundaries of event management and event studies research and become truly interdisciplinary if we are to gain holistic pictures of what is happening in our societies and wider communities.

In our introductory chapter we highlighted the importance of the margins and the marginalised and also provided discourse on some of the frame conditions that create the two phenomena such as: age, religious beliefs, sexuality, race/ethnicity, socio-economic status, disability, refugee/migrant status and geographic location.

We then went onto to justify the importance of studying the margins and marginalisation in the context of events. We concluded that events could help cause marginalisation, help perpetuate it or help bring attention to marginalisation in order that it is resisted or overcome. It is obvious from our earlier work in this area that marginalisation is an outward manifestation of power or hegemonic relationships within planning processes – whether consciously or subconsciously. If we understand the power relationships within our societies, and we give marginalised communities the opportunity to represent themselves then it is more probable that these relationships can be challenged or resisted. If successful, then inclusive planning processes can become a more prominent feature of contemporary cultural events and thus the chances of marginalising groups or subgroups in society are greatly reduced.

The conclusions given here are our attempt to bring together the outstanding research from our contributing scholars under the overarching themes of: identity, cohesion, well-being and quality of life; empowerment, resistance and transformation; and managing events at the margins of life, death and the universe.

Identity, cohesion, well-being and quality of life

In Chapter 2, Paulo Cezar Nunes Junior and Ana Paula Cunha Pereira reveal that gentrification can occur within ticket sales and thus marginalise those who are unable to attend as a result of their socio-economic status. They also conclude that this has an impact on the movement of people in and around urban centres which results in a lack of community cohesion: quite the opposite of what community festivals and events should achieve. Mexfest in São Paulo, for example, is seen to be a control mechanism for governments to restrict marginalised cultural expressions into predetermined and restricted event spaces with limited cultural exchange due to placing a higher monetary value on 'cultural performances advertised for sale'. Nunes Junior and Pereira make an interesting and important comparison with respect to the Mexfest and the Virada Cultural, with the latter using locally marginalised artists to foster cultural inclusion in the programme events and promote cultural tolerance in peripheral areas of Lisbon.

Yet interestingly the cultural output is controlled to exist only in peripheral areas rather than granting autonomy to gain a wider audience and further promote integration in major areas of the city. Organisers of these events are unknowingly following the 'social production' of power and in doing so have applied the spatial dynamics of power or 'sites of power' (Westwood, 2002: p. 135) as a form of social and cultural control.

Trudie Walters makes a valuable contribution in Chapter 3 with her research into the perceptions of the South D Street Festival in New Zealand, an inwardly focussed festival for the community and by the community. Walters concludes that if events in marginalised communities are to be successful they must be differentiated from other types of community events. Moreover, events need to be inwardly focussed, authentic and relatable, and meet the needs of the community. As was the case with Nunes Junior and Pereira's research in Chapter 2, being mindful of the socio-economic status of those attending the event is crucial to its authenticity and success.

Rayna Sage and Erin Flores chapter on disability and rural events (Chapter 4) concluded that physical accessibility is the first step to inclusion, but that event planning should also be purposeful in avoiding practices that might be reproducing social and cultural patterns of exclusion or exploitation of people with disabilities. Sage and Flores are potentially the first authors to discuss the significance of rural events and the benefits they can bring to communities and in particular the empowerment of marginalised disabled people. Finally, Sage and Flores call for event organisers to extend the inclusivity of disabled access to events beyond the physical to create a more inclusive culture for disabled people. We believe this is an excellent idea to reduce the stigma surrounding types of disabilities and how those with disabilities lead their lives.

Allan Jepson's chapter on participatory arts events and the over 70s in rural Hertfordshire, the United Kingdom (Chapter 5) concludes that such events are ideally positioned to enrich and enhance the over 70s quality of life through the fostering of positive social interaction, increasing self-esteem, reducing loneliness and social isolation. Jepson's work also demonstrates the potential for powerful collective memories through co-creation of the arts and the potential for local governments to reconnect with and de-marginalise older people and improve their well-being and quality of life.

The first four chapters of our book have clearly demonstrated that inclusivity in the event planning process (see Jepson, 2009) is vital to celebrate identity and improve the cohesion, well-being and quality of life of marginalised communities. So essentially, we should be concerned to develop events 'with' the local community and not 'for' it.

Empowerment, resistance and transformation

As we may be aware, power can be manifest in many forms: it has the potential to marginalise, but also to de-marginalise. In Chapter 6, Jared Mackley-Crump and Kirsten Zemke provide an excellent case study on the FAFSWAG Ball in Auckland, New Zealand. In doing so they reveal much about the interplay of power relationships and the progress of FAFSWAG to decentralise power through ball culture in which social inclusion and diversity have been used effectively to rightly promote counter-narratives to exclusion, racism and hetero-centricity.

Sudiipta Shamalii Dowsett's investigation into the transformative effects of hip-hop events in Khayelitsha, South Africa in Chapter 7 reveals much about how local events and their deeply embedded culture and habitus foster community building through storytelling, social commentary and the exchange of ideas. This embeddedness in the everyday helps transform the experience of the township, through remaking space and countering negative stereotypes.

Nicholas Wise, in Chapter 8, assessed the potential of the European Capital of Culture (ECoC) to integrate refugees in Matera, Italy. Wise rightly suggests that there is an inherent concern with respect to migration and mobility, and how this impacts place identities. The ECoC in the case of Matera offers migrants a unique opportunity to both display their own culture and to integrate and assimilate into their new country of permanent residence within an inclusive, impartial and artistically tolerant programme of events. Wise also calls for future research into the role of events as a platform for immigrants to integrate through arts and culture, and the benefits they can bring to their new country.

Amanda Ford, Jennifer Laing and Warwick Frost draw everyone's attention to the tension and spatial conflicts of interest between a large city driving forward an international events portfolio and disadvantaged groups in society (Chapter 9). Ford, Laing and Frost's research demonstrates the multipurpose nature of events as protest (see Spracklen & Lamond, 2014 for further examples). Homelessness has been largely ignored and consists of strategies that merely shift the problem to other urban areas. It could and should be argued that event producers and those marketing them need to think not just of events, but of events and society, looking at how events can be of benefit to marginalised groups in society. Although far and few between, examples are beginning to materialise such as the Homeless World Cup (https://homelessworldcup.org). This chapter also demonstrates the need for governments to be more transparent in their approach to dealing with social issues and policies within their constituencies as they are projected to international audiences.

Finally in this section, Willem Coetzee and Xiang Liu explored the potential of Gay Ski Week (GSW) to be transformative on individual attendees (Chapter 10). They put forward an argument for the transformative potential of events for marginalised communities: as a result of the interactions between individuals and hosts, the local community further embraces diversity, reduces stereotypes and judgement. This then allows the LGBTQ community to feel welcome, comfortable and able to be gay in a way that may not be possible for them at home.

This second set of chapters presents evidence of the influence of events in helping communities resist or overcome marginalisation and of the transformative possibilities for individuals. Indeed, it is argued that broader social benefits such as integration and skills development can also be achieved through careful event conceptualisation. However, there are also examples where this is not necessarily the case. Valuable insights are provided into how local governing bodies and/or event organisers can be cognisant of the effects of events on marginalised groups and how to mitigate these.

Managing events at the margins of life, death and the universe

The final theme of our book investigated the management of events at the margins of contemporary life, death and the universe, and all chapters in this section provided theoretically sound recommendations that will help event organisers to overcome issues of marginalisation.

Amanda Elliott and Rebecca Finkel investigated deeply rooted issues in the fashion industry and its events in Chapter 11. They did so by analysing both the physical and psychological barriers to access that plus-size women face when making the decision to attend fashion events. Plus-size women are marginalised through under-representation in the marketing of fashion events resulting in a psychological barrier to attendance: and physically as a result of event producers' inability to accommodate them in appropriate seating. Thus, event producers are unethical, morally wrong and insensitive in their noninclusive approach to the production of fashion events. Further, they are also significantly ignoring the economic potential of this market. It could be argued that the current and potentially future inability of the global fashion industry to adapt to changing bodies and represent marginalised plus-size consumers can only serve to be psychologically detrimental. Pockets of resistance and protest with greater frequency are vital in order that the power, hegemony and traditional hierarchy of the fashion industry are challenged so that inclusivity within fashion events can be achieved.

Madeleine Orr and Anna Baeth (Chapter 12) used safe space theory to unpack the negotiation of constraints to participation for women in the Marathon of Afghanistan. They found that without political support, the other four dimensions of safe space would not have been possible. However, it was the intentional building of relationships that was fundamental to all dimensions of safe space and enabled the event organisers to gain political support. Orr and Baeth conclude with the sound practical advice for event managers: begin building relationships that will create safe space for events, particularly those held in conflict zones or other areas with social inequities where safety is a concern.

In Chapter 13, Christina Ballico examined how event promoters overcame the challenges associated with staging these music festivals in peripheral and geographically isolated locations in Western Australia. The festival format is a cost-effective means of bringing music to isolated places, as it engages a range of performers, uses large-scale facilities and therefore attracts large audiences. Nevertheless, hosting music festivals 'out west' incurs a higher financial investment, and changes in the nature of music events (the inclusion of art exhibitions, luxury camping facilities, skate parks, audience fatigue), coupled with increasing competition, have led to some festivals becoming unviable. She concluded that overcoming geographical isolation may be increasingly difficult due to these factors.

The final chapter by Chantal Laws and Katie Deverell (Chapter 14) turns the focus to everyone's final event but one which is largely overlooked in the event studies arena: the funeral. End of life events are a growing area of the modern events industry, and as society changes so does our conceptualisation of funerals. Marginalisation around deathscapes is both literal and symbolic, and relates to general attitudes towards ageing (as discussed by Jepson in Chapter 5), dying and the grieving process. However, funerals are imbued with meaning and Laws and Deverell show that they are becoming increasingly personalised experiences. Celebrants need to respond to these changing expectations and demand for their services. The chapter includes a vignette that provides celebrants with ideas about how to enhance funerals through layout, staging and flow.

Thus again in this final section of the book, event organisers and critical event studies scholars alike are given insights into a variety of ways in which marginalisation takes place in events and in which to improve event delivery to be more inclusive.

Finally, we hope that you have enjoyed this edited collection of research as much as we have enjoyed the editorial, and it is our wish that this text will be the first of many to explore areas of marginalisation within events and wider societies.

References

Jepson, A. S. (2009) *Investigating cultural relationships within the festival planning and construction process in a local community festival context*, Unpublished PhD dissertation. Derby, University of Derby. Available from: www.academia.edu/919255/Investigating_cultural_relationships_within_the_festival_planning_and_construction_process_in_a_local_community_festival_context [Accessed 19th August 2018].

Spracklen, K. & Lamond, I. (2016) *Critical event studies*. Abingdon, Routledge.

Westwood, S. (2002) *Power and the social*. London, Routledge.

Index